Tacitus Annals XVI

Also available from Bloomsbury in the Latin Texts series

Tacitus: Annals I, edited by N. P. Miller
Tacitus: Annals XIV, edited by E. C. Woodcock
Tacitus: Annals XV, edited by N. P. Miller
Tacitus: Dialogus de Oratoribus, edited by William Peterson
Ovid, Metamorphoses X, edited by Lee Fratantuono
Pliny the Elder: The Natural History Book VII (with Book VIII 1–34),
edited by Tyler T. Travillian

Tacitus Annals XVI

Edited by
Lee Fratantuono

Bloomsbury Academic
An imprint of Bloomsbury Publishing Plc

B L O O M S B U R Y
LONDON · OXFORD · NEW YORK · NEW DELHI · SYDNEY

Bloomsbury Academic
An imprint of Bloomsbury Publishing Plc

50 Bedford Square   1385 Broadway
London   New York
WC1B 3DP   NY 10018
UK   USA

www.bloomsbury.com

**BLOOMSBURY and the Diana logo are trademarks of
Bloomsbury Publishing Plc**

First published 2018

© Lee Fratantuono, 2018

British Library Cataloguing-in-Publication Data
A catalogue record for this book is available from the British Library.

ISBN: PB: 978-1-3500-2351-2
        ePDF: 978-1-3500-2353-6
        epub: 978-1-3500-2352-9

Library of Congress Cataloging-in-Publication Data
Names: Fratantuono, Lee, 1973- editor.
Title: Tacitus Annals XVI / edited by Lee Fratantuono.
Other titles: Bloomsbury Latin texts.
Description: London : Bloomsbury Academic, 2017. | Series: Bloomsbury Latin
texts | Includes bibliographical references and index.
Identifiers: LCCN 2017024383 | ISBN 9781350023512 (pbk.) |
ISBN 9781350023529 (epub)
Subjects: LCSH: Tacitus, Cornelius. Annales. Liber 16–Commentaries.
Classification: LCC PA6705.A9 T33 2017 | DDC 937/.07–dc23
LC record available at https://lccn.loc.gov/2017024383

Cover design: Terry Woodley
Cover image: traveler1116/Getty Images

Typeset by Integra Software Services Pvt. Ltd.
Printed and bound in Great Britain

To find out more about our authors and books visit www.bloomsbury.com. Here
you will find extracts, author interviews, details of forthcoming events and the
option to sign up for our newsletters.

For Professor Robert Penella

Figure 1 Nero bust in Pierides Museum, Larnaca, Cyprus. © Katelyn McGarr.

Contents

List of Figures

Preface

The present edition of the last book of the surviving *Annales* of Tacitus is designed to be of particular help to undergraduate students who are approaching the author for the first time, though it has been drafted with the intention that more experienced undergraduate and graduate student readers of Tacitus may also find it to be of use. As such it is very much an example of that genre known as the "school commentary," even if along the way an attempt has been made to offer some comment on Tacitus' program and plan in the *Annales* that may be of interest to scholars of the Neronian books, and also to those interested in the intertextual relationship of the *Annales* with earlier Latin literature (especially the epic poetry of Virgil and Lucan).[1]

There has always been a relative dearth of editions of Tacitus that are suitable for college and university use, in part because of the perceived difficulty of the author and the resultant question of his suitability for the beginning stages of Latin instruction.[2] Tacitus remains, however, one of the most popular authors for study in English translation in courses on Roman imperial history, and alongside Suetonius' lives of the Caesars his *Annales* is one of the most widely read works of the so-called "Silver Age" of Latin literature—again, at least in translation. The rewards of encountering Tacitus' work in the original are many and rich, and this edition seeks to make the imperial historian's abundant treasures more easily accessible to a new audience.[3]

Why Book XVI of the *Annales*? One reason certainly is the relative lack of separate treatment of the book, especially for use in schools.[4] But beyond the utility of having "complete coverage" of the *Annales* for availability in Latin undergraduate education, there is the intrinsically interesting, even

---

[1] The advice of Salvador Bartera has been remembered, however: " ... the commentator on the *A.* cannot, and should not, draw a line between classroom use and a more philological approach. T. is too complex a writer to be reduced to an exact category." (In C. S. Kraus and C. Stray, *Classical Commentaries*, Oxford, 2016, p. 130).

[2] Two anthologies that deserve mention are Steven H. Rutledge's *A Tacitus Reader: Selections from the Annales, Historiae, Germania, Agricola, and Dialogus (BC Latin Readers)*, Mundelein, IL: Bolchazy-Carducci Publishers, Inc., 2013, and F. B. Marsh and H. J. Leon, *Tacitus: Selections from His Works*, New York: Prentice-Hall, Inc., 1936 (reprinted with some corrections, etc., Oklahoma, 1963).

[3] Tacitus' Latin has received a significant array of critical and grammatical aids, many of them designed to highlight the creative features by which the historian describes events and provides commentary on the intimate level of his language and syntax.

[4] Salvador Bartera's work is the most detailed available on the problems of Book XVI.

hauntingly mysterious quality of "Tacitus' last book." *Annales* XVI is relatively brief due to its unfinished or at least lost nature; its thirty-five paragraphs or chapters represent a reasonably brief compass of Latin for students to aspire to complete in a semester or term, and it comes as the *de facto* conclusion of a work that may have been intended originally to continue for another two books.

Annales XVI is the last of Tacitus' Neronian books, and it provides invaluable insight into major themes of what would prove to be the closing years of Nero's tumultuous reign—a tenure that would mark the end of the great dynasty of the Julio-Claudian rulers or *principes*. In *Annales* XVI we meet Nero the stage performer and aspiring artist-poet; we find detailed coverage of the aftermath of the so-called Pisonian conspiracy of A.D. 65; we encounter the unforgettable death scene of the famous novelist Gaius Petronius, the author of the *Satyrica*.[5] We explore the tensions and debates of representatives of rival schools of philosophy, as well as religious, theological reflections; we find one of the rare authorial interventions in the *Annales*, as Tacitus discusses certain of the moral and artistic goals of his *magnum opus*. In short, *Annales* XVI is an ideal text for a student of Tacitus' work; a reader of Book XVI will acquire a good sense of the style and technique of later Tacitus, while acquiring a reasonably comprehensive view of the problems (both historiographical and interpretive) of the waning years of Neronian tyranny. Book XVI also affords the reader an opportunity to study Tacitean consideration of the problem of Roman identity as the children of the Trojan exiles under Aeneas and his son Iulus—the "founder," as it were, of the dynasty of the Caesars of which Nero was the last—and of the depiction of such problems of identity in poetry and prose. The "Troy theme" may well have been hackneyed in literature by the time of Nero, Lucan, and Gaius (or Titus) Petronius—but at the very least it mattered much that the *princeps* was obsessed with the question of the Julian *gens* and the Roman descent from Troy, and so it may well be the case that the ludicrous is possible— the Nero we meet in the opening paragraphs of Tacitus' *Annales* XVI really is credulous enough to think that Caesellius has found the gold hoard of Carthage's queen Dido. What remains of *Annales* XVI—whether or not the historian ever continued or finished the book—is a priceless window into a period in which Roman history was experiencing a process of transformation

---

[5] "Though the date at which the *Satyricon* was composed has been hotly debated since the Renaissance, virtually all modern critics have now concluded that its author is identical with the Petronius of the Neronian age, unforgettably portrayed in a thumbnail sketch by Tacitus." (P. G. Walsh, *Petronius: The Satyricon, A New Translation* (Oxford World's Classics), Oxford, 1997, p. xiii).

that was soon to explode into a new unleashing of the all too familiar Roman horror of civil war.

The introduction, commentary, and bibliography of this edition attempt to provide an introductory student of Tacitus with material to spur further reading and research on the author.[6] While this edition is not a primer or introductory survey of Tacitus, it does seek to point the interested student in helpful directions for further study. Prejudice has been accorded throughout to scholarship in English, though references are given to several important works in other languages (not least the major, German commentary of Koestermann on the whole of the *Annales*). Due to the multiplicity of grammars on the market, there has been an avoidance of citation of references to this or that edition. Particular use has been made, however, of the first volume of Harm Pinkster's *Oxford Latin Syntax*. Lexical notes throughout cite the *Oxford Latin Dictionary* for the convenience of anglophone students; while there is a glossary of words provided for the sake of user convenience, students are strongly encouraged to engage in the profit of using a standard dictionary like the *Oxford Latin Dictionary*. Textual notes are found throughout the commentary, out of a belief that students should be made aware as early as possible in their reading of Latin literature that our knowledge of texts is sometimes imperfect and a matter for scholarly debate.[7]

I am indebted to a number of colleagues and friends for their assistance in the production of this volume. Alice Wright is an indefatigable, learned, and eminently judicious editor. Salvador Bartera generously agreed to read an early draft of the commentary and introduction, and every page of the finished volume bears a debt to his erudition and judgment; all errors that remain are entirely my own responsibility. The encouragement of Blaise Nagy is a constant source of paternal wisdom and patient guidance. I have profited immensely from the Tacitean scholarship of Caitlin Gillespie and Timothy Joseph. Shadi Bartsch-Zimmer, Alden Smith, and Richard Thomas are generous and supportive sources of inspiration and support. My Classics student Sarah Rosalind Foster is a talented young Latinist whose first undergraduate author course was on Tacitus; she has been a greatly appreciated help in the department and in my research. Elise Baer, vice

---

[6]   Of particular value to the Tacitean neophyte are the three exemplary volumes of collected papers edited by Rhiannon Ash (*Oxford Readings in Tacitus*), Anthony Woodman (*The Cambridge Companion to Tacitus*), and Victoria Pagán (the *Blackwell Companion to Tacitus*). For general introduction to the author, the Bristol Classical Press reprint of Ronald Martin's *Tacitus* is of particular value, as is Rhiannon Ash's *Tacitus* for the same press's *Ancients in Action* series.

[7]   The text of *Annales* XVI contained in this edition is taken from Fisher's Oxford text in part for the convenience of students who may be using the OCT; notes are given throughout, however, to the readings of the Teubner texts of Heubner, and of Wellesley.

president of the Delta Delta Delta sorority and gifted researcher, has been a most appreciated and loyal assistant.

I am especially indebted to Katie McGarr, freelance photographer and writer, for her photographic contributions that have enriched the present volume. Katie has traveled extensively in Tacitus' native Provence, and in areas relevant to the study of Neronian Rome; it is a privilege to benefit from her talent and insight.

Gerard Lavery introduced me to Tacitus at Holy Cross in an undergraduate seminar that focused on the Tiberian *Annales*. I read Tacitus in graduate school at Fordham with Professor Robert Penella in a stimulating and rewarding seminar on the major and minor works. It is a pleasure to offer this small token of gratitude to Professor Penella on the occasion of his retirement from Fordham University.

Tacitus lived at a moment in history when it was possible to gaze back on the long progress of the reigns of the Julio-Claudians, and to take stock of the reception and expenditure of the inheritance Rome had received from Caesar and Augustus. His *Annales* were written in the wake of a professional and political life lived under the spell of the second of Rome's imperial dynasties, the Flavian. The historian lived to see the dawn of what may well have seemed the chance for a new beginning under Nerva and Trajan, only, just possibly, to witness the fear that troubles might return again. The *Annales* are at one and the same time a profoundly detached and emotionally intimate work; there are those who rightly consider it to represent the summit of Roman historiography, even of Latin literature.[8] It is hoped that this edition of the last of the extant books of Tacitus' enigmatic prose epic of image, reality, and the often blurred lines between the two will serve to elucidate some of the mysteries posed by its author.[9]

[8] And a work of enduring influence and continuing challenge: for a start to approaching the vast field of the the *Nachleben* or "afterlife" of *Annales*, see Ronald Mellor's survey in his *Oxford Approaches to Classical Literature: Tacitus* volume, Oxford, 2010, pp. 196–225.

[9] Cf. B. M. Williams, *Image and Reality in Tacitus' Annals*, Dissertation Monash, 1992, to which the author is indebted for its careful and illuminating treatment of important aspects of Tacitean style and agenda.

Introduction

Figure 2 Forum of Augustus, Rome, Italy. © Katelyn McGarr.

Tacitus is often awarded the crown of "Rome's greatest historian," as the supreme artist of Roman historiography and historical analysis—the Roman Thucydides.[1] His most extensive surviving work is the *Annales*, a massive treatment of Roman history from the aftermath of the death of Augustus to

[1] Tacitus was one of the greatest historians, though not very influential in antiquity, when only a few authors seem to have taken any notice of him, as e.g. Ammianus Marcellinus, Sulpicius Severus, or Orosius, and even less influential in the Middle Ages: For he was known in the Carolingian age, but disappeared after that for centuries ... It was only in the fourteenth century that his histories were read again, and during the following centuries, especially after 1570 and the work of Muretus and Lipsius, he became more and more popular, mainly in France ...

(C. J. Classen, "Tacitus: Historian between Republic and Principate," in *Mnemosyne* 41.1/2 (1988), pp. 93–116).

the death of Nero that probably encompassed eighteen books in its original
edition (either composed or at least conceived).[2] Students and scholars
today can read the opening books in their entirety (I–IV), the slenderest
of remains of Books V–VI, then a significant portion of Book XI, and all
of Books XVI–XV; Book XVI is perhaps half finished. What we have, then,
covers much of the Tiberian reign (Books I–VI) and a fair amount of the
Claudian (Books XI–XII) and Neronian (Books XIII–XVI) texts; missing
entirely is the Tacitean treatment of Gaius Caligula. It appears that Tacitus
arranged his material in groups of six books, the so-called hexads (cf. the
"pentads" of division of Livy's monumental *Ab Urbe Condita*); the first
hexad (Books I–VI) would have concerned Tiberius, the second Caligula
and Claudius (Books VII–XII), and the third Nero (Books XIII–XVIII).[3]
The "halfway" point of Tacitus' historical epic is thus missing, as is the
putative conclusion; we have no way of knowing for certain if Tacitus ever
lived to complete his mammoth undertaking.[4]

Tacitus' *Annales* thus displays a tripartite structure; there were four
principes or emperors with whom he was concerned, though Caligula reigned
for but four years and could only with difficulty be stretched into a full hexad.
The first book opens in the immediate aftermath of Augustus' death, and
contains certain "preliminaries" before the commencement of Tiberius' reign

[2] Many anglophone students will encounter the 1906 Oxford Classical Texts edition of the
Annales by C. D. Fisher; better is Heinrich Heubner's revised Teubner (Stuttgart) text of
1994. There is also a Leipzig Teubner edition of Kenneth Wellesley (1986; second edition
1998) for Books XI–XVI, and of Stephanus Borzsák (1992) for the first hexad. The
Cambridge *Greek and Latin Classics* collection, and the *Classical Texts and Commentaries*
series, both contain significant editions of Tacitus; the former offers editions of *Historiae*
I and II, the *Agricola*, the *Dialogus*, and *Annales* IV; the latter has *Annales* I–III and
XI, with planned editions of Books IV (Woodman); V–VI (Woodman); XII (Malloch);
Lavan-Whitton (XIV); Ash (XV); and Bartera (XVI). The fullest commentary on the
entire *Annales* is that of Erich Koestermann, in four volumes (German). There is a two-
volume Oxford edition with commentary by Henry Furneaux; the second volume was
revised by Pelham and Fisher (Oxford, 1907).

[3] On the question of hexadic structure, with reference to the possible imitation of both
the Virgilian *Aeneid* and the *Annales* of Quintus Ennius, see E. Baynham, *Alexander the
Great: The Unique History of Quintus Curtius*, Ann Arbor: The University of Michigan
Press, 1998, p. 135; also T. D. Barnes, *Ammianus Marcellinus and the Representation of
Historical Reality*, Ithaca-London: Cornell University Press, 1998, p. 24; R. C. Blockley,
"Tacitean Influence upon Ammianus Marcellinus," in *Latomus* 32.1 (1973), pp. 63–78 .
The *Aeneid* can certainly be studied as having a fundamental division into two halves,
but it also has important three and four book units; further, one might expect to find
parallels in Tacitus between *Annales* XVI and IV, and XVI and XIII and XVI, for example.

[4] A classic study of the question of why and how exactly Tacitus decided to approach
his grand enterprise is R. Syme's "How Tacitus Came to History," in *Greece & Rome* 4.2
(1957), pp. 160–167, which is something of a tantalizing preface to his monumental two-
volume *Tacitus* (Oxford, 1958), a bewildering, dense monument of classical scholarship,
oftentimes composed in a style that bespeaks Tacitean *imitatio*.

proper; we can only speculate more or less blindly on how exactly the work would have ended.[5] From the start, the *Annales* is cast in epic terms—the famous opening line *Urbem Romam a principio reges habuere* constitutes a verse of dactylic hexameter, however lacking in what some might consider the refined quality of the poetry of an epic master. The *Annales* is nothing less than the epic of the transformation of Rome in the wake of the death of the great Augustus; it is the narrative epic and history of the Julio-Claudian principate,[6] a dramatic account of the changing fortunes of the house of the Caesars that comes to a climactic end with the suicide of the prince-artist Nero, the last emperor of the dynasty.[7] It is an epic story, to be sure—a prose masterpiece that at one and the same time engages in an enterprise of moralistic commentary, historical analysis and investigation, and in an attempt at the conferral of some hope of immortality on past deeds, both famous and infamous.[8] Even on the level of language and style, it conveys something of the Tacitean judgment on the nature of the imperial principate, a period in which titles and vocabulary experienced both losses and mutations of meaning.[9] And it is a time when the shifting and changing meanings of words and images, indeed the construction of a veil or mask over events and

[5] Important for the interplay of the Augustan and Tiberian material in the first hexad is E. Cowan, "Tacitus, Tiberius, and Augustus," in *Classical Antiquity* 28.2 (2009), pp. 179–210.

[6] It is also a metahistorical work, in which the emperors have certain affinities to historians; cf. E. O'Gorman, "On Not Writing about Augustus: Tacitus' *Annals* Book I," in *Materiali e discussioni per l'analisi dei testi classici* 35 (1995), pp. 91–114.

[7] It is also, too, an epic about the problem of Roman history writing and the place of the historian in the society of the Caesars; see here especially J. Marincola, "Tacitus' Prefaces and the Decline of Imperial Historiography," in *Latomus* 58.2 (1999), pp. 391–404.

[8] The *Annales* is a sequel to the *Aeneid* in the sense that it reveals the unfolding of the aftermath of the Augustan, imperial vision of the poet's treatment of the would-be new Golden Age after Actium; with benefit of hindsight it puts on display what happened in the decades after the establishment of the Augustan regime and the new manipulation of republican institutions and Roman political life. The dynasty of the Julio-Claudians ended with a *princeps* who, like Julius Caesar, had particular interest in the lore of Troy and the mythic origins of the *gens Iulia*; Tacitus' composition is very different from whatever Nero produced on the fall of Troy. "Troy lore" also figures significantly in the surviving portions of the Petronian *Satyrica* (on which note V. Rimell, *Petronius and the Anatomy of Fiction*, Cambridge, 2002, pp. 60 ff.; also E. Courtney, *A Companion to Petronius*, Oxford, 2001, pp. 133 ff.).

[9] For a convenient introduction to Tacitean Latin, see S. P. Oakley, "Style and Language," pp. 195–211 in the *Cambridge Companion*; note also F. R. D. Goodyear, "Development of Language and Style in the *Annals* of Tacitus," in *The Journal of Roman Studies* 58, Parts 1 and 2 (1968), pp. 22–31 . On the strong influence of the Roman rhetorical tradition on Tacitus' prose, see D. Sullivan, "Innuendo and the 'Weighted Alternative' in Tacitus," in *The Classical Journal* 71.4 (1976), pp. 312–326; cf. D. Whitehead, "Tacitus and the Loaded Alternative," in *Latomus* 38.2 (1979), pp. 474–495, and the classic treatment of I. Scott Ryberg, "Tacitus' Art of Innuendo," in *Transactions and Proceedings of the American Philological Association* 73 (1942), pp. 383–404.

deeds, also serve to call into question the very meaning of what we might call the reliability or trustworthiness of the historian, especially the historian who actively enacts the irony and doublespeak of the times in artfully composed, often bewitchingly sarcastic prose.[10]

All too often we must admit that we know relatively little for certain about the storied giants of Latin literature; Tacitus is no exception.[11] We cannot be sure how much the third-century A.D. Roman emperor Marcus Claudius Tacitus knew about his supposed ancestor; already by the time of the Emperor Tacitus, it seems that the historian was fairly little read, and we may owe a significant debt of gratitude to the man who ruled Rome from the autumn of 275 to the late spring/early summer of 276 for the preservation and dissemination of Tacitus' histories. The historian might have taken some pleasure in the knowledge that his descendant was the last emperor in Roman history who was elected by the senate.

We cannot be sure of where and when Cornelius Tacitus was born, though it was certainly during the Claudian reign, perhaps in 56 or 57; he was either a northern Italian or from the south of France. His first name or *praenomen* was apparently either Publius or Gaius (some have thought Sextus or Quintus, but with precious little to support the suggestion). He was certainly a senator; at *Annales* XI, 11 he refers to being praetor in 88, and to holding a quindecimviral priesthood—one of those precious tidbits of authorial information about career and trajectory. He was *consul suffectus*

---

[10] Cf. K. Wellesley, "Can You Trust Tacitus?," in *Greece & Rome* 1.1 (1954), pp. 13–33.

> Tacitus begins the *Annals* with his famous boast that he writes "without anger or partiality, any reasons for which I keep at a distance" ... In this he follows Cicero and Sallust in their pious protestations that truth must be the highest goal for an historian. Of course, even though Tiberius and Nero were long dead, Tacitus shows considerable animosity toward them. So when we indeed find hostility and favoritism throughout his writings, we must assess whether they come from Tacitus' own biases or from those of his sources.

(R. Mellor, *Oxford Approaches to Classical Literature: Tacitus' Annals*, Oxford, 2010, p. 23). On Tacitean impartiality cf. also J. Marincola, *Authority and Tradition in Ancient Historiography*, Cambridge, 1997, pp. 166 ff. There is also helpful material in K. Murphy and A. Traninger, eds., *The Emergence of Impartiality*, Leiden-Boston, 2014 on "the prehistory of impartiality." T. J. Luce, "Ancient Views on the Causes of Bias in Historical Writing," in *Classical Philology* 84.1 (1989), pp. 16–31, takes as its starting point Tacitus' remarks on the subject. On how Tacitus never mentions the word "truth," see A. J. Woodman, *Rhetoric in Classical Historiography: Four Studies*, London-New York: Routledge, 1988, pp. 73–74 . On the historian's use of wit and sarcastic anecdote and commentary as part of his critique and analysis of moral and political life, see P. Plass, *Wit and the Writing of History: The Rhetoric of Historiography in Imperial Rome*, Wisconsin, 1988.

[11] Cf. here A. R. Birley, "The Life and Death of Cornelius Tacitus," in *Historia: Zeitschrift für alte Geschichte* 49.2 (2000), pp. 230–247.

in 97, the fateful year after the assassination of Domitian; he delivered the funeral oration for the celebrated Verginius Rufus, while he prosecuted the corrupt Asian governor Marius Priscus. He was a friend of the epistolographer Pliny the Younger, to whom we owe some information about the historian's life.[12] He married the daughter of Gnaeus Julius Agricola, the governor of Britain who is the subject of his son-in-law's laudatory, quasi-biographical work, the *Agricola*. The origin of the cognomen *Tacitus* is unknown; the Latin adjective *tacitus* means "silent," and some have found a sense of irony with respect to Tacitus' oratorical, political, and historical work. Tacitus certainly benefited from the Flavian dynasty that replaced the Julio-Claudian; he owed his career and advancement to Vespasian and his sons Titus and Domitian, who reigned respectively from 69–79, 79–81, and 81–96. He was eventually granted the governorship of Asia, which he held in 112 or 113. His date of death is unknown; much has been made of his reference at *Annales* II, 61 to the expansion of Roman power to the *mare rubrum* or Red Sea, and some have taken this to mean that the passage must date to 116–117 on account of political and military decisions taken by Trajan and Hadrian—but at best it seems that we have a so-called *terminus post quem* for dating the historian.[13] One could speculate that he lived as late as, say, 130—but speculation is all we have.[14] We have no clear sense of what Tacitus completed of his historical corpus; he tells us that he planned a treatment of Augustus, and one of his own times—but no shred of these works exists.

We cannot be sure of the intended title of Tacitus' work; the name *Annales* comes from the so-called annalistic nature of the history, that is, the year-by-year treatment of events (Book XVI, for example, opens with a continuation of events from 65, and includes the consular dating for the start of 66). The title may have been *Ab Excessu Divi Augusti Historiarum Libri*: the "Books of Histories from the Death of the Divine Augustus" (cf. Livy's work *ab urbe condita*, "from the founding of the city"). The date of commencement of the composition of the work is unknown. An annalist could, of course, in theory

---

[12] On the relationship between the two peers see R. Gibson and R. Morello, *Reading the Letters of Pliny the Younger: An Introduction*, Cambridge, 2012, pp. 136 ff.; there is also a wealth of useful material in I. Marchesi, *The Art of Pliny's Letters: A Poetics of Allusion in the Private Correspondence*, Cambridge, 2008 (in particular on the question of the "voice of Pliny" in Tacitus' prose).

[13] See further K. Wellesley, "The Date of Composition of Tacitus, *Annals* II," in *Rheinisches Museum für Philologie* 98.2 (1955), pp. 135–149.

[14] For a convenient summary of the different views, see C. S. van den Berg, *The World of Tacitus' Dialogus de Oratoribus*, Cambridge, 2014, pp. 30–31 . Some have speculated that certain events in the early days of Hadrian's reign may have engendered the idea in Tacitus that the troubled times of Domitian were doomed to recur; on the executions of four ex-consuls early in his imperial career, see A. R. Birley, *Hadrian: The Restless Emperor*, London-New York: Routledge, 1997, pp. 86–87.

merely record events, without any comment or interpretive, editorializing work; it might well be all too easy for some to embellish and "enhance" the bare record of events with more or less elaborated prose.[15]

Saint Jerome's commentary on the prophet Zechariah includes the detail that thirty books of Tacitus' histories were extant in his day; an old view was that this referred to sixteen books of the *Annales* and fourteen of the *Historiae*, though it seems impossible to imagine that Tacitus intended to finish his narrative of Nero's last two years in what would likely have been a massive Book XVI.[16]

Tacitus had storied predecessors, both Greek and Latin, whose works served as both challenge and inspiration.[17] Certainly, there were the examples of both Livy and Sallust. The latter composed a history of Rome that survives only in fragments; it appears to have been a continuation of the lost work of Lucius Cornelius Sisenna. More famous are the surviving Sallustian monographs on the Catilinarian conspiracy of 63 B.C. and the war with Jugurtha; these in particular afford evidence to demonstrate the great influence on Tacitus of not only the republican historian, but also of the mutually inspirational Greek historian Thucydides. We do well to remember that relatively little Roman historiography survives; other than Sallust and Livy and some fragmentary remains of greater or lesser length,[18] there is no surviving historical work of the late republic and early empire other

---

[15] The field of early Roman historical writing is highly contentious and the province of vigorous debate; the surviving evidence has been subjected to rigorous study and scholarly argumentation. Invaluable are the two three-volume collections of the fragmentary historians by Martine Chassignet in the French Budé series, and by T. J. Cornell for Oxford University Press (with extensive commentary).

[16] See here also J. N. Adams, "Were the Later Books of Tacitus' *Annals* Revised?," in *Rheinisches Museum für Philologie* 117.3/4 (1974), pp. 323–333, with particular to the much studied question of the apparent changes in style and vocabulary in the later movements of the *Annales*; cf. the same author's "The Language of the Later Books of Tacitus' *Annals*," in *The Classical Quarterly* 22.2 (1972), pp. 350–373.

[17] A useful start for reference here is Andrew Feldherr's *The Cambridge Companion to the Roman Historians* (Cambridge, 2009), with chapters by John Dillery on the intertexts between Roman and Greek historians; also by Caroline Vout on representations of the emperor in Roman history; and by Gavin Kelly on the debt of Ammianus Marcellinus to Tacitus.

[18] Gary Forsythe sums up the problem well:

> Livy's first ten books are by far our single most important ancient source for early Roman history, but Livy's account of early Rome was itself the culmination of a complex historiographical process that spanned nearly 200 years. Although there survive numerous fragments from the lost histories of Livy's annalistic predecessors, the material is far from complete, so that more often than not we are left to deal with Livy's account of a particular episode that can sometimes be supplemented by the parallel narrative of Dionysius of Halicarnassus or information from Plutarch, Cicero, or some other source.

(G. Forsythe, *Livy and Early Rome: A Study in Historical Method and Judgment*, Stuttgart: Franz Steiner Verlag, 1999, p. 12).

than the *Historiae Romanae* of Velleius Paterculus, the early-first-century A.D. composer of a history from Rome's origins down to his own, Tiberian times—and it too is incomplete.[19] And, too, there were the rather different works of Gaius Julius Caesar, his so-called *commentarii* on the Gallic and civil wars; these are not histories in the strict sense, or at least, we might say, in the sense of Livian or Tacitean histories—but they, too, exercised an incalculable influence on the author of the *Annales*.[20]

The *Historiae* begin with the account of the so-called Long Year, that is, A.D. 69—the dramatic sequence of civil conflicts that befell Rome in the wake of the downfall of Nero. This was the infamous year of the four emperors: Galba, Otho, Vitellius, and finally the ultimate victor, the Flavian Vespasian. The plan of the *Historiae* was to continue to the assassination of Domitian, we might think; it would, in short, have been a Flavian successor to the Julio-Claudian *Annales*, and following in much the same pattern (with the drama of the death of a dynasty in the wake of Domitian's assassination as its likely close).[21] We possess Books I–IV, and an all too brief part of Book V; what we have covers the year 69 and part of 70—a quarter century or so remained for Tacitus to cover. Whether it was intended to be in twelve or more books is impossible to determine definitively. There was possibly an attempt in the fourth century at a continuation of the work by Ammianus Marcellinus, perhaps in thirty-six books; eighteen survive, which cover the difficult years 353–378 and provide an invaluable source for the history of that otherwise poorly served and attested period.[22]

---

[19] Uncertain is the relationship between Tacitus' work and the imperfectly preserved Alexander history of Quintus Curtius Rufus, which is of uncertain (but probably first century A.D.) date. On this see further A. B. Bosworth, "Mountain and Molehill? Cornelius Tacitus and Quintus Curtius," in *The Classical Quarterly* 54.2 (2004), pp. 551–567.

[20] Alain Gowing observes that:

Sallust ... writes on the cusp of the transition from Republican to imperial historical writing ... Livy ... is arguably the first imperial historian ... In Sallust Tacitus found an entirely congenial personality, and really the first Roman historian who may be said to have exercised considerable and readily observable influence on him. We should not underrate the importance to Tacitus of Caesar the author ... but, if Tacitus admired Caesar's authority ... the author whom he most revered for his skill as a writer was Sallust, identified in the *Annals* as "the most brilliant author in Roman history," "rerum Romanarum florentissimus auctor." (*A.* 3.30.2)

(A. M. Gowing, "From the Annalists to the *Annales*: Latin Historiography Before Tacitus," in A. J. Woodman, ed., *The Cambridge Companion to Tacitus*, Cambridge, 2009, p. 22).

[21] Cf. here E. O'Gorman, "Shifting Ground: Lucan, Tacitus, and the Landscape of Civil War," in *Hermathena* 158 (1995), pp. 117–131 (with consideration of the organization of the *Historiae* and speculation on how it may have been intended to end).

[22] See further G. Kelly, *Ammianus Marcellinus: The Elusive Historian*, Cambridge, 2008; note L. E. Wilshire, "Did Ammianus Marcellinus Write a Continuation of Tacitus?," in *The Classical Journal* 68.3 (1973), pp. 221–227.

The *opera minora* or "minor works" of Tacitus are three: the aforementioned *Agricola*, as well as the *Germania* and the *Dialogus de oratoribus*. The *Germania* or (more fully) *De origine et situ Germanorum* is an invaluable ethnographic treatment of Rome's northern neighbors, just as the *De vita et moribus Iulii Agricolae* offers insights into the history and culture of Roman Britain.[23] The *Dialogus* is a treatise on the art of rhetoric or public speaking; it stands apart from the rest of the Tacitean corpus not least in subject matter.[24]

The Neronian *Annales* is one of the most important surviving sources of information for the reign of the last of the Julio-Claudians.[25] Nero had a lengthy reign of some fourteen years (54–68), though he spent the first five in the shadow of his mother Agrippina. Born on December 15, 37, Nero was only seventeen when his adopted father Claudius was poisoned; he would die before his thirty-first birthday. Tacitus' *Annales* and the later biography of Suetonius offer what has become the unforgettable account of an increasingly mad despot, of a man consumed with artistic pretensions and aspirations and overwhelmed by anxiety and fear for the security of his reign. Scholars

[23] The bibliography on both works is extensive. For the *Agricola*, there is a Cambridge "green and yellow" commentary of Woodman and Kraus (Cambridge, 2014); the Clarendon Ancient History series has a volume on the *Germania* by J. B. Rives (Oxford, 1999). For the harrowing story of the misappropriation of the *Germania* through history, see C. B. Krebs, *A Most Dangerous Book: Tacitus' Germania from the Roman Empire to the Third Reich*, New York-London: W. W. Norton & Company, 2011.

[24] For an argument that the *Dialogus* presents a carefully constructed account of the development of literature, see D. S. Levene, "Tacitus' *Dialogus* as Literary History," in *Transactions of the American Philological Association* 134.1 (2004), pp. 157–200. There is a "green and yellow" edition of the *Dialogus* by Roland Mayer (Cambridge, 2011).

[25] The bibliography is extensive. Michael Grant's *Nero: Emperor in Revolt* (New York: American Heritage, 1970) is a well-written, popular general guide. Miriam Griffin's *Nero: The End of a Dynasty* (London: B. T. Batsford Ltd., 1984; reprinted edition 1996) provides a more scholarly appraisal. Edward Champlin's *Nero* (Cambridge, Massachusetts: Harvard University Press, 2005; original publication, 2003) "is a glittering achievement badly in need of a subtitle" (Paul Roche in *Bryn Mawr Classical Review*), a work of learning and sensitive analysis that adds immeasurably to our understanding of this perennially fascinating figure. Important on the dramatic interplay of senate and aristocracy with Nero the stage actor is Shadi Bartsch's *Actors in the Audience: Theatricality and Double-Speak from Nero to Hadrian*, Cambridge, MA: Harvard University Press, 1994. Anthony Barrett's *Agrippina: Sex, Power, and Poliics in the Early Roman Empire*, New Haven, CT: Yale University Press, 1996, has much of interest and value. The Suetonian life of Nero has received a commentary by B. H. Warmington (*Suetonius: Nero*, Bristol Classical Press, 1977); this can be useful in league with the same author's 1969 *Nero: Reality and Legend* (London: Chatto and Windus). More detailed is K. R. Bradley's *Suetonius' Life of Nero: An Historical Commentary*, Bruxelles: Editions Latomus, 1978 . E. Mary Smallwood's volume *Documents Illustrating the Principates of Gaius, Claudius, and Nero* (Cambridge, 1967) gathers various important texts and inscriptions, though without translations; it has been reprinted as part of the Cambridge paperback reprint program. Note too the Blackwell Companion to the Neronian Age edited by Emma Buckley and Martin Dinter (2013).

have sometimes been tempted to identify "turning points" in the rule of the young *princeps* that mark this or that more or less irrevocable tendency toward tyranny; certainly, the death of Agrippina by imperial matricide in 59 is one such a balefully fateful moment, and so too the progress and exposing of the Pisonian conspiracy of 65 that led to the enforced suicides of the authors Lucan, Seneca, and Petronius. The Nero we meet in Tacitus' last extant book is still very much preoccupied with the aftermath of the threat to his rule from the recently revealed Pisonian plot; the climate in Rome is one of dread and sycophancy, resignation and righteous indignation in the face of an evermore oppressive atmosphere of threats to republican freedom and Roman *libertas*.

In a perverse sense, Nero was the most "literary" of the Julio-Claudians, certainly in the realm of poetry and drama and the patronage of writers. His interests were in verse, not in the lengthy histories that attracted his stepfather Claudius; his passion was epic and lyric competition, not to mention the world of athletic competition, of horse and chariot racing. In the poetic arena, he was confronted with the poetic rival Lucan; his tutor Seneca—the uncle of the poet of the civil war of Caesar and Pompey—was a distinguished man of letters, with an impressive corpus of tragic works to his name. Lucan's theme for his own *magnum opus* was arguably a risky one; he endeavored to write an epic on the internecine conflict between the republican hero-martyr Pompey and the assassinated luminary of the Julian *gens*, the adoptive father of the great Augustus and the first of the Caesars, as it were.[26]

Annales XVI is incomplete; it constitutes Tacitus' final surviving words on Nero. When the book opens, the emperor has found time amid the prosecutions and trials of Pisonian conspirators and sympathizers to be lost in a world of mythological fancy and ancient lore: he has learned that the gold of the Carthaginian queen Dido has been discovered in North Africa.[27] Acquisition of the gold would not only secure Nero's difficult financial

---

[26] And Tacitus, too, is a poetic artist, indeed a consummate master of poetic tricks in the art of historical composition. Cf. the observation of Ronald Mellor:

> Tacitus not only provides dramatic vignettes; he includes in his history the devices familiar from Greek tragedy ... He makes dramatic use of silence: the silence of shame, the silence of terror, or the ominous silence of abandonment ... Omens and portents foreshadow future events, while the weather and other natural phenomena reflect human conflicts ... The Olympian gods of Homer or Vergil have no place in such an intrinsically skeptical writer; only Fortune appears as Nemesis might in Greek tragedy.

(*Tacitus*, London-New York: Routledge, 1993, p. 121).

[27] Cf. here V. Rimell, *The Closure of Space in Roman Poetics: Empire's Inward Turn*, Cambridge, 2015, p. 67 : "We start from a revision of Dido's dream ... which in Tacitus comes to stand for deceptive, seductive composition of stories ..."

prospects in the wake of his penchant for excessive spending, but would also make his name in terms of the antiquarian history of Rome and the Julian family—and, not least, in the world of the romance of poetry and epic. Dido's gold was a treasure that evoked the splendor of the Virgilian *Aeneid*, that instant classic of Roman verse; its discovery and recovery would place the *princeps* Nero in the tradition of his Julian ancestor Aeneas and his divine mother Venus. The poet Lucan described a visit of Caesar to the site of the once great city of Troy in the ninth book of his epic; North Africa had been the scene of victories of Caesar over the Pompeians who survived the battle at Pharsalus. Now Nero would take his place in the history of the Julians and of Rome by seizing the gold that had once been buried by the great Elissa or Dido, the founder of the city that would prove to be Rome's inveterate enemy through disaster and war. And with the boon and windfall of gold would come the dawn of another new Golden Age, a rebirth of peace and prosperity for a Rome united under the power of its poet-prince.[28] The Golden Age motif was central to the literary and artistic propaganda of the Augustan revival; it would recur under Nero, though with the benefit of Tacitean hindsight, by 66 Nero was steadily drawing nearer to the end.

The Didonian gold, no surprise, was a farce; Nero was the victim of the caprice of Fortune and his own gullibility. The rest of what survives of Book XVI is concerned principally with the continuing persecution of perceived enemies of the state; it reaches noteworthy heights of memorable narrative and dramatic stage setting in the suicides of Petronius and Thrasea Paetus. Indeed, in some regards it is a book of suicide, of the grim catalogue of those who were forced to take their own lives in a world where exile and loss of property rights was a comparatively mild form of punishment. The victims of Nero's purge are mostly senators and equestrians—men of the same rank and status as Tacitus and his friend Pliny—and also the wives and daughters of the luckless men. Rome is mired in something of a civil war; there are soldiers and armed guards outside the *curia* of the senate, and both military and civil officials—centurions and quaestors—are sent on missions to give the order to this or that noble man to choose his *arbitrium mortis* or choice of manner of death.

And amid the seemingly endless catalogue of deaths and executions, suicides and despair there are the questions of philosophy and theology: the

---

[28] Throughout Book XVI of his *Annales*, Tacitus alludes to the poetic and performative escapades of the *princeps*; it is thought that one of the favorite themes of the emperor was the fall of Troy—the subject of the second book of Virgil's epic, and a story of particular attraction to a descendant of the Julian *gens*. For the scattered, very slender, indeed, remains of Nero's verse, see E. Courtney, *The Fragmentary Latin Poets*, Oxford, 1993 (corrected paperback edition, 2003).

ultimate destiny of the human soul and its fate after the death of the body, and the reaction of the immortals to the scene that is unfolding in the capital of the world. The debates of Stoics, Epicureans, Cynics, and Skeptics are on display, too; the apparent wrath of the gods in the face of the degradation of an evermore decadent Rome—or, chillingly, perhaps in league with the work of the would-be god Nero—is glimpsed even in tempestuous weather and natural disaster.[29] It was an age where a daughter could be forced to take her own life for the crime of having consulted a magician about the destiny of her doomed father; it was a time where the Roman virtue of *pietas* or loyalty to family and friends could be given ample opportunity for display and ultimate devotion. The characteristic virtue of Virgil's Aeneas has been transformed in the course of the long history of the Julio-Claudians; in *Annales* XVI *pietas* now means inquiring into the horoscope and destiny of one's father in a desperate, futile hope for his salvation, and dying together with one's relatives, in one bedroom and with one dagger.

Tacitus' last surviving book stands forth along the way as a narrative of rival poets and dramatists, of this or that imperiled victim of Nero emerging as a theatrical threat to the artistic preeminence of the violent, furious *princeps*. In a time when the *exempla* or "examples" of constancy and devotion to honor and loyalty were both needed and in abundance, Nero is upstaged again and again in a series of dramatic death *tableaux*, stage-managed suicides and deaths that impress themselves on the memory of the reader more effectively than the citharoedic escapades of a madman. The book opens with Fortune making sport of the *princeps* in a context of mythological mystery and the ancient legends and history of Rome and her Mediterranean neighbors; at once it continues with the image of Nero taking the stage and wishing to compete in the theatrical contests and events of his Neronian or quinquennial games. The senate is depicted as trying to dissuade Nero from indulging his artistic fetishes; the concern was to maintain some modicum of decency and respect for his office, especially in the wake of the great embarrassment about Dido's treasure. Nero, of course, will have none of it, and insists on performing and continuing his dramatic pursuits—but

---

[29] Tacitus deftly eludes any attempt to impose a rigid system of classification on his theology or divine machinery. "Tacitus' use of such phrases [as *ira deum*], as well as terms like *fatum* and *fors*, is indeed erratic, and is determined most of all by the terms' value to a given context in his narrative" (T. A. Joseph, *Tacitus the Epic Successor: Virgil, Lucan, and the Narrative of Civil War in the Histories*, Leiden-Boston, 2012, p. 67). One of the historian's consistent points of the reference is the image of the emperor as god; Nero and Jupiter, for example, can be seen to be conflated into one eminently ironic deity in the closing moments of Thrasea Paetus' life. In the criticism of Nero's pursuit of luxury and wealth, there may be an echo of the Epicurean condemnation of the same.

what the rest of the surviving Book XVI reveals is a series of rival dramas that threaten the artistic crown of the doomed emperor.

The *Annales*, like so much of Tacitus' work, is also an epic history of the power of memory. The historian—like the epic poet—recalls the events of the past and offers vivid commentary on the contemporary world of politics and foreign affairs, and moral *exempla* for individual contemplation and consideration. "The verb Tacitus must often uses to denote what he is doing is *memorare*."[30] At the close of the second chapter[31] of his *Agricola*, Tacitus notes hauntingly:

> dedimus profecto grande patientiae documentum; et sicut vetas aetas vidit quid ultimum in libertate esset, ita nos quid in servitute, adempto per inquisitiones etiam loquendi audiendique commercio. memoriam quoque ipsam cum voce perdidissemus, si tam in nostra potestate esset oblivisci quam tacere.

> We have provided then a great testimony to endurance: and just as a bygone age saw the ultimate in liberty, so we have seen the ultimate in slavery, with even commerce in speaking and listening taken away by investigative inquiries. We would have lost memory also along with voice, were it as much in our power to forget as to remain silent.[32]

Tacere, perhaps, was chosen as the crowning word of the sentiment out of a sense of irony, given his own name.[33] Tacitus refers here to the experience

---

[30] A. M. Gowing, *Empire and Memory: The Representation of the Roman Republic in Imperial Culture*, Cambridge, 2005, p. 12.

[31] "Chapter" is a convenient, if inaccurate and potentially misleading, designation for the individual "paragraphs" of Tacitus' text, divisions that do not date back to the author, but rather to his Renaissance and later editors. See further here S. Bartera, "Commentary Writing on the *Annals* of Tacitus," in C. S. Kraus and C. Stray, eds., *Classical Commentaries: Explorations in a Scholarly Genre*, Oxford, 2016, p. 120n44 . Bartera's chapter is a masterful survey of Tacitean commentaries (both "school" and "scholarly"), with exhaustive detail and judicious remarks.

[32] Translation my own. There are complete editions of Tacitus in the Penguin Classics and Oxford World's Classics Series; in the latter set, the 2008 *Annales* of J. C. Yardley (with introduction and notes by Anthony Barrett) provides a reliable rendering and useful commentary (including valuable appended material on Roman institutions).

[33] the issue of silence is emphasized in Tacitus' relationship to his sources, in his decision to talk about what others have left unrecorded, and even in his own style of writing. The theme is finally elevated to a virtual principle of his historical method. The connection between silence and anger, or oppression, provides the motivation for his practice of history and is illustrated in his accounts of earlier historians who spoke unmentionable truths and suffered the consequences.

(C. W. Hedrick,Jr., *History and Silence: Purge and Rehabilitation of Memory in Late Antiquity*, Austin: The University of Texas Press, 2000, p. 162).

of the Domitianic tyranny, when silence could purchase not only survival, but also career success, relative security, and advancement; the persistence of memory becomes a powerful incentive to historical inquiry and reflection, as well as to emotions of guilt and self-recrimination.[34] Book XVI of the *Annales* contains a powerful authorial comment on the perception that his lengthy and repetitive record of just such *inquisitiones* may bring tedium; chapter sixteen of the book has its fair share of interpretive difficulties, but the historian seems clearly enough to be asking the indulgence of his audience if he cannot bring himself to hate those who quietly went to their deaths as if slaves to imperial will and wrath.[35] One of the key questions of the *Annales* is the degree to which memory can be translated or converted into history.[36] The very repetitive nature of the senatorial and equestrian *inquisitiones* of the period after the Pisonian conspiracy serves as a mnemonic device that preserves the *exempla* of great constancy and fortitude in the face of the oppression and suppression of *libertas*; for Tacitus, there is no need of a Muse to recall the events of the Tiberian or Neronian reigns, since he saw much the same thing under Domitian. And we do well to remember that just as the "ultimate" in servility and slavery can be a bad thing, so too can the ultimate in freedom and liberty—as the student of the history of the Roman Republic learns all too quickly and well.[37]

Tacitus will be the voice of the memory of the experience of servility: *non tamen pigebit vel incondita ac rudi voce memoriam prioris servitutis ac praesentium bonorum composuisse (Agricola, c. 3).*[38] And it may well be that

---

[34] Memory is also linked by Tacitus with the visual; there will be several instances that highlight this connection in *Annales* XVI, most notably at the very end of the extant book. See further J. Grethlein, *Experience and Teleology in Ancient Historiography: "Futures Past" from Herodotus to Augustine*, Cambridge, 2013, pp. 139 ff.

[35] On the relationship of the *Agricola* to the author's later works, note D. Sailor, "Becoming Tacitus: Significance and Inconsequentiality in the *Agricola*," in *Classical Antiquity* 23.1 (2004), pp. 139–177.

[36] Cf. here E. O'Gorman, *Irony and Misreading in the Annals of Tacitus*, Cambridge, 2000, p. 177 . The Tacitean Petronius will implicate the *princeps* in a veritable confrontation of memory in his sending to Nero a detailed account of the names and acts of *flagitia* of which he was made aware.

[37] For a good overview of the vast problems associated with Tacitean use of *exempla* and the composition of what we might call a "moral history," see D. J. Kapust, *Republicanism, Rhetoric, and Roman Political Thought: Sallust, Livy, and Tacitus*, Cambridge, 2011, pp. 111 ff. On the Tacitean portrayal of liberty and slavery with respect to the emperor and his court, see J. Percival, "Tacitus and the Principate," in *Greece & Rome* 27.2 (1980), pp. 119–133.

[38] "Even while Tacitus was putting the finishing touches to the *Dialogus*, he must have been contemplating the nature of his next project. There is a hint as early as the *Agricola* that he was aiming at a historical narrative as the culmination of his literary career." (R. Ash, *Ancients in Action: Tacitus*, London: Bristol Classical Press, 2006, p. 52). On the

the reference to *incondita ac rudi voce* is not merely an artistic aim at self-deprecation, but rather a nod to the idea that a composition about the depths of servile behavior might require language that reflects the debased state of aristocratic slavery.

There is ample scope for consideration of servility in the *Annales*, and also for glimpses of resistance and *exempla* of fierce opposition to tyranny, scenes that help to explain something of the persistent afterlife of the work. The extant portion of Book XVI closes with a scene of suicide that includes a pointed commentary for the few witnesses of the last moments of the Stoic Thrasea Paetus. The dying senator pours out blood from his open veins, and sprinkles the gore on the ground with a word of offering to Jupiter in his capacity as liberator and bringer of freedom. The act of offering and words of seeming defiance to Nero are an imitation of moments from the death scene of Seneca that offered a dramatic high point in the preceding book; it is also presented as an implicit challenge to the young quaestor who witnesses it. The minor official had been sent to bring the news of the senatorial deliberations and decrees to the condemned man; Tacitus notably does not even bother to provide his name or any hint as to his identity—he is merely another functionary in a long line of imperial servants. He is offered a front row seat, as it were, for the drama of Thrasea Paetus, who dramatically invites his guest to gaze on the scene: *specta, iuvenis*. The spectacle is an implicit challenge for those who would remain silent in the face of oppression, let alone to those who—like the *quaestor*—were in greater or lesser ways actively collaborative in Neronian rule; Tacitus himself would, after all, be a quaestor in the reign of Nero's eventual successor Vespasian. In this, as often in the *Annales*, there is cathartic self-commentary and reflection, we might think, from the historian who lived and even prospered under his own madman.

---

value of the *Agricola* in understanding better Tacitus' later program, see R. Ash, "Tacitus and the Battle of Mons Graupius: A Historiographical Route Map?," in J. Marincola, *A Companion to Greek and Roman Historiography*, Malden, MA: Wiley-Blackwell, 2011 (paperback reprint of the 2007 original), pp. 434 ff.

Text

Figure 3 Inside the Théâtre Antique, Arles, France. © Katelyn McGarr.

1. Inlusit dehinc Neroni fortuna per vanitatem ipsius et promissa Caeselli Bassi, qui origine Poenus, mente turbida, nocturnae quietis imaginem per spem haud dubiae rei traxit, vectusque Romam, principis aditum emercatus, expromit repertum in agro suo specum altitudine immensa, quo magna vis auri contineretur, non in formam pecuniae sed rudi et antiquo pondere. lateres quippe praegravis iacere, adstantibus parte alia columnis; quae per tantum aevi occulta augendis praesentibus bonis. ceterum, ut coniectura demonstrabat, Dido Phoenissam Tyro profugam condita Carthagine illas opes abdidisse, ne

novus populus nimia pecunia lasciveret aut reges Numidarum, et alias infensi, cupidine auri ad bellum accenderentur.

2. Igitur Nero, non auctoris, non ipsius negotii fide satis spectata nec missis per quos nosceret an vera adferrentur, auget ultro rumorem mittitque qui velut paratam praedam adveherent. dantur triremes et delectum remigium iuvandae festinationi. nec aliud per illos dies populus credulitate, prudentes diversa fama tulere. ac forte quinquennale ludicrum secundo lustro celebrabatur, ab oratoribusque praecipua materia in laudem principis adsumpta est. non enim solitas tantum fruges nec confusum metallis aurum gigni, sed nova ubertate provenire terram et obvias opes deferre deos, quaeque alia summa facundia nec minore adulatione servilia fingebant, securi de facilitate credentis.

3. Gliscebat interim luxuria spe inani consumebanturque veteres opes quasi oblatis quas multos per annos prodigeret. quin et inde iam largiebatur; et divitiarum expectatio inter causas paupertatis publicae erat. nam Bassus effosso agro suo latisque circum arvis, dum hunc vel illum locum promissi specus adseverat, sequunturque non modo milites sed populus agrestium efficiendo operi adsumptus, tandem posita vaecordia, non falsa ante somnia sua seque tunc primum elusum admirans, pudorem et metum morte voluntaria effugit. quidam vinctum ac mox dimissum tradidere ademptis bonis in locum regiae gazae.

4. Interea senatus propinquo iam lustrali certamine, ut dedecus averteret, offert imperatori victoriam cantus adicitque facundiae coronam qua ludicra deformitas velaretur. sed Nero nihil ambitu nec potestate senatus opus esse dictitans, se aequum adversum aemulos et religione iudicum meritam laudem adsecturum, primo carmen in scaena recitat; mox flagitante vulgo ut omnia studia sua publicaret (haec enim verba dixere) ingreditur theatrum, cunctis citharae legibus obtemperans, ne fessus resideret, ne sudorem nisi ea quam indutui gerebat veste detergeret, ut nulla oris aut narium excrementa viserentur. postremo flexus genu et coetum illum manu veneratus

sententias iudicum opperiebatur ficto pavore. et plebs quidem urbis, histrionum quoque gestus iuvare solita, personabat certis modis plausuque composito. crederes laetari, ac fortasse laetabantur per incuriam publici flagitii.

5. Sed qui remotis e municipiis severaque adhuc et antiqui moris retinente Italia, quique per longinquas provincias lascivia inexperti officio legationum aut privata utilitate advenerant, neque aspectum illum tolerare neque labori inhonesto sufficere, cum manibus nesciis fatiscerent, turbarent gnaros ac saepe a militibus verberarentur, qui per cuneos stabant ne quod temporis momentum impari clamore aut silentio segni praeteriret. constitit plerosque equitum, dum per angustias aditus et ingruentem multitudinem enituntur, obtritos, et alios, dum diem noctemque sedilibus continuant, morbo exitiali correptos. quippe gravior inerat metus, si spectaculo defuissent, multis palam et pluribus occultis, ut nomina ac vultus, alacritatem tristitiamque coeuntium scrutarentur. unde tenuioribus statim inrogata supplicia, adversum inlustris dissimulatum ad praesens et mox redditum odium. ferebantque Vespasianum, tamquam somno coniveret, a Phoebo liberto increpitum aegreque meliorum precibus obtectum, mox imminentem perniciem maiore fato effugisse.

6. Post finem ludicri Poppaea mortem obiit, fortuita mariti iracundia, a quo gravida ictu calcis adflicta est. neque enim venenum crediderim, quamvis quidam scriptores tradant, odio magis quam ex fide: quippe liberorum cupiens et amori uxoris obnoxius erat. corpus non igni abolitum, ut Romanus mos, sed regum externorum consuetudine differtum odoribus conditur tumuloque Iuliorum infertur. ductae tamen publicae exequiae laudavitque ipse apud rostra formam eius et quod divinae infantis parens fuisset aliaque fortunae munera pro virtutibus.

7. Mortem Poppaeae ut palam tristem, ita recordantibus laetam ob impudicitiam eius saevitiamque, nova insuper invidia Nero complevit prohibendo C. Cassium officio exequiarum, quod primum indicium mali. neque enim in longum dilatum est, sed Silanus additur, nullo crimine nisi quod Cassius opibus vetustis et gravitate morum, Silanus

claritudine generis et modesta iuventa praecellebant. igitur missa ad senatum oratione removendos a re publica utrosque disseruit, obiectavitque Cassio quod inter imagines maiorum etiam C. Cassi effigiem coluisset, ita inscriptam "duci partium": quippe semina belli civilis et defectionem a domo Caesarum quaesitam; ac *ne* memoria tantum infensi nominis ad discordias uteretur, adsumpsisse L. Silanum, iuvenem genere nobilem, animo praeruptum, quem novis rebus ostentaret.

8. Ipsum dehinc Silanum increpuit isdem quibus patruum eius Torquatum, tamquam disponeret imperii curas praeficeretque rationibus et libellis et epistulis libertos, inania simul et falsa: nam Silanus intentior metu et exitio patrui ad praecavendum exterritus erat. inducti posthac vocabulo indicum qui in Lepidam, Cassii uxorem, Silani amitam, incestum cum fratris filio et diros sacrorum ritus confingerent. trahebantur ut conscii Vulcacius Tullinus ac Marcellus Cornelius senatores et Calpurnius Fabatus eques Romanus; qui appellato principe instantem damnationem frustrati, mox Neronem circa summa scelera distentum quasi minores evasere.

9. Tunc consulto senatus Cassio et Sillano exilia decernuntur: de Lepida Caesar statueret. deportatusque in insulam Sardiniam Cassium, et senectus eius expectabatur. Silanus tamquam Naxum deveheretur Ostiam amotus, post municipio Apuliae, cui nomen Barium est, clauditur. illic indignissimum casum sapienter tolerans a centurione ad caedem misso corripitur; suadentique venas abrumpere animum quidem morti destinatum ait, sed non remittere percussori gloriam ministerii. at centurio quamvis inermem, praevalidum tamen et irae quam timori propiorem cernens premi a militibus iubet. nec omisit Silanus obniti et intendere ictus, quantum manibus nudis valebat, donec a centurione vulneribus adversis in pugna caderet.

10. Haud minus prompte L. Vetus socrusque eius Sextia et Pollitta filia necem subiere, invisi principi tamquam vivendo exprobrarent interfectum esse Rubellium Plautum, generum Luci Veteris. sed initium

detegendae saevitiae praebuit interversis patroni rebus ad accusandum Fortunatus libertus, adscito Claudio Demiano, quem ob flagitia vinctum a Vetere Asiae pro consule exolvit Nero in praemium accusationis. quod ubi cognitum reo seque et libertum pari sorte componi, Formianos in agros digreditur: illic eum milites occulta custodia circumdant. aderat filia, super ingruens periculum longe dolore atrox, ex quo percussores Plauti mariti sui viderat; cruentamque cervicem eius amplexa servabat sanguinem et vestis respersas, vidua inpexa luctu continuo nec ullis alimentis nisi quae mortem arcerent. tum hortante patre Neapolim pergit; et quia aditu Neronis prohibebatur, egressus obsidens, audiret insontem neve consulatus sui quondam collegam dederet liberto, modo muliebri eiulatu, donec princeps immobilem se precibus et invidiae iuxta ostendit.

11. Ergo nuntiat patri abicere spem et uti necessitate: simul adfertur parari cognitionem senatus et trucem sententiam. nec defuere qui monerent magna ex parte heredem Caesarem nuncupare atque ita nepotibus de reliquo consulere. quod aspernatus, ne vitam proxime libertatem actam novissimo servitio foedaret, largitur in servos quantum aderat pecuniae; et si qua asportari possent, sibi quemque deducere, tres modo lectulos ad suprema retineri iubet. tunc eodem in cubiculo, eodem ferro abscindunt venas, properique et singulis vestibus ad verecundiam velati balineis inferuntur, pater filiam, avia neptem, illa utrosque intuens, et certatim precantes labenti animae celerem exitum, ut relinquerent suos superstites et morituros. servavitque ordinem fortuna, ac seniores prius, tunc cui prima aetas extinguuntur. accusati post sepulturam decretumque ut more maiorum punirentur, et Nero intercessit, mortem sine arbitrio permittens: ea caedibus peractis ludibria adiciebantur.

12. Publius Gallus eques Romanus, quod Faenio Rufo intimus et Veteri non alienus fuerat, aqua atque igni prohibitus est. liberto et accusatori praemium operae locus in theatro inter viatores tribunicios datur. et menses, qui Aprilem eundemque Neroneum sequebantur, Maius Claudii, Iunius Germanici vocabulis mutantur, testificante Cornelio

Orfito, qui id censuerat, ideo Iunium mensem transmissum, quia duo
iam Torquati ob scelera interfecti infaustum nomen Iunium fecissent.

13. Tot facinoribus foedum annum etiam dii tempestatibus et morbis
insignivere. vastata Campania turbine ventorum, qui villas arbusta
fruges passim disiecit pertulitque violentiam ad vicina urbi; in qua omne
mortalium genus vis pestilentiae depopulabatur, nulla caeli intemperie
quae occurrret oculis. sed domus corporibus exanimis, itinera funeribus
complebantur; non sexus, non aetas periculo vacua; servitia perinde
et ingenua plebes extingui, inter coniugum et liberorum lamenta, qui
dum adsident, dum deflent, saepe eodem rogo cremabantur. equitum
senatorumque interitus quamvis promisci minus flebiles erant,
tamquam communi mortalitate saevitiam principis praevenirent.

Eodem anno dilectus per Galliam Narbonensem Africamque et
Asiam habiti sunt supplendis Illyricis legionibus, ex quibus aetate
aut valetudine fessi sacramento solvebantur. cladem Lugdunensem
quadragies sestertio solatus est princeps, ut amissa urbi reponerent;
quam pecuniam Lugdunenses ante obtulerant urbis casibus.

14. C. Suetonio Luccio Telesino consulibus Antistius Sosianus, factitatis
in Neronem carminibus probrosis exilio, ut dixi, multatus, postquam
id honoris indicibus tamque promptum ad caedes principem accepit,
inquies animo et occasionum haud segnis Pammenum, eiusdem loci
exulem et Chaldaeorum arte famosum eoque multorum amicitiis
innexum, similitudine fortunae sibi conciliat, ventitare ad eum nuntios
et consultationes non frustra ratus; simul annuam pecuniam a P.
Anteio ministrari cognoscit. neque nescium habebat Anteium caritate
Agrippinae invisum Neroni opesque eius praecipuas ad eliciendam
cupidinem eamque causam multis exitio esse. igitur interceptis Antei
litteris, furatus etiam libellos, quibus dies genitalis eius et eventura
secretis Pammenis occultabantur, simul repertis quae de ortu vitaque
Ostorii Scapulae composita erant, scribit ad principem magna se et
quae incolumitati eius conducerent adlaturum, si brevem exilii veniam
impetravisset: quippe Anteium et Ostorium imminere rebus et sua

Caesarisque fata scrutari. exim missae liburnicae advehiturque propere
Sosianus. ac vulgato eius indicio inter damnatos magis quam inter reos
Anteius Ostoriusque habebantur, adeo ut testamentum Antei nemo
obsignaret, nisi Tigellinus auctor extitisset monito prius Anteio ne
supremas tabulas moraretur. atque ille hausto veneno, tarditatem eius
perosus intercisis venis mortem adproperavit.

15. Ostorius longinquis in agris apud finem Ligurum id temporis erat:
eo missus centurio qui caedem eius maturaret. causa festinandi ex
eo oriebatur quod Ostorius multa militari fama et civicam coronam
apud Britanniam meritus, ingenti corpore armorumque scientia
metum Neroni fecerat ne invaderet pavidum semper et reperta nuper
coniuratione magis exterritum. igitur centurio, ubi effugia villae clausit,
iussa imperatoris Ostorio aperit. is fortitudinem saepe adversum
hostis spectatum in se vertit; et quia venae quamquam interruptae
parum sanguinis effundebant, hactenus manu servi usus ut immotum
pugionem extolleret, adpressit dextram eius iuguloque occurrit.

16. Etiam si bella externa et obitas pro re publica mortis tanta casuum
similitudine memorarem, meque ipsum satias cepisset aliorumque
taedium expectarem, quamvis honestos civium exitus, tristis tamen et
continuos aspernantium: at nunc patientia servilis tantumque sanguinis
domi perditum fatigant animum et maestitia restringunt. neque aliam
defensionem ab iis quibus ista noscentur exegerim, quam ne oderim
tam segniter pereuntis. ira illa numinum in res Romanas fuit, quam
non, ut in cladibus exercituum aut captivitate urbium, semel edito
transire licet. detur hoc inlustrium virorum posteritati, ut quo modo
exequiis a promisca sepultura separantur, ita in traditione supremorum
accipiant habeantque propriam memoriam.

17. Paucos quippe intra dies eodem agmine Annaeus Mela, Cerialis
Anicius, Rufrius Crispinus, C. Petronius cecidere, Mela et Crispinus
equites Romani dignitate senatoria. nam hic quondam praefectus
praetorii et consularibus insignibus donatus ac nuper crimine
coniurationis in Sardiniam exactus accepto iussae mortis nuntio semet

interfecit. Mela, quibus Gallio et Seneca parentibus natus, petitione honorum abstinuerat per ambitionem praeposteram ut eques Romanus consularibus potentia aequaretur; simul adquirendae pecuniae brevius iter credebat per procurationes administrandis principis negotiis. idem Annaeum Lucanum genuerat, grande adiumentum claritudinis. quo interfecto dum rem familiarem eius acriter requirit, accusatorem concivit Fabium Romanum, ex intimis Lucani amicis. mixta inter patrem filiumque coniurationis scientia fingitur, adsimilatis Lucani litteris: quas inspectas Nero ferri ad eum iussit, opibus eius inhians. at Mela, quae tum promptissima mortis via, exolvit venas, scriptis codicillis quibus grandem pecuniam in Tigellinum generumque eius Cossutianum Capitonem erogabat quo cetera manerent. additur codicillis, tamquam de iniquitate exitii querens ita scripsisset, se quidem mori nullis supplicii causis, Rufrium Crispinum et Anicium Cerialem vita frui infensos principi. quae composita credebantur de Crispino, quia interfectus erat, de Ceriale, ut interficeretur. neque enim multo post vim sibi attulit, minore quam ceteri miseratione, quia proditam C. Caesari coniurationem ab eo meminerant.

18. De C. Petronio pauca supra repetenda sunt. nam illi dies per somnum, nox officiis et oblectamentis vitae transigebatur; ut alios industria, ita hunc ignavia ad famam protulerat, habebaturque non ganeo et profligator, ut plerique sua haurientium, sed erudito luxu. ac dicta factaque eius quanto solutiora et quandam sui neglegentiam praeferentia, tanto gratius in speciem simplicitatis accipiebantur. proconsul tamen Bithyniae et mox consul vigentem se ac parem negotiis ostendit. dein revolutus ad vitia seu vitiorum imitatione inter paucos familiarium Neroni adsumptus est, elegantiae arbiter, dum nihil amoenum et molle adfluentia putat, nisi quod ei Petronius adprobavisset. unde invidia Tigellini quasi adversus aemulum et scientia voluptatum potiorem. ergo crudelitatem principis, cui ceterae libidines cedebant, adgreditur, amicitiam Scaevini Petronio obiectans, corrupto ad indicium servo ademptaque defensione et maiore parte familiae in vincla rapta.

19. Forte illis diebus Campaniam petiverat Caesar, et Cumas usque progressus Petronius illic attinebatur; nec tulit ultra timoris aut spei moras. neque tamen praeceps vitam expulit, sed incisas venas, ut libitum, obligatas aperire rursum et adloqui amicos, non per seria aut quibus gloriam constantiae peteret. audiebatque referentis nihil de immortalitate animae et sapientium placitis, sed levia carmina et facilis versus. servorum alios largitione, quosdam verberibus adfecit. iniit epulas, somno indulsit, ut quamquam coacta mors fortuitae similis esset. ne codicillis quidem, quod plerique pereuntium, Neronem aut Tigellinum aut quem alium potentium adulatus est, sed flagitia principis sub nominibus exoletorum feminarumque et novitatem cuiusque stupri perscripsit atque obsignata misit Neroni. fregitque anulum ne mox usui esset ad facienda pericula.

20. Ambigenti Neroni quonam modo noctium suarum ingenia notescerent, offertur Silia, matrimonio senatoris haud ignota et ipsi ad omnem libidinem adscita ac Petronio perquam familiaris. agitur in exilium tamquam non siluisset quae viderat pertuleratque, proprio odio. at Minucium Thermum praetura functum Tigellini simultatibus dedit, quia libertus Thermi quaedam de Tigellino criminose detulerat, quae cruciatibus tormentorum ipse, patronus eius nece immerita luere.

21. Trucidatis tot insignibus viris ad postremum virtutem ipsam exscindere concupivit interfecto Thrasea Paeto et Barea Sorano, olim utrisque infensus et accendentibus causis in Thraseam, quod senatu egressus est cum de Agrippinae referretur, ut memoravi, quodque Iuvenalium ludicro parum spectabilem operam praebuerat; eaque offensio altius penetrabat, quia idem Thrasea Patavi, unde ortus est, ludis cetastis a Troiano Antenore institutis habitu tragico cecinerat. die quoque quo praetor Antistius ob probra in Neronem composita ad mortem damnabatur, mitiora censuit obtinuitque; et cum deum honores Poppaeae decernuntur sponte absens, funeri non interfuerat. quae oblitterari non sinebat Capito Cossutianus, praeter animum ad flagitia praecipitem iniquus Thraseae quod auctoritate eius concidisset, iuvantis Cilicum legatos dum Capitonem repetundarum interrogant.

22. Quin et illa subiectabat, principio anni vitare Thraseam sollemne ius iurandum; nuncupationibus votorum non adesse, quamvis quindecimvirali sacerdotio praeditum; numquam pro salute principis aut caelesti voce immolavisse; adsiduum olim et indefessum, qui vulgaribus quoque patrum consultis semet fautorem aut adversarium ostenderet, triennio non introisse curiam; nuperrimeque, cum ad coercendos Silanum et Veterem certatim concurreretur, privatis potius clientium negotiis vacavisse. secessionem iam id et partis et, si idem multi audeant, bellum esse. "ut quondam C. Caesarem" inquit 'et M. Catonem, ita nunc te, Nero, et Thraseam avida discordiarum civitas loquitur. et habet sectatores vel potius satellites, qui nondum contumaciam sententiarum, sed habitum vultumque sectantur, rigidi et tristes, quo tibi lasciviam exprobrent. huic uni incolumitas tua sine cura, artes sine honore. prospera principis respuit: etiamne luctibus et doloribus non satiatur? eiusdem animi et Poppaeaem divam non credere, cuius in acta divi Augusti et divi Iuli non iurare. spernit religiones, abrogat leges. diurna populi Romani per provincias, per exercitus curatius leguntur, ut noscatur quid Thrasea non fecerit. aut transeamus ad illa instituta, si potiora sunt, aut nova cupientibus auferatur dux et auctor. ista secta Tuberones et Favonios, veteri quoque rei publicae ingrata nomina, genuit. ut imperium evertant libertatem praeferunt: si perverterint, libertatem ipsam adgredientur. frustra Cassium amovisti, si gliscere et vigere Brutorum aemulos passurus es. denique nihil ipse de Thrasea scripseris: disceptatorem senatum nobis relinque.' extollit ira promptum Cossutiani animum Nero adicitque Marcellum Eprium acri eloquentia.

23. At Baream Soranum iam sibi Ostorius Sabinus eques Romanus poposcerat reum ex proconsulatu Asiae, in quo offensiones principis auxit iustitia atque industria, et quia portui Ephesiorum aperiendo curam insumpserat vimque civitatis Pergamenae prohibentis Acratum, Caesaris libertum, statuas et picturas evehere inultam omiserat. sed crimini dabatur amicitia Plauti et ambitio conciliandae provinciae ad spes novas. tempus damnationi delectum, quo Tiridates accipiendo

Armeniae regno adventabat, ut ad externa rumoribus intestinum scelus obscuraretur, an ut magnitudinem imperatoriam caede insignium virorum quasi regio facinore ostentaret.

24. Igitur omni civitate ad excipiendum principem spectandumque regem effusa, Thrasea occursu prohibitus non demisit animum, sed codicillos ad Neronem composuit, requirens obiecta et expurgaturum adseverans, si notitiam criminum et copiam diluendi habuisset. eos codicillos Nero properanter accepit, spe exterritum Thraseam scripsisse, per quae claritudinem principis extolleret suamque famam dehonestaret. quod ubi non evenit vultumque et spiritus et libertatem insontis ultro extimuit, vocari patres iubet.

25. Tum Thrasea inter proximos consultavit, temptaretne defensionem an sperneret. diversa consilia adferebantur. quibus intrari curiam placebat, securos esse de constantia eius disserunt; nihil dicturum nisi quo gloriam augeret. segnis et pavidos supremis suis secretum circumdare: aspiceret populus virum morti obnoxium, audiret senatus voces quasi ex aliquo numine supra humanas: posse ipso miraculo etiam Neronem permoveri: sin crudelitati insisteret, distingui certe apud posteros memoriam honesti exitus ab ignavia per silentium pereuntium.

26. Contra qui opperiendum domi censebant, de ipso Thrasea eadem, sed ludibria et contumelias imminere: subtraheret auris conviciis et probris. non solum Cossutianum aut Eprium ad scelus promptos: superesse qui forsitan manus ictusque per immanitatem ausuri sint; etiam bonos metu sequi. detraheret potius senatui quem perornavisset infamiam tanti flagitii et relinqueret incertum quid viso Thrasea reo decreturi patres fuerint. ut Neronem flagitiorum pudor caperet inrita spe agitari; multoque magis timendum ne in coniugem, in filiam, in cetera pignora eius saeviret. proinde intemeratus, impollutus, quorum vestigiis et studiis vitam duxerit, eorum gloria peteret finem. aderat consilio Rusticus Arulenus, flagrans iuvenis, et cupidine laudis offerebat se intercessurum senatus consulto: nam plebei tribunus erat. cohibuit

spiritus eius Thrasea ne vana et reo non profutura, intercessori exitiosa inciperet. sibi actam aetatem, et tot per annos continuum vitae ordinem non deserendum: illi initium magistratuum et integra quae supersint. multum ante secum expenderet quod tali in tempore capessendae rei publicae iter ingrederetur. ceterum ipse an venire in senatum deceret meditationi suae reliquit.

27. At postera luce duae praetoriae cohortes armatae templum Genitricis Veneris insedere; aditum senatus globus togatorum obsederat non occultis gladiis, dispersique per fora ac basilicas cunei militares. inter quorum aspectus et minas ingressi curiam senatores, et oratio principis per quaestorem eius audita est: nemine nominatim compellato patres arguebat quod publica munia desererent eorumque exemplo equites Romani ad segnitiem verterentur: etenim quid mirum e longinquis provinciis haud veniri, cum plerique adepti consulatum et sacerdotia hortorum potius amoenitati inservirent. quod velut telum corripuere accusatores.

28. Et initium faciente Cossutiano, maiore vi Marcellus summam rem publicam agi clamitabat; contumacia inferiorum lenitatem imperitantis deminui. nimium mitis ad eam diem patres, qui Thraseam desciscentem, qui generum eius Helvidium Priscum in isdem furoribus, simul Paconium Agrippinum, paterni in principes odii heredem, et Curium Montanum detestanda carmina factitantem eludere impune sinerent. requirere se in senatu consularem, in votis sacerdotem, in iure iurando civem, nisi contra instituta et caerimonias maiorum proditorem palam et hostem Thrasea induisset. denique agere senatorem et principis obtrectatores protegere solitus veniret, censeret quid corrigi aut mutari vellet: facilius perlaturos singula increpantem quam nunc silentium perferrent omnia damnantis. pacem illi per orbem terrae, an victorias sine damno exercituum displicere? ne hominem bonis publicis maestum, et qui fora theatra templa pro solitudine haberet, qui minitaretur exilium suum, ambitionis pravae compotem facerent. non illi consulta haec, non magistratus

aut Romanum urbem videri. abrumperet vitam ab ea civitate cuius caritatem olim, nunc et aspectum exuisset.

29. Cum per haec atque talia Marcellus, ut erat torvus ac minax, voce vultu oculis ardesceret, non illa nota et celebritate periculorum sueta iam senatus maestitia, sed novus et altior pavor manus et tela militum cernentibus. simul ipsius Thraseae venerabilis species obversabatur; et erant qui Helvidium quoque miserarentur, innoxiae adfinitatis poenas daturum. quid Agrippino obiectum nisi tristem patris fortunam, quando et ille perinde innocens Tiberii saevitia concidisset. enimvero Montanum probae iuventae neque famosi carminis, quia protulerit ingenium, extorrem agi.

30. Atque interim Ostorius Sabinus, Sorani accusator, ingreditur orditurque de amicitia Rubelli Plauti, quodque proconsulatum Asiae Soranus pro claritate sibi potius accommodatum quam ex utilitate communi egisset, alendo seditiones civitatium. vetera haec: sed recens et quo discrimini patris filiam connectebat, quod pecuniam magis dilargita esset. acciderat sane pietate Serviliae (id enim nomen puellae fuit), quae caritate erga parentem, simul imprudentia aetatis, non tamen aliud consultaverat quam de incolumitate domus, et an placabilis Nero, an cognitio senatus nihil atrox auferret. igitur accita est in senatum, steteruntque diversi ante tribunal consulum grandis aevo parens, contra filia intra vicesimum aetatis annum, nuper marito Annio Pollione in exilium pulso viduata desolataque, ac ne patrem quidem intuens cuius onerasse pericula videbatur.

31. Tum interrogante accusatore an cultus dotalis, an detractum cervici monile venum dedisset, quo pecuniam faciendis magicis sacris contraheret, primum strata humi longoque fletu et silentio, post altaria et aram complexa "nullos" inquit 'impios deos, nullas devotiones, nec aliud infelicibus precibus invocavi quam ut hunc optimum patrem tu, Caesar, vos, patres, servaretis incolumem. sic gemmas et vestis et dignitatis insignia dedi, quo modo si sanguinem et vitam poposcissent. viderint isti, antehac mihi ignoti, quo nomine sint, quas artes exerceant:

nulla mihi principis mentio nisi inter numina fuit. neque tamen miserrimus pater et, si crimen est, sola deliqui.'

32. Loquentis adhuc verba excipit Soranus proclamatque non illam in provinciam secum profectam, non Plauto per aetatem nosci potuisse, non criminibus mariti conexam: nimiae tantum pietatis ream separarent, atque ipse quamcumque subiret. simul in amplexus occurrentis filiae ruebat, nisi interiecti lictores utrisque obstitissent. mox datus testibus locus; et quantum misericordiae saevitia accusationis permoverat, tantum irae P. Egnatius testis concivit. cliens hic Sorani et tunc emptus ad opprimendum amicum auctoritatem Stoicae sectae praeferebat, habitu et ore ad exprimendam imaginem honesti exercitus, ceteram animo perfidiosus, subdolus, avaritiam ac libidinem occultans; quae postquam pecunia reclusa sunt, dedit exemplum praecavendi, quo modo fraudibus involutos aut flagitiis commaculatos, sic specie bonarum artium falsos et amicitiae fallacis.

33. Idem tamen dies et honestum exemplum tulit Cassii Ascleopiodoti, qui magnitudine opum inter Bithynos, quo obsequio florentem Soranum celebraverat, labantem non deseruit, exutusque omnibus fortunis et in exilium actus, aequitate deum erga bona malaque documenta. Thraseae Soranoque et Serviliae datur mortis arbitrium; Helvidius et Paconius Italia depelluntur; Montanus patri concessus est, praedicto ne in re publica haberetur. accusatoribus Eprio et Cossutiano quinquagies sestertium singulis, Ostorio duodecies et quaestoria insigna tribuuntur.

34. Tum ad Thraseam in hortis agentem quaestor consulis missus vesperascente iam die. inlustrium virorum feminarumque coetus frequentis egerat, maxime intentus Demetro Cynicae institutionis doctori, cum quo, ut coniectare erat intentione vultus et auditis, si qua clarius proloquebantur, de natura animae et dissociatione spiritus corporisque inquirebat, donec advenit Domitius Caecilianus ex intimis amicis et ei quid senatus censuisset exposuit. igitur flentis queritantisque qui aderant facessere propere Thrasea neu pericula sua miscere cum sorte damnati hortatur, Arriamque temptantem mariti suprema et

exemplum Arriae matris sequi monet retinere vitam filiaque communi subsidium unicum non adimere.

35. Tum progressus in porticum illic a quaestore reperitur, laetitiae propior, quia Helvidium generum suum Italia tantum arceri cognoverat. accepto dehinc senatus consulto Helvidium et Demetrium in cubiculum inducit; porrectisque utriusque brachii venis, postquam cruorem effudit, humum super spargens, propius vocato quaestore "libamus" inquit "Iovi liberatori. specta, iuvenis; et omen quidem dii prohibeant, ceterum in ea tempora natus es quibus firmare animum expediat constantibus exemplis." post lentitudine exitus gravis cruciatus adferente, obversis in Demetrium ***

Commentary

Figure 4 Under Le Ponte Vieux, Carcassone, France. © Katelyn McGarr.

Chapter one: Fortune's tricks and Dido's gold

Inlusit dehinc: The sixteenth book of the *Annales* opens (amid an account of the continuing events of A.D. 65) with the odd story of Fortune's deception of Nero in the matter of the alleged discovery of the gold of the Carthaginian queen Dido. The passage follows on the detail at the close of Book XV that Nero had rejected the proposal of the consul-designate Anicius Cerealis that a temple should be erected in his honor as a new Roman god—the *princeps* was afraid that such a gesture might portend his death (*Annales* XV, 74). One might think that such a rejection of the honor of a temple demonstrated a certain rational, sober act of judgment on Nero's part—but at once Tacitus paints a portrait of Nero as pawn of Fortune and credulous, gullible believer in a wild tale of gold beyond anyone's dreams or imagination. Book XVI would have opened the last triad of the Neronian *Annales*; on the likely eighteen book length of the original work, see H. W. Benario, "The *Annals*," in V. E. Pagán, *A Companion to Tacitus*, Malden, Massachusetts: Wiley-Blackwell, 2012, p. 104. For general commentary on Tacitus' approach to historiography and methodological practice in his later books, see M. Morford, "Tacitus' Historical Methods in the Neronian 'Annals,'" in W. Haase and H. Temporini, eds., *Aufstieg und Niedergang der römischen Welt (ANRW), Teil II: Principat, Band 33.2*, Berlin-New York: Walter de Gruyter, 1990, pp. 1582–1627.

The deception of Nero is described also by Suetonius (*Vita Neronis* 31.3-32.1). Dido's gold (along with silver) is referenced by Virgil (*Aeneid* I, 357–364), as the disguised goddess Venus describes to her son Aeneas how Dido made her escape to North Africa with a tremendous store of precious metals. The powerful opening verb *inlusit* highlights at once the change in Nero's luck; Furneaux notes that *dehinc* implies that until now, Nero had known mostly good fortune and success. On the relative importance of the story, see D. Braund, "Treasure-Trove and Nero," in *Greece & Rome* 30.1 (1983), pp. 65–69; cf. P. Murgatroyd, "Dido's Treasure at Tacitus, *Annals* 16.1-3," in *Mnemosyne* 231 (2002), pp. 131–134. For a detailed analysis of this episode and subsequent chapters of the book, see V. Rudich, *Political Dissidence Under Nero: The Price of Dissimulation*, Oxford-New York: Routledge, 1993, pp. 132 ff. "The gold of Bassus is another of the *rumores* which contributed to Nero's ruin …" (S. Bartera, *A Commentary on Tacitus, Annals 16.1-20*, Dissertation Virginia, 2008, *ad* XVI, 1). On the significance of rumors in Tacitus, see P. Hardie, *Rumour and Renown: Representations of Fama in Western Literature*, Cambridge, 2012, pp. 273 ff.; also B. J. Gibson, "Rumors as Causes of Events in Tacitus," in *Materiali e discussioni per l'analisi dei testi classici* 40 (1998), pp. 111–129; also I. Shatzman, "Tacitean Rumors," in *Latomus* 33.3 (1974), pp. 549–578.

> The most savage comment on the pretentious hypocrisies that always threaten to topple the whole ideology comes from Tacitus, in his account of Nero's reign. He seizes on an opportunity to work with the friction between the various associations of gold when he opens *Annals* 16 … In accordance with his usual strategy of associating Nero with the spurious allure of the Virgilian myths, Tacitus makes this crackpot a second Dido, for she too had a significant dream about treasure in the earth … Nero's dream of a new Golden Age is wickedly made literal with this vision of physical hunks of unworked bullion lying underground, and

the impossibility of Nero's fantasies is made real when Bassus' fantasies are dispelled.

(D. Feeney, *Caesar's Calendar: Ancient Time and the Beginnings of History*, Berkeley-Los Angeles-London: The University of California Press, 2007, pp. 135-136). For allusions to Virgil in Tacitus, advanced students may wish to consult the extensive treatment of R. T. S. Baxter, *Virgil's Influence on Tacitus*, Dissertation Stanford, 1968; "Virgil's Influence on Tacitus in Book 3 of the *Histories*," in *CPh* 66.2 (1971), pp. 93-107; and "Virgil's Influence on Tacitus in Books 1 and 2 of the *Annals*," in *CPh* 67.4 (1972), pp. 246-269. On Bassus note R. Ash, "At the End of the Rainbow: Nero and Dido's Gold (Tacitus *Annals* 16.1-3)," in R. Ash *et al.*, eds., *Fame and Infamy: Essays on Characterization in Greek and Roman Biography and Historiography*, Oxford, 2015, pp. 269-284.

Book XVI of the *Annales* is the likely commencement of the last third of the third hexad of the complete epic history; at once Tacitus plunges into a scene that is redolent with the spirit of the Virgilian account of the long journey of Aeneas and his men from Troy to Italy, and the fateful stopover in Dido's Carthage. It may have had particular resonance in light of Nero's own Trojan epic compositional aspirations; it is a story that is ultimately a trick and delusion of Fortune, even as Nero moves inexorably toward his own doom. The Carthaginian Dido brought emotional grief and turmoil to the Trojan Aeneas, and her amatory affair with him—while relatively brief—had the lasting consequence of the legacy of the Punic Wars. The Julian Nero will now be cheated out of his hope to win the long lost gold of Africa's queen.

Neroni: Dative with a compound verb (*inlusit*). The Medicean manuscript has the genitive *Neronis* here. Nero is deceived both by his own *vanitas* or readiness to believe whatever suits his fancy (the root of the noun conveys a notion of "emptiness," cf. the English "vanity"), and by the promises of Caesellius Bassus. Bassus merely provides the catalyst to stir up what was already a weakness of Nero.

What is referred to in this commentary as the "Medicean manuscript" by way of convenience refers to what is more properly the "second" Medicean, a manuscript in the Laurentian Library in Florence that probably dates to the eleventh century. To it we owe our text of the later books of Tacitus, that is, *Annales* XI–XVI and the *Historiae*. "At the end of Book 16 a little more than a page and a half is left blank ..." (C. Mendell, *Tacitus: The Man and His Work*, New Haven, Connecticut: Yale University Press, 1957, p. 296). Mendell provides a careful account of the manuscripts and early editions of

Tacitus that remains a useful *précis*; Malloch also provides an account of this Codex Laurentianus Mediceus 68.2 in the introduction to his major edition of *Annals* XI:

> Uncertainty attends the origin of the exemplar from which it was copied. The suggestion that *Annals* 11–16 and *Histories* 1–5 had been in Italy since antiquity has failed to win many converts … and the more common explanation is that the exemplar came from Germany … perhaps from Fulda at some point before the middle of the eleventh century.

ipsius: That is, Nero.

Caeselli Bassi: In Suetonius, the source of the story of the gold is referred to as a *Romanus eques* or "Roman knight." Nothing is known of Caesellius Bassus, who appears nowhere else in Tacitus' surviving works. He may have been of African origin, but this is uncertain.

origine: Ablative of source, or perhaps of respect (though the difference is not so great; Bassus was either Punic in origin or with respect to his origin). The ablative case expresses separation (cf. "ablative" from *ablatus*, the perfect passive participle of *auferre*).

Poenus: "Punic" or "Carthaginian." The Carthaginians were traditionally condemned for mendacity and a penchant for deceit and trickery (on which see further R. M. Sheldon, *Intelligence Activities in Ancient Rome: Trust in the Gods But Verify*, London-New York: Routledge, 2004, pp. 41–42); from the start the whole subsequent story is identified as being of questionable legitimacy.

mente turbida: Not only is Bassus Carthaginian and thus likely a liar—he is also mentally unstable.

nocturnae quietis imaginem: That is, a dream; cf. *Annales* IV, 4.4-5, of the fatal dream of a defendant during Claudius' reign. The dream image could be said to belong to the "quiet of the night"; the genitive expresses the relationship between two nouns (and thus often expresses possession).

spem: "Expectation."

haud dubiae rei traxit: The text printed is the result of the scholar Döderlein's correction of the manuscript reading *haud dubie retraxit*, where the "e" in the adverb is written in an erasure. The verb conveys the idea that the deranged Bassus had literally "dragged" Nero along "through the expectation of a scarcely doubtful thing," that is, in his fantastic dream of having discovered the legendary Carthaginian queen's gold. Bassus persuaded Nero to have hope or belief in a "scarcely doubtful thing"; the language expresses both the credulity of Nero and the powerfully persuasive lure of Bassus' seductive story. Heubner prints *re<I>traxit*.

Romam: The accusative expresses the place to which Bassus traveled; no preposition is used with the name of the city.

principis aditum: "Access to the *princeps*," that is, an audience with Nero; the genitive is objective. In this case, the access was bought (*emercatus*), a detail that raises the question of bribery as a means of obtaining access to the *princeps*, and more generally the corrupt workings of the Neronian imperial court.

expromit: Historic present. The verb is particularly appropriate for use in describing Bassus' story of how gold could be extracted from a subterranean cave.

repertum … specum: Accusative in indirect discourse after *expromit*.

altitudine immensa: The ablative describes a quality or aspect of the cave: the cave was of immense depth. The reference to the vast depth of the grotto conveys a sense of how much gold must be contained in its recesses.

contineretur: Imperfect subjunctive in a subordinate clause in indirect discourse. The imperfect tense conveys the idea that the action of the subordinate verb was occurring at the same time as that of the main verb in secondary sequence. The verb can refer to that which is kept safe or preserved (*OLD* s.v. 5b).

rudi et antiquo pondere: Once again the ablative expresses the quality of the gold.

lateres … praegravidas: The gold exists both in "bricks" or "ingots" (*OLD* s.v. b, a usage that goes back to Plautus) and, we learn at once, also in standing columns or "stacks" (so Marsh and Leon). The prefix *prae-* expresses the great weight of the bars of gold.

augendis praesentibus bonis: Literally, "for present good things/benefits to be increased," that is, "to increase present benefits." *Augendis* is the future passive participle or gerundive, here used in a dative of purpose construction. In Bassus' crazy account and reckoning, the gold was hidden in the earth for so long so that the joy and benefit to Nero's reign could be all the greater. *Bonis* is used as a substantive.

ut coniectura demonstrabat: The Medicean manuscript has the present *demonstrat* here, which Halm corrected to the imperfect; Heubner prints the imperfect marker *ba* in angle brackets (<>) in consequence, as an indicator of something he thinks was lost from the text. *Coniectura* literally conveys the notion of tossing out an idea; Bassus suggests that the hidden store of gold is that of Dido and her original Carthaginian exile colonists. The noun is most likely ablative, not nominative. The verb describes the tale that Bassus wove for Nero; the story is heavily indebted to Virgil's account of the queen and her early experiences in North Africa, and may have been of particular appeal to a *princeps* with literary interests and ambitions (not to say pretentions). On the emperor's literary pretensions and the depiction thereof in Tacitus, see especially E. E. Keitel, "Is dying so very terrible? The Neronian Annals," in A. J. Woodman, ed., *The Cambridge Companion to Tacitus*, Cambridge, 2009, pp. 127–143. *Coniectura* basically means the inference of one fact from another so as to draw a conclusion; it can also refer to prophecy and dream prognostication (*OLD* s.v. 3 and 3b).

Dido Phoenissam: Subject accusative in indirect discourse. *Didonem* is also found as a form of the accusative of the queen's name. Dido is the subject of the infinitive *abdidisse*, which is introduced by the main verb *demonstrabat*.

Tyro: The ablative describes the place from which Dido and her companions departed ("from Tyre").

profugam: "Exile," with a notion of flight from harm and peril.

condita Carthagine: Ablative absolute; the concealing of the wealth came after the queen had fled from Tyre and had founded her new North African city, Carthage.

abdidisse: Perfect infinitive in indirect discourse.

ne … lasciviret: Negative clause of purpose with imperfect subjunctive in secondary sequence. The verb *lascivire* has a rich range of meanings, most basically to "frisk" or "frolic," from which derive the senses of acting without control or restraint, to have no sense of order or maintenance (often in erotic contexts; cf. *OLD* s.v. 3b). Biting irony, since Nero was known for his *lascivia*.

nimia pecunia: Ablative of cause; Dido is imagined as worrying that her people would come to live a life of indulgence and wanton expenditure if they had access to a seemingly inexhaustible repository of gold. The adjective *nimius* can refer to that which transgresses the bounds of good taste and legal limit, that which is intemperate and extravagant, even of persons in the sense of being overeager and overzealous for something (*OLD* s.v. 3b).

reges Numidarum: "The kings of the Numidians." The poetic reminiscences continue, in this case of King Iarbas, the suitor of Dido in Virgil's fourth *Aeneid*.

et: Likely an adverb and not a conjunction.

alias: "Otherwise."

cupidine auri: Another causal ablative, or, perhaps better, ablative of means.

accenderentur: Imperfect subjunctive.

Chapter two: Fantasy exaggerated: The false lure of a new golden age

auctoris: That is, Bassus.

ipsius negotii: "The very affair/business," that is, the story of the gold. Nero did not consider either the trustworthiness of the source, or the inherent plausibility of the tale. *Negotium* can refer to an occupation or business, or to any sort of annoyance or trouble that might be connected to labor (*OLD* s.v. 3).

fide … spectata: Ablative absolute. *Fides* here describes the plausibility or reliability of the story (cf. *OLD* s.v. 9, "the quality of being worthy of belief"); Nero did not bother to subject it to careful investigation. The noun can also describe trust and confidence more generally (*OLD* s.v. 12), indeed "the range or possibility of belief" (*OLD* s.v. 13).

missis: Substantive use of the adjective, this time used in another ablative absolute; Nero did not even try to send anyone who could investigate the truth of Bassus' claims. The compressed language expresses the hurried, rushed atmosphere of the proceedings. The Medicean adds the rare word *visoribus* after the participle; this may be a gloss (Heubner admits it to his text, though in square brackets that reflect his judgment that it was introduced as a gloss). Cf. *oblatis* at XVI, 3 below.

nosceret … adferrentur: First, an imperfect subjunctive in a relative clause of purpose; then an imperfect subjunctive in an indirect question. *An* should be translated as "whether."

auget ultro: Nero gullibly accepted the truth of Bassus' tall tale, *and* he freely and of his own volition made a bad situation worse by exaggerating the claims of the Carthaginian madman. *Ultro* conveys the sense that Nero needed no help in exacerbating the opportunity for mockery.

qui … adveherent: Relative clause of purpose. The language follows on the force of *missis* above; men were sent to North Africa, but with orders to take the gold, which is assumed to be in Bassus' cave exactly as he described. The antecedent of *qui* = the men who were sent after the gold.

velut paratam praedam: The sailors are sent to convey back the gold as if it were plunder simply waiting for Nero to have it fetched back to Rome. The Medicean reading *partam* was perceptively corrected by Acidalius, the sixteenth-century German critic and poet; on his Tacitean work see S. J. V. Malloch, "Acidalius on Tacitus," in R. Hunter and S. P. Oakley, eds., *Latin Literature and Its Transmission*, Cambridge, 2016, pp. 225 ff.

dantur triremes: "Triremes are provided." The verb = historic present. On ancient merchant galleys see L. Casson, *Ships and Seamanship in the Ancient World*, Princeton, 1971, pp. 157 ff. The vessels that are commissioned here were likely imperial naval galleys that were dispatched by Nero for the purpose of securing the gold; size of ship and military watch over the gold were the pressing needs.

iuvandae festinationi: Another gerundive in a dative of purpose construction; the triremes and select crew of sailors to man the oars is delegated to "help along the haste" of the mission: the credulous and avaricious Nero wants the gold now. *Festinatio* can describe any sort of speed or "undue haste" (cf. *OLD* s.v. 2).

nec aliud: "No other thing." The fantastic tale of Dido's gold dominated the attention of the populace, to the exclusion of all else.

populus … prudentes: We might interpet that the "rabble" believed in the story just as readily as Nero, while the *prudentes* (implicitly fewer in number) had a very different reaction (as expressed by the ablative *diversa fama*): a typically Tacitean weighted alternative. *Prudentes* is Boxhorn's conjecture for the manuscript reading *prodentis*.

diversa fama: The implication is that the prudent hearers of the story not only disbelieved it, but also heaped ridicule on the idea that Dido's gold had been found, or that Nero's venture would lead to any successful infusion of wealth into the treasury.

tulere: That is, *tulerunt*.

quinquennale ludicrum: "Quinquennial Games." These games are referred to as the "Neronia" by Suetonius (XII, 3; cf. XXI.1) and by Dio Cassius (epitome of Book LXII, 21 of his *Roman History*); note also Tacitus, *Annales* XIV, 20 and XVI, 4 below. Musical competitions, athletic events, and chariot racing were all held as part of the great festival of the arts and sport. In Tacitus' arrangement and description of material, the story of Bassus—with its elements of romance and the evocation of the Dido of myth and legend—leads soon enough into the narrative of Nero as stage actor (XVI, 4–5). "Nero was the ultimate player-king among Roman emperors; he performed for all fourteen years of his reign, in public and in private, on stage and off. Theatricality was, of course, in his blood." (R. Mellor, *Tacitus' Annals (Oxford Approaches to Classical Literature)*, Oxford, 2010, p. 184). *Ludicrum* describes any source of entertainment or relaxation; from this derives the specialized sense of a public game or spectacle (*OLD* s.v. 2), such as the famous *ludicrum Troiae* that commemorated the fall of Priam's (and Aeneas') city. On Nero's musical interests and phihellenic character, see A. Wallace-Hadrill, *Suetonius*, London: Bristol Classical Press, 1995 (second edition of the 1983 original), pp. 181 ff.

secundo lustro: A *lustrum* referred to a period of five years; Nero had taken power in A.D. 54 and had instituted the Neronia in A.D. 60. A *lustrum* was a particular ceremony of purification and cleansing; cf. the traditional rites for the dedication of a church or cathedral. It could refer to the censor's five-year tenure in office (*OLD* s.v. 2); Lucretius and Manilius use it to describe the period of time in which a celestial object completes its rotation (*OLD* s.v. 5). Nero would not live to see to the celebration of a third set of "quinquennial" games. On certain problems of interpretation of what exactly the "Quinquennial Games" refer to in terms of frequency of celebration and start date, see J. D. P. Bolton, "Was the Neronia a Freak Festival?," in *The Classical Quarterly* 42.3/4 (1948), pp. 82–90; D. W. MacDowall, "The Numismatic Evidence for the Neronia," in *The Classical Quarterly* 8.3/4 (1958), pp. 192–194; F. A. Lepper, "Some Reflections on the Quinquennium Neronis," in *The Journal of Roman Studies* 47.1/2 (1957), pp. 95–103; M. K. Thornton, "The Enigma of Nero's 'Quinquennium': Reputation of Emperor Nero," in *Historia: Zeitschrift für alte Geschichte* 22.3 (1973), pp. 570–582; J. G. F. Hind, "Is Nero's Quinquennium an Enigma?," in *Historia: Zeitschrift für alte Geschichte* 24.4 (1975), pp. 629–630; also A. Momigliano, "Literary Chronology of the Neronian Age," in *The Classical Quarterly* 38.3/4 (1944), pp. 96–100. The problem of determining years and recurring anniversaries stems from the question of whether one counts inclusively or not.

celebrabatur: The Medicean reads the present *celebratur* here; Heubner restores the *ba* in his text, in angle brackets.

ab oratoribus: The Medicean has *avaratoribus oratoribusque*, which is unintelligible.

praecipua: "Exceptional." The adjective describes that which belongs to someone or something to the exclusion of all else, as a peculiar and proper possession or characteristic; it denotes a paramount state of exceptionalism (cf. *OLD* s.v. 3).

in laudem principis: "In praise of the *princeps*." The artists of the Neronia present the story of the gold as ultimately redounding to the praise of the glorious prince in whose reign the blessings of the gods were bestowed so generously.

tantum: "Only."

confusum metallis aurum: The thoughtful deities of this Neronian Golden Age are imagined as having ensured that no one needs to waste their time with sifting through veins of inferior metal in quest for gold. *Metalla* can refer either to metals or to the mines when they are excavated; Nipperdey conjectured that *aliis* should be added after *metallis*, while Furneaux interprets the passage as meaning that there was more than "mere gold ore in the mines." Following Draeger, Heubner prints *confusum in metallis*.

provenire: The earth was coming to life, as it were, with a novel richness of bounty and treasure.

obvias opes deferre deos: A mark of the Golden Age; there is no need for labor, since the gods provide all that one could want for the sustaining and enjoyment of life. *Obvius* can describe that which is merely in front of something or someone, or that which is situated in front of one to render assistance in the case of attack or hostile action; it can mean that which is veritably "commonplace" because it is right in front of one's sight at all times (*OLD* s.v. 6b).

quaeque ... servilia: Tacitus builds up to the keyword *servilia*. The image is one of the creation of fawning panegyrics and testimonials to the greatness of the emperor under whose auspices the new Golden Age had come.

summa facundia ... minore adulatione: The language employs an effectively biting juxtaposition of ideas: the *facundia* or "eloquence" of the orators was of the highest quality, and the adulation with which they praised Nero with the "slavish" (*servilia*) creations of their arts displayed a sycophancy that matched their supreme skill in wordplay.

fingebant: The imperfect tense can convey a sense of durative or repetitive action; what the orators and performers did, they did over and over again in a constant display of both their eloquence and their praise of the *princeps*. The orators were just as readily given to made up stories as Bassus. For a provocative study of the Tacitean use of imagery of fashioning and the power of belief, with particular attention to the use of the verbs *fingere* and *credere*, see H.

Haynes, *Tacitus on Imperial Rome: The History of Make-Believe*, Berkeley-Los Angeles-London: The University of California Press, 2003, pp. 7–19. We do well to remember, too, that "no criticism and scarcely any mention of Tacitus' historical style survives to suggest what its effect were on ancient readers" (K. Gilmartin, "Tacitean Evidence for Tacitean Style," in *The Classical Journal* 69.3 [1974], pp. 216–222); we can mostly engage only in speculation as to the effects (dazzling or otherwise) of his verbal play in the judgment of his peers. *Fingere* has a wide range of meanings, rooted in the sense of shaping something from clay or fashioning it in the manner of a potter; it can refer equally, however, to the work of sculptors (*OLD* s.v. 3) and of poets and authors (*OLD* s.v. 6a). It can describe something that is conjured by the creative energy of the mind, even the intangible (*OLD* s.v. 8); it can have a negative sense of that which is deliberately crafted to be hypocritical and mendacious (i.e., lying words).

securi: "Confident" (with *de*; cf. *OLD* s.v. 3).

facilitate: "Readiness." Nero was reliably able to be expected to trust a fantastic yarn.

credentis: That is, Nero. The paragraph closes with another reminder of the emperor's ready assent to the truth of the nonsensical lore; the emphasis throughout is on credulity and the question of what is worthy of belief.

Chapter three: The shattering of the illusion and the end of Bassus

Gliscebat interim luxuria: The imperfect is probably inceptive as well as durative; Nero's *luxuria* and wastrel lifestyle both began to increase and continue, as it were, as a result of the expectation of his newfound wealth. The implication is that the previous heights of Nero's self-indulgence were now far surpassed, with nary a concern for when (let alone if) the money would actually be at hand to pay for the newly incurred debts. On *luxuria* cf. P. Kragelund, "Nero's *Luxuria*, in Tacitus and in the *Octavia*," in *The Classical Quarterly* 50.2 (2000), pp. 494–515, with consideration of the meaning and implication of the judgment of the emperor's successor Galba that *luxuria* was a major factor in Nero's undoing (*Historiae* I, 16). The root meaning of *gliscere* is to become swollen or distended, from which comes the sense of growing in power and even violence, of becoming a more feverish and impassioned emotion or sense (*OLD* s.v. 4); cf. Virgil's *accenso gliscit violentia Turni* (*Aeneid* XII, 9), of the increasing emotive anger of Aeneas' arch rival.

spe inani: Ablative of cause. The expectation for the immense riches of the phantom gold was devoid of any substance. The adjective and its related noun refer originally to an empty space or void (cf. Lucretius' description of matter and the void in the realm of nature and the universe); from this comes the sense of that which is worthless or illusory, indeed of reports that are unjustified or groundless (*OLD* s.v. 12), and to promises that are not fulfilled (*OLD* s.v. 11b). It is sometimes applied to the insubstantial shades in the underworld.

oblatis: Perfect passive participle from *offerre*. Another compressed ablative absolute (cf. *missis* at XVI, 2 above); Nero acted as if the promised wealth of Bassus' Didonian gold had already been offered and presented to him to make up for the tremendous expense losses incurred through so many years of lavish spending.

prodigeret: Imperfect subjunctive (from *prodigo, prodigere, prodegi, prodactum*) in a relative clause of characteristic (i.e., a generic relative clause), also of purpose. The basic meaning of the verb is to drive out; from this comes the sense of wasting and squandering one's resources (*OLD* s.v. 2).

quin: "Even." Nero not only spent old treasure, but he began to use the money that was not yet in hand.

inde: That is, from the alleged newly discovered source of revenue.

divitiarum expectatio ... erat: A typical Tacitean paradox; the expectation of riches was among the reasons for public poverty.

effosso: Perfect passive participle from *effodere*; Bassus had his own property thoroughly excavated (the prefix *ex* is intensive), as well as the surrounding land.

hunc vel illum: The demonstrative adjectives are deictic, that is, they indicate that Bassus kept "pointing" to this or that place as the location of the buried hoard.

promissi specus: "the promised cavern," which of course contained the promise of untold riches. A *specus* can be any sort of cave or grotto, indeed even a hole or other manmade, excavated cavity (cf. *OLD* s.v. 1b; 2); it has a particular use with reference to mines.

adseverat: Pluperfect third-person singular indicative from *adseverare*. Bassus kept swearing and asserting that this or that place was the location of the promised underground trove. The verb describes the act of laying hands on something, of claiming something; it is a particularly appropriate verb for the action of Bassus as he tries to point out where exactly the hoard is. It can also be used in contexts of alleging or asserting something to be true (cf. *OLD* s.v. 6).

populus agrestium: The rustic folk or people from the local farmland. The inhabitants of the neighboring fields are impressed into service, one might imagine, by the deputation of soldiers sent by Nero. The apparently impressive collection of labor is insufficient to the task of finding the imaginary treasure hoard.

efficiendo operi: The gerundive in another dative of purpose.

adsumptus: To be taken with *populus*; the local population was drafted/ enlisted in the enterprise of digging up the whole area to find the gold.

tandem: The adverb effectively expresses how the charade was at last finished.

posita vaecordia: Ablative absolute. Tacitus does not make clear the exact nature of Bassus' delusion, or just how and why the insanity was put aside. *Vaecordia* is an old word (it is found in Livius Andronicus, Pacuvius, and Terence); it was used by Tacitus' model Sallust in both his *Catiline* and *Jugurtha*, but had a somewhat archaic ring and flavor; it is of infrequent occurrence in extant Latin (though it does appear in both Livy and Ovid). It describes a disordered state of the mind, a deranged or demented state of being.

somnia: "Dreams."

admirans: Bassus was in shock that his prophetic dreams were, for once, proven to be false, and that he had been deceived with respect to his own expectation of unearthing Dido's gold. Nipperdey emended the participle to *affirmans*, while Furneaux argues that Bassus was sincere in his belief that the gold would be discovered. The present participle expresses the same time as the main verb.

elusum: Perfect participle from *eludere*; the referent is Bassus.

pudorem: The concept of "shame" is important in the Virgilian Dido story as well, in the question of the queen's willingness to forsake the memory of her dead husband Sychaeus by commencing an affair with Aeneas. Bassus' noblest act from the Roman perspective is his suicide in the face of shame and fear; he is another victim of the Neronian regime, though solely through his own actions. *Pudor* can refer not only to a sense of shame, but also to a recognition that certain traits or styles of behavior are more seemly and proper than others (cf. *OLD* 2); *Pudor!* and *pro pudor!* can be used as exclamations in the sense of the English, "for shame!" (*OLD* s.v. 5).

morte voluntaria: That is, by suicide. The detail may evoke the memory of Dido, whose suicide provides a dramatic climax to Virgil's fourth *Aeneid*.

quidam: "Certain men."

vinctum: From *vincire*, "to bind." Bassus either committed suicide, or he was arrested and then later set free by Nero, though with the loss of his confiscated property. One imagines that the wealth of Bassus (even if considerable) could not possibly meet the debts incurred by Nero, though certainly the *princeps* would have tried to recoup as much of his losses as he could. Was Bassus treated with relative mercy because Nero was sympathetic to the purveyor of such a romantic, poetic tale? Furneaux notes that the language of the entire passage serves to indicate Tacitus' lack of faith in this version; the suicide is the likelier outcome of the tale of the crazed Carthaginian—exactly as in Virgil.

tradidere: That is, *tradiderunt*. The basic meaning of the verb is to hand over; in Tacitus and other historians, the meaning is often "to record" or "to say," that is, to hand over to posterity.

in locum regiae gazae: "In place of the royal treasure." *Gaza* is a relatively rare word that connotes Eastern luxury and decadence. Fittingly, the story ends with a word that sums up what Nero had most desired, and the dream of the fabulous wealth associated both with Dido's Tyre and Priam's Troy.

Chapter four: The response of the senate to the shame, and Nero's artistic endeavors

propinquo iam lustrali certamine: Ablative absolute. The time for the Quinquennial Games was now drawing near/at hand. If the episode of Dido's fake gold were a source of embarrassment, Nero would soon provide even more opportunities for shame in the matter of his stage career. The adjective refers to that which is related to ritual purification and cleansing; here it is applied to what which has to do with the quinquennial games (cf. *OLD* s.v. 2).

averteret: Imperfect subjunctive in a clause of purpose. The goal of the senate to avert the shame (*dedecus*) of the stage performance in the wake of the farce with the Carthaginian gold; the problem of the fake treasure leads straight on to the question of Nero's appearing on stage as an actor. He has already served as a character in the Bassus farce, an episode rooted in the lore and drama of the tragic queen Dido.

imperatori: Properly of a military commander; the martial origins of the word contrast deliberately with the world of singing and the stage in which Nero seeks to conquer and to achieve victory.

qua: Ablative of means.

ludicra deformitas: Yardley translates this phrase as "scandalous stage performance." The senate decided to offer Nero the crown of victory in both singing and eloquence so as to keep him from giving a performance on the stage. *Ludicra* is an old adjective (Plautus), found in Cicero, Livy, and in the poetry of Virgil and Horace; cf. *Aeneid* XII, 763–765 *quinque orbis explent cursu totidemque retexunt/huc illuc, neque enim levia aut ludicra petuntur/praemia, sed Turni de vita et sanguine certant.* Tacitus has it in the *Dialogus* and Book I of the *Annales*; not surprisingly, it is most prevalent, however, in the Neronian books. It can refer to that which has to do with the stage and the life of the theater (*OLD* s.v. 2); the basic meaning (as with the related noun *ludicrum*) is that which has to do with sport and play.

velaretur: Another imperfect subjunctive in a purpose clause. The verb continues the Tacitean expression of the theme of truth, falsehood, *species*, and concealment; the senate hopes to cover up the shame of the *princeps'* dramatic aspirations, to throw a veil, as it were, over the spectacle of shame.

nihil … opus esse: Nero claimed that "there was no need" of either the *ambitus* or the *potestas* of the senate. The idiom can take an ablative (a type of ablative of means).

ambitu … potestate: The first noun conveys the notion of favor and influence, the second of authority and power (legal and otherwise). The paragraph opens with the senate; it will draw to a close with the plebeians. The former seeks to avoid the spectacle of having Nero on stage, while the latter is described as having no serious problem with the sight of their *princeps* in the guise of a theater performer.

religione iudicum: Nero says that he will win the praise he deserves by virtue of the scrupulous observance of the judges. *Religio* refers to the idea of binding and restraint; the judges will be constricted by the demands of the proper execution of their task. In context the word may carry something of a ridiculous air.

meritam laudem: "Praise that has been earned/merited." The phrase is not without a certain irony, at least from Tacitus' point of view.

adsecuturum: The form is future active participle. The *esse* is regularly omitted from the construction of the periphrastic infinitive.

carmen in scaena recitat: Tacitus is silent as to the subject of the poem, which may have been Nero's *Troica*, or perhaps a *Niobe*. On the subjects of Nero's songs, and the vexed question of whether or not the games of 65 were actually a postponed event from 64, see E. Champlin, *Nero*, Cambridge, Massachusetts: Harvard University Press, 2003, pp. 74–75.

We know very little about Nero's poetic production and output, despite the plethora of references to his artistic ambitions and pretenses. Dio (LXII, 29) is a source for the existence of the emperor's poem on the Trojan War; cf. the reference to the *Halosin Ilii* or "Sack of Ilium" at Suetonius, *Nero c.* 38, which Nero is said to have recited during the great fire "*in illo suo scaenico habitu.*" Seneca's *Naturales Quaestiones* (I, 5.6) preserves some of the paltry remains we have of actual Neronian verse, along with the scholia to Lucan's *Bellum Civile* (*apud* III, 261, with three verses on the Tigris). Cf. M. Dewar, "Nero on the Disappearing Tigris," in *The Classical Quarterly* 41.1 (1991), pp. 269–272. We know somewhat more about the roles that Nero was fondest of performing on stage in dramatic productions: Thyestes, Oedipus, Orestes (cf. Dio LXIII, 9; 10; Suetonius, *cc.* 21; 39; 46—though admittedly in Dio the citations are from a speech of the rebellious Vindex, a clearly critical source).

flagitante vulgo: Ablative absolute, "with the mob demanding." Suetonius notes in his life of Vitellius (*c.* 4) that the future emperor was responsible for calling Nero back to compete among the citharodes when the *princeps* was perhaps feigning an unwillingness to participate.

omnia studia sua: Literally, "all his passions" or objects of zealous pursuit.

haec enim verba dixere: By way of a parenthetical aside, Tacitus underscores the point that these were the very words of the crowd. The point is to highlight the disgrace of how the *vulgus* was encouraging Nero in his bad behavior.

dixere: For *dixerunt*.

cunctis citharae legibus: "All the laws of the lyre." Nero follows all the protocols and customs that were associated with the best stage performances. The dative is with the compound verb *obtemperans*.

ne fessus resideret: Nero was careful to observe the convention that one did not sit down on stage when fatigued.

indutui: From *indutus, indutus*, m.; the noun is quite rare. It literally means "a putting on," that is, a garment. The dative expresses purpose; Nero did not wipe away the perspiration of his brow except with that garment which he was using for a covering.

nulla oris aut narium excrementa: The language is vividly graphic, and serves to highlight the implicit contrast between the world of high art and Nero's attempts to insert himself among the ranks of poetic and dramatic greats. *Narium* = "nostrils" (genitive plural).

viserentur: The Medicean has the active *viserent*, with the audience as the implied subject. Heubner brackets the passive ending here, indicating his judgment on how the text should be corrected.

genu: This could be ablative (of means) or accusative (of respect). Furneaux follows Nipperdey in taking it as the latter ("of part concerned"). For the ablative one might note that *manu* rather balances *genu* (Bartera rightly reminds me, however, that Tacitus is fond of *variatio* or variation of expression); Nero is bent at the knee, and with his hand he salutes the *iudices*. The image is one of Nero as a virtual statue of an artist, awaiting the results of the judges.

veneratus: From *venerari*; supply *est*. The omission of forms of the verb "to be" is very common in Tacitus and may be a poetic usage; see further H. Pinkster, *Oxford Latin Syntax, Volume I: The Simple Clause*, Oxford, 2015, p. 131. "After the classical period omission of forms of *sum* becomes a stylistic device, exploited extensively by Tacitus" (p. 135).

opperiebatur: Deponent. Once again the imperfect imbues the description of the scene with a certain vividness, as Tacitus constructs his image of Nero *scaenicus*. The verb describes the act of waiting for something, and can refer in particular to the awaiting of the outcome a given event (*OLD* s.v. 3).

ficto pavore: "With feigned fear." Nero knows that he will be awarded the prize for his performance.

histrionum: Genitive plural. The noun (which is apparently of Etruscan origin) refers to an actor; it can have a more specialized meaning of the performer in a pantomime (*OLD* s.v. b).

solita: "Accustomed."

certis modis: "According to certain modes," that is, in measured manner.

plausuque composito: "Orchestrated clapping" (Yardley); the whole spectacle is one of pseudo-elegance and abject flattery of the despot.

crederes: Potential subjunctive; the imperfect expresses past potentiality ("you might have believed ..."). The passage closes on a note of thinly veiled contempt for the *plebs*; the plebeians are described as being accustomed to applaud even for actors on the stage (the profession was not held in particularly high regard or repute), and perhaps as even actually rejoicing for Nero (*ac fortasse laetabantur*)—another weighted alternative. We are reminded here that there were many who were quite happy with the lavish spectacles and entertainments of the Neronian reign; on the possible connection between this celebration and the matter of Dido's gold, see R. C. Beacham, *Spectacle Entertainments of Early Imperial Rome*, New Haven, Connecticut: Yale University Press, 1999, p. 229.

incuriam: "Lack of concern." Cf. *securi* at the end of XVI, 2. The Medicean has *iniuriam* here.

publici: In pointed relationship to *plebs*. The plebeians, one might think, should be particularly concerned with public disgrace (*flagitii*). The noun *flagitii* with which the paragraph ends highlights the shame; it recalls *flagitante vulgo* above, as the crowd was demanding that Nero perform his entire repertoire—a classic example of the depths to which the common people are said to have sunk in the presence of the *princeps*.

Three chapters on the fiasco of Bassus' alleged Didonian gold hoard transition seamlessly into the image of *Nero scaenicus*. If Nero performed anything from his *Troica* (cf. *Annales* XV, 39; Suetonius *c.* 38) as part of the entertainment, the connection to the Dido lore is especially pointed. If the emperor performed a *Niobe* (cf. Suetonius *c.* 21), then the point would be at least implicitly to underscore the angry vengeance of Apollo—the god with whom the *princeps* was increasingly to be associated.

Chapter five: Diverse theater reactions, and a glimpse of a future emperor

Sed: The conjunction introduces a different sort of audience, as those from more distant locales are not at all impressed by what they see on the stage. Bartera wonders if there is a self-reference to Tacitus here, since he would have been one of those coming from afar.

remotis e municipiis: Furneaux distinguishes these towns of Italy to municipalities in the provinces (whose inhabitants are described next). The implicit contrast throughout this paragraph is between the decadent life of Rome and the more traditional, morally observant life of the towns.

severaque adhuc et antiqui moris retinente Italia: The Medicean has *severamque adhuc et antiqui moris retinentes Italiam*. The genitive after *retinente* is good Tacitean Latin, as Furneaux notes (citing *Annales* II, 38); in either case, the emphasis is on the Italy that still holds fast to the *antiquus mos* and the "severe," more restrained life.

quique: Tacitus proceeds to his mention of the provincials who happened to be in Rome at the time of the Neronia.

lascivia inexperti: "Inexperienced in wantonness." The Medicean has *experti*, which makes little sense here.

officio legationum aut privata utilitate: Ablatives of cause. Some visitors were present on official legations, while others had come for some private reason or other. A good example of Tacitean *variatio*.

aspectum illum: "That sight," that is, of their emperor on stage.

neque labori inhonesto sufficere: The visitors to the competitions were not "up to the task," one might say, of the ignoble effort of pretending to endorse Nero's performances. *Inhonestus* refers to that which is ignoble and shameful, to something that is degrading and beneath one's dignity (cf. *OLD* s.v. c).

manibus nesciis: The country and provincial guests did not know how to clap and applaud in rhythm; they were unskilled in the business of being in attendance at the absurd theater that was the Neronian stage.

fatiscerent: Imperfect subjunctive in a *cum*-causal construction. The verb means to "droop" or to become weary (a transferred sense; cf. *OLD* 3); literally "gapes" began to appear in the applause as the unpracticed hands were unable to follow the measure and mode of the crowd's adulation of Nero.

turbarent gnaros: The visitors to Rome disturbed those who knew exactly how to behave during the Neronian performance; Tacitus plays on the idea that the spectators were themselves part of the spectacle, and that the audience was expected to behave and to function according to a set of rules just as strict as those observed by the performers on stage. *Gnarus* refers to a state of having either experience or knowledge; it can be used with passive force to refer to that which is familiar (*OLD* 2).

cuneos: Literally a "wedge," with reference to the wedge-shaped sections of the Roman amphitheatral seating. The soldiers were stationed throughout the theater to ensure that the audience acted in accordance with the wishes of the *princeps*, and as a sign of intimidation. Throughout this section there may be a hint of the idea that the soldiers would have been better off on a foreign expedition, in pursuit of an expansionist, imperialist policy (rather than serving as a *de facto* police force for the emperor); see further here I. Kajanto, "Tacitus' Attitude to War and the Soldier," in *Latomus* 29.3 (1970), pp. 699–718.

impari clamore: The thunder of the applause needed to be even and in proper measure; the soldiers were charged with making sure that no moment of time went by (*praeteriret*) without fit praise of Nero's performance.

silentio segni: Not only did the applause have to be measured and according to what was now no doubt considered the most artful practice, but there could also be no awkward moments of "sluggish" or "lazy silence." The adjective *segnis* describes that which is slothful and lacking in energy and vigor; it can describe a process that is slow in operation and conduct (*OLD* s.v. 4).

constitit: From *constare*. The meaning is that it was agreed upon. The basic sense of the verb is to stand together or to stand firm; by extension it can convey the idea that the authorities stand together on a certain point. The Medicean manuscript reads *consistit* here.

obtritos: Supply *esse*; the participle is from *obterere*. Furneaux cites the present passage as evidence that Suetonius was incorrect in his assertion that no one was allowed to leave the theater during Nero's performances; of course in Tacitus, those who did were trampled in the narrow entrances by the multitude of incoming spectators. The verb describes the crushing or destruction of something by trampling and like action; it can mean to wipe something out utterly, and by extension even to talk ill of someone in the most vicious of ways (*OLD* 3).

sedilibus: Furneaux notes the ablative of place.

continuant: The spectators were expected to stay for prolonged periods of time.

morbo exitiali correptos: The adjective means "fatal" or "deadly." The exact nature of the illness or sickness is not specified, and there may be a degree of rhetorical embellishment, though Tacitus memorably and effectively depicts the scene of the strong encouragement for the spectators to remain in place for inordinate periods of time (and seemingly interminable performances). Again, supply *esse* with the participle.

defuissent: Pluperfect subjunctive to express past contrafactuality in the protasis of a mixed conditional sentence.

nomina ac vultus: Not only the names, but also the faces of the spectators were investigated. The conjunction *ac* often conveys the sense of "and, what is more."

coeuntium: "of the ones coming together."

scrutarentur: Imperfect subjunctive to express purpose.

inrogata: The verb (*inrogare*) has the legal meaning of a proposal in opposition to something; here the meaning is that the punishments (*supplicia*) were "inflicted" or "imposed" at once (*statim*).

inlustris: The more illustrious or famous citizens. High birth and noble lineage had the benefit only of delaying, not of escaping the fate of the disinterested and the unimpressed.

dissimulatum: Tacitus is frequently concerned with the notion of appearance and of truth and falsehood. The hatred (*odium*) of Nero and his sycophants was never really gone; in some cases there was merely a temporary pretense that it had abated or been put aside. The root meaning of *dissimulare* is to give something a false appearance or identity by making it appear to be like to something else; it can mean to pretend that something is what it is not, or to conceal the more or less obvious reality of something (cf. *OLD* s.v. 2).

ferebantque Vespasianum: "And they said/used to say that Vespasian ..." Tacitus turns to the future *princeps*, the ultimate victor in the wars of succession that would follow the suicide of Nero. The historian thus enhances the scope of the whole spectacle by mention of Nero's successor (after the interim reigns, as it were, of Galba, Otho, and Vitellius); the opening of the book (and of the likely second part of Tacitus' Neronian hexad) is thus shaded with the approaching end of the *princeps* by his own more or less "voluntary death."

coniveret: The verb means to close the eyes (sometimes to blink or to wink). Vespasian was "nodding off" during the performance.

Phoebo liberto: The name is cited in a Latin inscription and is also mentioned in Dio Cassius. Vespasian's freedman is named after the god of the sun; in this case there might be a fortuitous play on the notion of the sun working to rouse slumberers from their rest.

aegre ... obtectum: Vespasian was defended by the prayers of the *meliores*—but their action was just barely able to do the job.

maiore fato: That is, his becoming emperor in his own right, at the close of the so-called Long Year (A.D. 69). Vespasian would have been one of the *inlustres* who were sooner rather than later marked down for destruction; Tacitus ascribes his salvation to the "greater destiny" or fate of his imminent reign, a *fatum* that was more *imminens* than the *pernicies* he faced at the hands of Nero. The ablative is of cause.

effugisse: Perfect infinitive in indirect discourse. The last word of the paragraph dramatically describes of the flight of the man who would soon enough be *princeps*.

Chapter six: The death of Poppaea

Poppaea: Poppaea Sabina was Nero's second wife after Claudia Octavia; they were wedded in A.D. 62. Previously she had been married to the future emperor Otho. Perhaps the most famous example of her afterlife in the arts is the opera of Claudio Monteverdi, *L'incoronazione di Poppea*, which was performed during the Venetian *Carnevale* of 1643. P. Oxy. LXXVII 5105, preserves hexameter verses on the apotheosis of Poppaea; the Greek poem is perhaps to be dated some two centuries after the death of Nero.

mortem obiit: Literally, "went to meet her death"; the phrase appears in the historian Velleius Paterculus, and in comedy.

fortuita mariti iracundia: Ablative of cause. *Fortuita* indicates that the wrath of Nero was not planned or orchestrated; he was merely angered enough one day to injure his wife fatally. The adjective highlights the almost random nature of the event; it was a haphazard act of violence that ended Poppaea's life (cf. *OLD* s.v. 3).

gravida: "Pregnant." If Poppaea had actually died of a miscarriage, the reputation of Nero could easily have seen the whole story converted into one of violence and domestic abuse.

ictu calcis: "By a blow of the heel of the foot." *Calcis* is from *calx, calcis*, f.; cf. the verb *calcare*, to "tread." A *calque* is a verbatim, "word for word" translation—something that literally follows in the very footsteps of its exemplar.

crediderim: The perfect subjunctive can be used to express present or future potentiality. Tacitus here inserts his own personal judgment on the matter; in his view there is no good reason to suspect that Nero had Poppaea poisoned (*venenum*). Poppaea's fate is rather different in the 1951 film *Quo Vadis*, where she is Nero's last victim just before his suicide, strangled to death by her husband with the dramatically uttered words, "You are my evil genius!" On the end of Nero's wife see R. Mayer, "What Caused Poppaea's Death?," in *Historia: Zeitschrift für alte Geschichte* 31.2 (1982), pp. 248–249.

quidam scriptores: "Certain writers," that is, of histories or other accounts of the Neronian period. Ancient source criticism did not demand that one cite the specifics of one's predecessors.

odio magis quam fide: "More from hatred than from trust." Tacitus ascribes the motives of those writers who claim malice aforethought to their hatred for the emperor, not to any actual belief in the story. This is another example of a weighted alternative, and of Tacitus' preoccupation with the notion of bias or editorializing judgment in the production of history. Here he indicts those who know better about the actual course of events, but who are willfully blinded by hatred for the subject of their historical inquiry.

quippe: "Surely" or "indeed," even "by all means." Tacitus makes clear in this passage that Nero both wanted children and was enamored of his wife.

liberorum cupiens: Genitive in an expression of want or desire.

amori: Dative after a compound adjective.

obnoxius: Here the meaning = "compliant" or "submissive"; one must take care in translating this adjective not to be misled by the English "obnoxious." *Obnoxius* can also mean "guilty" or "able to be punished," "vulnerable" or "in peril." The root is the noun *noxa* meaning offense, harm, injury, or crime. Tacitus may be playing on the idea that while Nero was *amori uxoris obnoxius*, it was Poppaea who was a victim to the fatal consequences of Nero's relationship with her.

abolitum: Supply *est*. Poppaea's body was not cremated, but rather embalmed. Furneaux notes that the verb is not found before Virgil and Livy.

ut Romanus mos: Tacitus' point here is to draw a sharp distinction between the habits and practices of Nero and his immediate circle and the traditions of "old Rome" and "severe Italy." Furneaux cites the evidence of the Elder Pliny that cremation was not actually an old Roman custom, but rather one that developed out of the need to dispose of the dead from foreign wars (i.e., they would be burned, and funerary urns brought back to Italy). Whatever the origin of the habit, Nero departs from the Roman way in his lavish treatment of the wife he inadvertently killed. On Roman funerary practices, J. M. C. Toynbee's *Death and Burial in the Roman World* (reprinted by the Johns Hopkins University Press, 1996) is an invaluable introduction.

regum externorum: "Foreign kings," for example in Egypt, with its famous embalming practices.

differtum: "Crowded" or "stuffed with" (from *dis-farcio*). There may be a contemptuous mockery of what Nero did to honor the body. In the BBC docudrama *Ancient Rome: The Rise and Fall of an Empire*, Episode 2 (*Nero*), the corpse of Poppaea is put on display. The adjective is not common; the fact that it occurs in the fragments of Cremutius Cordus, the historian and victim of Sejanus who is a key figure in the narrative of *Annales* IV, is perhaps coincidental. In Cremutius (fr. 1 Cornell), it refers to Antony' being "stuffed" with the slaughter of the proscriptions of the Second Triumvirate.

odoribus: Perfumes, spices rich in aroma, and the like. The funeral rites reflect the luxurious, decadent living of the honoree.

conditur: The verb *condire* can describe the dressing up of something, as with spices or myrrh (for preservation). Here it refers to the embalming of the body, as if Poppaea were "dressed/adorned" with perfumes and spices.

tumuloque Iuliorum: "In the tomb of the Julians." This is the Mausoleum of Augustus that had been constructed in 28 B.C. on the Campus Martius; both Claudius and his ill-fated son Britannicus were buried there. The mausoleum was not used for an emperor's burial after the death of Nerva in A.D. 98.

infertur: "She was buried."

ductae: Supply *sunt*; the funeral rites "were conducted." Since the body was "led out" for burial, *ducere* is appropriate to describe the action of the funeral liturgy.

exequiae: Funeral or requiem rites.

ipse: That is, Nero himself. We are reminded of the Nero who was so recently on stage; here he gives a performance of a rather different sort. *Laudavitque* is used here of a panegyric in praise of Poppaea.

apud rostra: The *rostra* was a speaker's platform, which took its name from the rams or beaks of warships. Six such bronzed prows had been captured in 338 B.C. by Duilius in the first great naval victory of the Romans; the originals were eventually replaced (ultimately with decorative and not authentic beaks).

formam: Her loveliness.

divinae: The child of the god would, of course, also be a god; the reference is also to the fact that the child is dead.

fuisset: Subjunctive in a clause of alleged reason after *quod*; Poppaea was the mother of a daughter who had been posthumously declared divine.

pro virtutibus: Nero praised the blessings of fortune and luck as if they were virtues of a heroic spouse. The mention of the alleged boons of fortune comes in the wake of the delusions of fortune that were the focus of the opening of the book.

Chapter seven: The case of Gaius Cassius

palam: "Openly."

tristem … laetam: A typical Tacitean antithesis; openly the mood of the funeral of Poppaea was sad and grim, but for those with the blessing (or curse) of memory, the whole affair was a happy one.

The death of Poppaea follows upon the narrative of the games and entertainment in which Nero figured prominently as performer and participant; now Tacitus transitions to the main focus of the rest of the extant book—the persecutions of senators and other leading citizens. The first of these episodes of imperial anger recalls the storied example of Cassius, the assassin of Julius Caesar, founder of the line of the Julian emperors, the would-be descendant of Venus, Aeneas, and Iulus.

recordantibus: Dative of reference. The root of the verb indicates that one kept something in one's heart, in this case the recollection of the deplorable behavior of Nero's late wife. Syme notes the verb *recordor* as an example of vocabulary that read appears in the *Annales* only in the later books (*op. cit.*, p. 741).

eius: That is, Poppaea's. On the striking role of women in the Claudian and Neronian *Annales*, see R. Syme, "Princesses and Others in Tacitus," in *Greece & Rome* 28.1 (1981), pp. 40–52.

nova insuper invidia: Ablative of means or instrument. Nero finished the funeral with a new display of resentment and envy over and above his previous exercise of this signal fault of his personality. *Invidia* has its etymological roots in looking askance at something (*in-videre*); one might recall folklore about the "evil eye" and other common associations of jealousy and envious ill-will. The paragraph opens with Nero's newest outburst of resentful prejudice and spite; it will end on a note of revolution (*res novae*).

complevit: Nero put the "finishing touches" on the funeral, as Yardley translates, as if the death of so wicked a woman demanded some final touch of cruelty from her surviving spouse.

prohibendo: The gerund is used here as an ablative of means or manner: Nero completed the funeral "by prohibiting" Gaius Cassius from attending. The mention of Poppaea's death in the wake of the Neronia leads at once to the resumed narrative of Nero's wrath in the wake of the Piso conspiracy. On the various plots against Nero in this period, Morgan notes: "These were invariably as unsuccessful as they were small. But the repercussions were widespread, or so the sources assert, echoing the claim that birth, wealth, and ability were criminal charges in Nero's eyes, and fatal to their possessors." (G. Morgan, *69 A.D.: The Year of Four Emperors*, Oxford, 2006, p. 11).

C. Cassium: Gaius Cassius, a jurist who was suffect consul in A.D. 30 and later proconsul of Asia; see further Furneaux's note on *Annales* XII, 12. Tacitus seems to have had a particular interest in Asia because of his proconsulship there; see further G. W. Bowersock, "Tacitus and the Province of Asia," in T. J. Luce and A. J. Woodman, *Tacitus and the Tacitean Tradition*, Princeton, 1993, pp. 3–10.

officio: Separative ablative. Cassius was barred from exercising the usual patrician right to "pay his respects" to the deceased wife of the *princeps*. The noun refers to one's "duty" or "obligation."

primum indicium mali: An ominous portending of imminent ruin: the funeral ban was the first mark or sign of the evil to come.

dilatum: From *differre*: the *malum* that was foreshadowed by the prohibition of attendance was not put off or differed for very long.

Silanus: Lucius Junius Silanus Torquatus, one of the ever dwindling number of surviving direct descendants of Augustus. See further here R.S. Rogers, "Heirs and Rivals to Nero," in *Transacttions and Proceedings of the American Philological Association* 86 (1955), pp. 190–212.

additur: Silanus was added to the roster of those presently on Nero's list of victims.

nullo crimine: Ablative of cause, or perhaps an ablative absolute. Silanus was added to the list of Nero's newest resentments not because of any guilt or crime except for the fact that … (*nisi quod*, etc.).

opibus vetustis: The first of four artfully balanced ablatives of respect or manner: Cassius was outstanding (*praecellebant*) because of his old money, as it were, and the severity of his morals and habits of living (i.e., he was eminently old-fashioned, a representative of the ancient customs of the Republic), while Silanus was famous for his (Augustan) lineage and the respectful, "modest" way in which he had conducted his youth. Tacitus' narrative thus ascribes the whole matter to one of true resentment on the part of Nero; he was jealous of these two men for the affront that their very existence posed to his own way of life and habits.

praecellebant: The two men are identified as excelling and surpassing their fellows by virtue of their noble bearing, manner, and heritage. The verb is indicative because Tacitus is giving not the alleged reason for something, but what he considers to be the actual cause of Nero's wrath. *Praecellere* describes being superior to others, that is, to be preeminent or to excel.

missa ... oratione: Yet another opportunity is thus afforded to Nero for the display of his rhetorical skills and flair. Here he sends a speech to the senate to alert them to his feelings in the matter of the two newest targets of his *invidia*.

removendos ... utrosque: "That both men had to be removed." The gerundive expresses obligation or necessity. *Utrosque* refers to Cassius and Silanus, and is the subject accusative in indirect statement introduced by *disseruit*.

disseruit: From *dissero, disserere, disserui, dissertum* (cf. "dissertation"); Nero "explained" or "arranged it that." Cf. *dissero, disserere, dissevi, dissitum*, "to scatter" or "sow seed abroad," that is, to plant or discuss an idea; cf. *semina* below. On the verb see G. Morgan, "*Disserere* and *edisserere* in Tacitus," in *Latomus* 62.3 (2003), pp. 642–647.

Cassio: Dative after a compound verb.

imagines maiorum: The reference is to the funeral masks of one's distinguished (in this case, arguably infamous) ancestors. For detailed consideration of the subject, see H. I. Flower, *Ancestor Masks and Aristocratic Power in Roman Culture*, Oxford, 2000. On how senatorial *imagines* were displayed less and less often in public, see S. Bartsch, *The Mirror of the Self: Sexuality, Self-Knowledge, and the Gaze in the Early Roman Empire*, Chicago, 2006, pp. 189–190.

C. Cassi: Gaius Cassius, the assassin of Julius Caesar. Cassius and Brutus were venerated as heroes by those with republican sentiments.

effigiem: Cf. English "effigy." The noun could refer to any type of portrait or image, a bust or statue.

coluisset: Pluperfect subjunctive in a *quod*-clause of alleged reason; Cassius was being condemned because he had kept or cherished the *effigies* of the assassin.

duci partium: Literally, "to/for the leader of the faction." The problem was likely the inscription more than the actual *effigies*. The faction or cause in this case would be those who sought to restore a republican system of government without the problem of the *princeps*.

semina belli civilis: Nero accuses Cassius of sowing the seeds of civil discord and internecine strife by having such a memorial to his ancestor.

defectionem: The noun has a wide rage of meanings, from a case of open revolt and rebellion (as here) to the "failing" or "eclipse" of the sun (*OLD* s.v. 2), or an individual's fainting spell or collapse. Its basic meaning is some sort of failing or flagging of energy of strength; from this comes the sense of desertion or abandonment of a particular person or cause/belief (*OLD* s.v. 3).

ne: This particle was added by Faërnus; the Oxford text italicizes it. Heubner accepts the emendation in his Teubner.

a domo Caesarum: "From the house of the Caesars." Cassius is accused of being all too true to the memory of his storied ancestor.

infensi nominis: The name of Cassius was hated by all those who loved and cherished the rule of the Caesars; there is a hint, too, of the hatred that would be owed to someone who was seen as betraying a benefactor.

ad discordias: One might translate, "for the fomenting of discord" (literally, the division of hearts). Accusative of purpose (a construction of which Tacitus is fond).

uteretur: The verb *utor, uti* takes the ablative (a sort of ablative of means), in this case *memoria*; Cassius is accused not only of using the memory of Gaius Cassius, but also the help of Lucius Silanus.

animo praeruptum: Silanus is characterized as being rash and bold, careless and "headstrong" (Yardley); *animo* is an ablative of respect.

novis rebus: "Revolution." To the conservative, traditionally minded Romans, "new things" meant revolution or revolt from the established order.

ostentaret: Cassius is accused of using Silanus as someone whose noble name and lineage would be useful in furthering the cause of those who would fight for the end of the house of the Caesars and the restoration of a "true" republic. There is also the hint that Silanus would be a better governor of the republic than Nero, whether as a caretaker until the old machinery of senatorial prerogative could be stored, or as a new *princeps* with a more favorable attitude toward the patricians. See further Furneaux's note here. *Ostentare* means to hold something up for an exhibition or display; it can refer to a display of particular "ostentation" or show (*OLD* s.v. 2); it can have a sense both positive and pejorative.

Chapter eight: Further Neronian accusations

increpuit: The root of the word describes a rattling or similar noise; the picture is of Nero repeatedly chiding or rebuking Silanus with bitter, stinging reproaches and protestations (cf. *OLD* s.v. 6, "to say by way of reproach, remark indignantly or scorn").

isdem quibus: Sc., for example, *verbis*. Nero attacked Silanus with the same words or charges with which he attacked Torquatus before him.

patruum: "Paternal uncle." A mother's brother was an *avunculus* (or the husband of a mother's sister, or a great uncle).

Torquatum: Decimus Iunius Silanus Torquatus, who was compelled to commit suicide in A.D. 64; he was a great-great-grandson of Augustus.

disponeret: Imperfect subjunctive after *tamquam* in a conditional clause of comparison. Silanus was charged "as if he were arranging" tasks for his freedmen that would be the emperor's prerogative to dispense (i.e., the *imperii curas*)

praeficeret: From *praeficere*, "to put someone in charge of something," literally "to make someone first or in front."

rationibus: Accounts or reckonings, as one would find in a ledger of transactions.

libellis: "Little books," that is, petitions.

inania simul et falsa: Tacitus returns to the theme of falsehood and illusion *vs.* reality. The charges against Silanus were trumped up and false; the *princeps* who had banked on the existence of phantom gold is now indulging in more unjust and dishonest charges against the object of his resentment. The phrase is in apposition to what precedes.

intentior metu et exitio patrui: In contrast to the description of this young man being headstrong and reckless. Silanus was more focused because of the ruin of his uncle; in *praecavendum* there is a note of careful thought and focus to try to stave off his own destruction. Silanus was more "intent" because of his fear, and he was terrified into taking precautions because of the ruin of his uncle. The emphasis of the entire passage is on the dread and abject terror of the young man. The Medicean has *intetior metu et etio* here.

praecavendum: Far from arranging offices and duties for freedmen as if he were already *princeps*, Silanus was taking care in advance that he would not fall victim to the emperor's wrath. *Praecavere* means to be on one's guard, to take steps to protect oneself from some threat (real or perceived); it can be either intransitive (as here) or transitive (cf. *OLD* s.v. 2).

exterritus erat: The prefix is intensive. Silanus could not have been more frightened.

inducti: This is Ferrettus' reading for the Medicean *inducit*.

vocabulo indicum: The men who were brought in to level accusations were called *indices* or "informers," literally those who would indicate what exactly had been done. They were, however, merely agents of Nero, not really impartial observers of wrongdoings. The emphasis is on the power of words and the contrast between what one does and what one claims to do, and on the motivations and enticements to action. On *vocabulo* see H. Haynes, "Tacitus' Dangerous Word," in *Classical Antiquity* 23.1 (2004), pp. 33–61.

Lepidam: Iunia Lepida. Julia the Younger was her maternal grandmother; she was thus descended from Augustus and Agrippa. Tacitus does not record what happened to her; a reasonable speculation is that she was killed in A.D. 65. For a complete account of the children of Aemilia Lepida (the fiancée of Claudius and daughter of Julia the Younger), see the detailed listing of the "Descendants of Agrippa" in L. Powell, *Marcus Agrippa: Right-hand Man of Caesar Augustus*, South Yorkshire: Pen & Sword Military, 2015.

amitam: "Paternal aunt."

incestum: Literally, that which was not *castus*. The Latin charge *incestum* encompassed a broader range of charges than the English "incest." Here, however, Lepida is charged with an illicit union with her nephew.

diros sacrorum ritus: What we might call "black magic" or the dark arts. The *lex Cornelia de sicariis et veneficiis* of 80 B.C. was concerned with the problem of deaths caused by invocations of infernal deities and magic potions and spells.

confingerent: The verb emphasized the cooperative nature of the action of the informants; the focus is once again on the fashioning and crafting of falsehoods and mendacious narratives.

conscii: That is, as being aware of the crimes of incest and magic. The force of *trahebantur* is that these new individuals were "dragged in" under threat of ruin and force; they would just barely escape the fate of their more important alleged co-conspirators.

Vulcacius Tullinus …: Very little is known of these two senators and one equestrian; Calpurnius Fabatus was a correspondent of Pliny the Younger. Lipsius conjectured that the reading *Tertullinus* is correct, based on the evidence of Tacitus, *Historiae* IV, 9.

appellato principe: Ablative absolute. Nero would have been the last possible hope for appeal in a criminal prosecution.

instantem damnationem: "The damnation that was standing right in front of them," that is, the imminent ruin.

frustrati: From the deponent *frustror*. Vulcacius Tullinus and the others "frustrated" their impending doom, that is, they tricked or cheated it of its victory.

circa summa scelera: *Circa* ("concerning") as a preposition takes an accusative object that indicates that extent of the action or state of being; the *summa scelera* refers to the prosecution of major figures.

distentum: Nero was "swollen" or "distended" in the matter of crimes of the highest magnitude, that is, in the punishment of Silanus and Cassius—he was preoccupied and anxiously busy. The adjective may have an added negative force of the stretched out and extended body of a glutton (so in Horace's *Sermones*). Nero is so focused on the ruin of his nobler victims that he cannot be bothered with lesser alleged criminals (and despite his apparent ravenous appetite for ruin). There is also a hint of the more famous deaths to come (Petronius, Thrasea).

minores: From the image of the ancestors, the *maiores*, we have moved to the trifling senators and knights who could escape the hazards and perils of Nero's reign precisely because they were not important enough to demand immediate destruction.

evasere: That is, *evaserunt*. The potential additional victims of the "scandal" escaped only because Nero was preoccupied with more serious victims of his wrath.

Chapter nine: Sentence of exile and the death of Silanus

consulto senatus: "By a decree of the senate." Nero's indignation against Cassius and Silanus was endorsed as if by the normal workings of senatorial governance.

Caesar: That is, Nero.

statueret: Imperfect subjunctive. The senate passed decrees of exile on Cassius and Silanus, and Nero (the subject of the verb) was left to determine a suitable punishment for Lepida; no extant source records her exact fate. For detailed consideration of the punishment of exile under Nero and Tiberius in particular, see M. V. Braginton, "Exile under the Roman Emperors," in *The Classical Journal* 39.7 (1944), pp. 391–407.

eius: That is, Cassius'.

expectabatur: It was anticipated that Cassius would soon enough die of old age on Sardinia, so that there was no need to order his execution. Cassius would have the last laugh; he survived into the reign of Vespasian, blind and aged though he was.

Naxum ... Ostiam: Accusatives of place to which without prepositions. Silanus was apparently sentenced to be exiled on the Greek island of Naxos; he was temporarily held at the great harbor of Ostia in preparation for his journey. *Ostiam* is the correction of Lipsius for the Medicean reading *ostia*. For a comprehensive study of Rome's great harbor district, see R. Meiggs, *Roman Ostia*, Oxford, 1960 (second edition, 1973).

Barium: The modern Bari in Apulia, on the Adriatic coast of Italy. It is not entirely clear how Silanus was transported from Ostia to Bari; it is likely that he was supposed to set off from the harbor at Ostia, but that the arrangements were changed for some unknown reason. The plan, however, was that he would never make it to the island (hence *tamquam*; once again there is an emphasis on show and pretense, the Neronian theater of the macabre). "Bari, on the Adriatic, about 70 miles N.W. of Brindisi; in the time of Horace, and probably of Nero, little more than a fishing-village, now a considerable city" (Jackson's Loeb notes *ad loc.*; cf. Horace, *Serm.* 1.5.97 *Bari moenia piscosi*).

indignissimum casum: "His most unworthy fall." Tacitus makes clear that Silanus did not deserve this end.

sapienter tolerans: Once again Silanus is depicted as being eminently thoughtful, reflective, and possessed of the highest sentiments of wisdom and philosophical contemplation.

centurione ad caedem misso: Nero's order is that the "exiled" Silanus will actually be executed before he ever makes it out of Italy. *Caedes* is a strong, poetic word for execution or slaughter.

suadenti: That is, the centurion.

venas abrumpere: "To cut his veins," that is, to commit suicide.

animum: Silanus had been described as being headstrong or spirited in his *animus* (XVI, 7); now the young man demonstrates just how determined in spirit he is.

destinatum: Supply *esse*.

percussori: "The executioner." Cf. *percutere*.

gloriam ministerii: "The glory of his ministry." Silanus sarcastically assures the centurion that he will not allow him to lose the chance to achieve glory in the "heroic" exploit of killing the helpless captive.

praevalidum: Tacitus continues to emphasize the notion of preeminence and exceptional fortitude. Silanus may have been unarmed, but all the same he was outstanding in his valor and strength. *Praevalidus* describes that which is of outstanding strength; it can have a particular meaning with respect to that which is exceptional in the military and political arenas (*OLD* s.v. 2).

irae quam timori propiorem: "Nearer to anger than to fear." At last, in the face of his imminent death, Silanus is free of the fear that had earlier possessed him.

a militibus: The centurion orders that Silanus be slain by the soldiers; there is an implicit contrast between the brave mien and nobility with which the Neronian victim meets his end, and the unwillingness of the centurion to dispatch him in what would already be an uneven single combat against an unarmed man.

obniti: Present infinitive of the deponent *obnitor*.

intendere ictus: The verb means to stretch out something or to strain toward something; it can be used metaphorically of the turning of the mind to some object of attention, or to describe one's mental focus on a given task or subject (cf. the English "to intend"). Silanus is fiercely fighting to the end; he strains against the blows of his assassins.

quantum ... valebat: "As much as he was able." The accusative expresses extent or duration.

manibus nudis: Silanus fought with his bare hands; the picture is one of both pathetic resistance and heroic defiance of Nero's minions.

vulneribus adversis: "With wounds facing/in front." Silanus never sought to escape the blows of his executioners; he died bravely, as if in the heat of battle (*tamquam in pugna caderet*).

caderet: Imperfect subjunctive after *donec*. The present or imperfect subjunctive can be used in such temporal clauses to express intention or will.

Chapter ten: Further victims and dramatic incidents

Haud minus prompte: Literally, "scarcely less promptly." A recurring theme is the alacrity with which certain outbursts of Neronian anger and resultant deaths occur; the expression is heavy with a sense of weariness and dry contempt for the times and the actions of the *princeps*.

Tacitus will now also prepare to introduce another element of the long and grim stories of imperial wrath: the displays of *pietas* that were made by the relatives of the condemned.

L. Vetus: Lucius Antistius Vetus, who had been consul in A.D. 55 (*Annales* XIII, 11), and who also served in Germany and Asia. For the early history of the Antistii, see R. Syme, *The Augustan Aristocracy*, Oxford, 1989, p. 426. Cf. also T. J. Cornell, *The Fragments of the Roman Historians*, Oxford, 2013, pp. 630–631:

> An L. Vetus is mentioned by Pliny *nat.* 1 among the sources for books 3–6, "*geographicorum*" ... Our author may be identical with L. Antistius Verus ... who committed suicide in 66 ...but he is not credited with any campaigns in Germany and is known only to have begun construction of a canal, which he was unable to complete (Tac. *Ann.* 13.53.2-4). He may have written on geography, engineering, or river management.

socrus: "Mother-in-law." The phrase *socrus Sextia et Pollitta filia* = chiasmus, a rhetorical figure of speech in which there is an inverted parallelism. The name is taken from the Greek word for a "crossing," or literally "the making of the letter X or chi." Nothing is known about Sextia other than what is found in Tacitus.

subiere: That is, *subierunt*.

invisi: "Hateful." Again the image is implicitly one of sight and vision; Nero cannot stand to see this family, because they constitute a living memory of one of his previous acts of violence.

vivendo: Gerund. The ablative is of means; Vetus and his family were an affront to Nero by virtue of their very existence. *Vivendo* is the correction of the Puteolanus edition for the Medicean reading *vincendo*.

exprobrarent: Imperfect subjunctive after *tamquam*. The verb means to "reproach" or to "upbraid" someone. As the paragraph opens, the family of Vetus is a powerful, silent reproach to the emperor; as it draws to a close, Pollitta will be loud and vocal in her criticism of Nero.

Rubellium Plautum: Gaius Rubellius Plautus, whose mother Julia was the granddaughter of the emperor Tiberius; she was executed in A.D. 43 during the Claudian reign as a victim of the notorious Messalina. Rubellius was killed in A.D. 62. See further V. Pagán, *Conspiracy Theory in Latin Literature*, Austin: The University of Texas Press, 2012, pp. 54–55:

> C. Rubellius Plautus was the great-great-grandson of Augustus ... According to Tacitus, Rubellius Plautus was accused in 55 on trading on his pedigree so as to marry Agrippina the Younger and thereby obtain rule and achieve a revolution ... Five years later the appearance of a comet gave people the chance to bandy about names of possible replacements for Nero; Rubellius Plautus was mentioned ... Rubellius' compliant withdrawal from Rome bought him but two years. In 62, at the instigation of Tigellinus ... Rubellius Plautus was marked for death on a pretext of fomenting a revolution; his head was brought to Nero (*Ann.* 14.59).
>
> Rubellius Plautus suffered the fatal flaw of belonging to the imperial lineage, bearing to the great Augustus the same relation as Nero did, great-great-grandsons both. A second damning trait was his high moral virtue, bearing-although young and wealthy-a stern countenance befitting his old-fashioned morals. Nero regarded the first as a personal threat and the second as a personal affront. Rubellius Plautus in turn took the prudent tack of withdrawing into secluded private life, having nothing whatever to do with any public affairs. Nero pursued him anyway. (J. T. Dillon, *Musonius Rufus and Education in the Good Life*, Lanham, Maryland: University Press of America, 2004, p. 52)

generum: "Son-in-law."

detegendae: Gerundive. The *saevitia* or "savagery" of Nero had to be exposed, as it were; the language is again reflective of the image of pretense and masks that do a poor job of obscuring the reality beneath the façade. The basic meaning of the verb is to remove the roof or covering from something; it can refer to the unsheathing of a weapon (as a sword from a scabbard; cf. *OLD* s.v. 2b); from these physical uses comes the sense of disclosing or revealing some detail.

interversis: Past participle of *intervertere*. The basic meaning of the verb is to turn something aside; by natural enough extension it comes to mean to cheat or defraud someone.

Fortunatus: Once again the freedman has an appropriate name; Fortunatus will provide the excuse that Nero needs to move against Rubellius' surviving family. Vetus' *libertus* was a disreputable criminal sort in matters of money; now he is graduated to informer and destroyer of lives. On the reputation of freedmen in Nero's time *vs.* the Claudian era, see F. Millar, *The Emperor in the Roman World (31 B.C.–A.D. 337)*, London: Duckworth, 1977 (second edition 1992).

accusandum: Gerund.

adscito: "Taken," in this case as a partner in conspiracy and crime.

vinctum: From *vincire*. Fortunatus had been imprisoned for embezzlement by his master during his proconsulship of Asia.

exolvit: That is, *exsolvit*. Nero had Claudius Demianus released from prison as a reward for his treachery against Vetus (*in praemium accusationis*). Once more the narrative of Nero's wickedness is populated by thoroughly disreputable agents and emissaries of wrongdoing.

reo: "The defendant," that is, Vetus.

pari sorte componi: As Furneaux observes, the implicit metaphor is from the world of the arena. Vetus realized that he and his freedman were now on equal terms; in theory a *libertus* should not be allowed to prosecute his former master. The historian's point is that the normal order of things has been inverted; if anything, life in Rome has become something akin to one of Nero's stage productions. For a comprehensive treatment of Roman *liberti*, see H. Mouritsen, *The Freedman in the Roman World*, Cambridge, 2011.

Formianos in agros: Formiae was about halfway on the journey between Rome and Naples.

occulta custodia: Vetus was surrounded by a "hidden guard." Again the emphasis is on secrecy, deception and illusion; everything seems more or less fine at Formiae, but in reality Vetus' every move is being watched.

super: "Over and above." Pollitta has had ample experience of Nero's horrors.

ingruens: Neuter participle in agreement with *periculum*. The verb *ingruere* means to attack or to assail; the peril of the charges against Vetus is the present danger that is threatening the family. The verb can be used with particular references to circumstances that are especially unwelcome or unwanted (*OLD* s.v. 3).

atrox: A quite strong adjective (cf. English "atrocious"). Vetus' daughter is seriously afflicted by the long sorrow of some three years now (i.e., since the death of her husband Rubellius). Furneaux renders the adjective as "exasperated." One word effectively captures what must have been the attitude of so many in the face of Nero's violent excesses and abuses of republican liberty.

viderat: The power of vision: Pollitta was an eyewitness to the bloody scene of Nero's *percussores* as they rushed in to slay her husband Rubellius.

cruentam cervicem: The assassins struck Rubellius in the neck, either to stab his jugular or to behead him.

ex quo: Sc. *tempore*: "from the time when."

eius: That is, Rubellius'.

amplexa: From *amplector, amplecti*.

servabat: The imperfect is durative; Rubellius' wife took care of the blood and bloodstained clothes of her husband as if they were sacred relics of the sort one might associate with martyrs and saints. Pollitta is depicted by Tacitus as being another classic example of an *univira*, that is, a woman devoted to one man; in widowhood Vetus' daughter is largely devoted to preserving the memory of her slain husband, and with fresher and more gruesome relics than Cassius had to do honor to his tyrannicide of an ancestor.

vestis respersas: The garments that were stained with the blood of Rubellius. Again, the description is rich with the image of the hagiography that was developing around those perceived to be victims of tyranny and despotism.

inpexa: "Uncombed." By extension the adjective can describe someone who is unsophisticated or unpolished; here the point is literally that Rubellius' widow is neglecting her appearance as a mark of grief. The word is a correction of Petavius for the reading *inplexa* of the Medicean.

luctu continuo: "In/with constant lament." Furneaux concludes that this ablative and *ullis alimentis* are probably ablatives of quality, though they could also be ablatives absolute.

alimentis: "Nourishment" (cf. the verb *alo, alere, alui, altum/alitum*); in anatomy, the "alimentary canal."

arcerent: "Stave off." She eats only that which is necessary to prevent death. *Arcere* refers to keeping something close or contained; it can also mean to prevent something else from approaching or drawing near (*OLD* s.v. 2); to rescue or protect someone or something; to dispel or keep away some physical state (e.g., sleep).

hortante patre: Ablative absolute. Tacitus does not make clear exactly why Vetus encouraged his daughter to travel to Naples; it is perhaps unlikely that he sent her there to intercede on his behalf.

Neapolim: Naples; the form is accusative (here without a preposition, as usually with the names of cities).

aditu: Separative ablative. We are reminded of the ease with which informers could gain access to the *princeps*; this noble Roman daughter and widow, in contrast, is unable to see her emperor.

egressus: Accusative (i.e., not a nominative participle). Rubellius' widow literally besieged the exits to Nero's residence; she insisted on an audience to intercede for her father.

insontem: "Innocent."

consulatus sui: "Of his own consulship." Pollitta begs that Nero might show respect and honor to the colleague with whom he shared the highest office in the *cursus honorum*.

dederet: From *dedo, dedere, dedidi, deditum*, "to surrender" or "hand over." The imperfect subjunctives *audiret* and *dederet* describe the actions that Pollitta wishes for Nero to take; they are dependent on *clamitabat* and function as virtual indirect commands.

quondam: "Once."

modo ... aliquando: "Now" ... "sometimes/at other times."

eiulatu: "Wailing" or "lamentation."

egressa: "She surpassed" or "went beyond" her gender (*sexum*). The participle comes soon after the related noun *egressus*; Tacitus enjoys this sort of wordplay and repetition in close sequence.

voce infensa: Pollitta has an understandable enough hatred for Nero, and sometimes the language of lament and petition is exchanged for that of angry reproach and open contempt.

clamitabat: The main verb is another durative imperfect, expressing well the repeated nature of the woman's pleas. *Clamitare* can have a particular sense of calling on someone repeatedly by name (*OLD* s.v. 2), or to proclaim something in an exceptionally loud voice, with repetition.

immobilem se: Nero was unmoved by her petitions, just as she was constant in her vigilance at his door. The whole scene is something of a perversion of the image of the elegiac lover at the door, here in a quite different context, through with equally ineffective cries for attention.

iuxta: Adverbial, "just as." Nero was deaf both to her petitions and to her own ill-will and enmity. We have moved from the *invidia* of the *princeps* to the rather more justified resentment of the brave woman.

ostendit: Once again the language may reflect the sense of the playing of roles in a theatrical drama; Nero "displays" himself as impervious either to criticism or to cajoling. The pose here is very different from that of XVI, 4 *flexus genu*, where the *princeps* awaited the verdict of the audience for his stage performance. For a study of how the Neronian hexad uses certain elements of theatrical, dramatic confrontation and gesture to provide authorial commentary on the *princeps*, see A. Betensky, "Neronian Style, Tacitean Content: The Use of Ambiguous Confrontations in the *Annales*," in *Latomus* 37.2 (1978), pp. 419–435.

Chapter eleven: A family suicide

nuntiat: The subject is Vetus' daughter Pollitta. The announcement she makes to her father is that he should cast away all expectation of reprieve or hope; the revelation that Vetus must commit suicide paves the way for a dramatic *tableau* of familial *pietas* in the face of imperial fury. If Nero fancied himself a Julian in the line of Aeneas and Iulus, then one might well think that some of his contemporaries, at least, took note of where the displays of Aeneas' signal quality of *pietas* were on display in the months after the Piso conspiracy.

uti: The verb *utor* takes an ablative object as usual. *Necessitate* refers to the fact that Vetus' life is over; his daughter urges him literally to "exercise necessity"—Vetus is encouraged to make his death as dignified and noble as possible. If Vetus had indeed sent her to Nero in the hope that she might win pardon or mercy for him, then now Pollitta exhorts her father to die in the storied tradition of so many other casualties of tyranny.

adfertur: The passive is impersonal; translate "It was reported to them that…"

cognitionem: An investigation or inquiry. A *cognitio* is literally the act of coming to know something; it can emphasize the process by which the knowledge is obtained, with a natural enough extension to the world of judicial processes and investigations (*OLD* s.v. 3). It has the specialized use in drama of the recognition of identity that is often central to a tragic plot.

trucem sententiam: The verdict is a foregone conclusion; the senate has been quite effectively co-opted by the *princeps*.

defuere: For *defuerunt*.

monerent: Imperfect subjunctive in a generic relative clause/relative clause of characteristic.

Caesarem: That is, Nero. "Caesar" and "heir" stand in apposition.

ita: "Thus, thereby, in this way."

quod aspernatus: Vetus would hear nothing of the suggestion that he should name Nero as his principal heir. Latin has a more marked fondness than English for commencing sentences with relative pronouns; *quod* is best translated with a demonstrative (e.g., Yardley's "this option").

proxime: Superlative adverb. Vetus had lived his life "very near" to freedom and *libertas*.

actam: *Agere* is one of the most versatile verbs in Latin; here the perfect passive participle is used with *vitam* to describe a "life lived" or "conducted": Vetus drove out his years, as it were, in a state of relative freedom—and he was determined to die in a manner that accorded with his life.

novissimo servitio: "The newest" moment of life is just before death; Vetus refuses to take on the yoke of slavery in his final moments.

foedaret: "Besmirch" or "stain." The verb and its related adjective *foedus*, *-a*, *-um* is another strong, sharp choice; Vetus concluded that it would be "disgusting" and "vile" for him to leave a bequest to Nero.

largitur: Deponent.

quantum aderat pecuniae: Literally, "as much as was present of money." *Pecuniae* functions as a partitive genitive or genitive of the divided whole. Whatever money he had at hand, he gave it to his slaves—this highlighting a marked contrast between his servants and his *princeps*.

qua: That is, *aliqua*. "After *si, nisi, num*, and *ne*, all the *ali*'s drop away." The pronoun is indefinite: whatever was at hand to be taken away, the slaves were to transport, be it goods or riches.

sibi quemque: "Each one for himself."

ad suprema: "For the last things," that is, for the suicide. Vetus acts here as a veritable stage director; the "crew" is free to remove everything from the platform except the three couches on which the drama of suicide will be performed. This is also rival theater: for the absurd madness of Nero's performances, this noble family will offer a substitute play.

eodem ... eodem: Tacitus emphasizes the shared nature of the deaths: the family used the same room and the same weapon for their exit from Nero.

singulis vestibus: "With a single garment." Each one is covered for the sake of modesty (*ad verecundiam*) with a single article of clothing as they are hastily (*properi*) taken to the baths.

balineis: Dative with a compound verb.

inferuntur: The family is carried into the bath; Tacitus plays throughout with forms of *fero, ferre*, given the image of burial and being carried out for a funeral.

avia: "Grandmother."

certatim: "Earnestly" and "avidly"; the adverb speaks to the idea of a competition. The "actors" urge each other on in a macabre drama of death—for each one wants to be left alive so that the other does not need to witness their death.

labenti animae: "For soul as it slips away." The participle is from *labor, labi, lapsum*. The verb is one of the more evocative and lovely in the language; its basic meaning is to glide or move with effortless, sliding motion. From this comes its use to describe the motions of celestial bodies and the stars of the heaven; also the behavior of liquids and (in a poetic sense), the passage of time (*OLD* s.v. 4). It can also mean to fall or to tumble, either of an individual or of the toppling of buildings and edifices; the body and its constituent parts can fall down and fail in death, injury, or fainting.

superstites et morituros: A marvelously expressed sentiment; they all wish to leave their relatives behind as survivors, though survivors who are (like all mortals), "about to die." *Morituros* is future active participle.

ordinem: Fortune preserved "order," that is, the old died first, the youngest last. It was considered a supreme blow of ill fortune for a parent to be compelled to witness the death of a child.

seniores: The Medicean manuscript has *seniore* here; Heubner prints *seniore <s>*.

cui prima aetas: "For whom the first age was at hand." The dative is one of possession or reference. Pollitta died last.

accusati: Supply *sunt*. Tacitus thrusts the reader back into the world of Nero's drama; the dead are reviled after their noble suicide, in what could be considered the emperor's personal verdict on their performance.

post sepulturam: Not just after death, but after burial; the detail adds to the ridiculousness of what Nero proceeds to do in the wake of the suicides.

more maiorum: The (ridiculous) decree was that the dead should be punished according to the "custom of the ancestors." In Suetonius' life of Nero (*c.* 49), Nero is informed that he has been condemned to death in the same way by a decree of the senate (*ut puniatur more maiorum*), and he is compelled to ask what exactly this means. He is told that the malefactor was stripped of his garments and fastened by the neck against pieces of wood, only then to be flogged or beaten to death with rods. Terror at such a prospect serves to hasten his own decision to commit suicide.

intercessit: Nero "interceded," that is, he annulled the decree of the (co-opted) senate, most likely in an attempt to appear merciful. The family would be allowed to die in any manner they wished. Tacitus savors the absurd ridiculousness of the scene.

sine arbitro: "Without an arbiter." The dead family was afforded a measure of freedom in how they could die.

ea ... laudibria: "Those reproaches/mockeries." The expression literally frames the words that describe the deaths; Nero throws insults on the noble dead. "There was no shortage of senators willing to turn up and condemn their peers" (M. T. Griffin, *Nero: The End of a Dynasty*, London-New York: Routledge, 2000, p. 170 (reprint of the 1984 B. T. Batsford Ltd. first edition).

caedibus peractis: "With the slaughter having been quite completed." The prefix is once again intensive; the family had already taken quite good care of what Nero and his senatorial collaborators had decided. One might compare the historically inaccurate but effectively hilarious scene in *Quo Vadis* after Seneca informs Nero of the suicide of Petronius; Peter Ustinov's Nero insists that all manner of abuse and punishment be heaped on Petronius for having committed suicide without Nero's order.

Chapter twelve: Another victim, and changes for the calendar

Publius Gallus: The identity of this Roman equestrian is unknown; Nipperdey wondered if the correct name should be "Rubrius" Gallus.

Faenio Rufo: After the death of Burrus, Faenius Rufus had been appointed praetorian prefect with Nero's henchman Tigellinus in A.D. 62; he had previously been prefect of the grain supply (*praefectus annonae*) from 55 to 62. He had fallen victim to the Pisonian conspiracy (cf. *Annales* XIV, 51 and XV, 50).

Veteri non alienus fuerat: The implied relationship need not have been particularly strong; cf. Yardley's "passing acquaintance." Gallus was a close associate of Rufus, and he was known to Vetus—more than enough to ensure his end in these days of Nero's reign. The verb is indicative because Tacitus is not giving the alleged, but rather the actual reason for Nero's enmity.

aqua et igni prohibitus est: This was a variety of sentence of exile, less severe than, for example, Cassius' being deported to the island of Sardinia. Publius Gallus could more or less depart for wherever he wanted, but he needed to flee Rome (and suffer a loss of property there).

liberto et accusatori: The freedman and accuser Fortunatus, we might think. The contrast is between the image of the *libertus* and that of the informer or betrayer of a former master.

the potential for betrayal was if anything greater in the high-status Roman household, which frequently incorporated many members not related by marriage or blood—slaves, most obviously, but also adopted sons, stepparents, and so on … Civil war reminded Romans of that fact as no other event could. In his preface to the *Histories* highlighting the features of the civil war of 68–69 AD, Tacitus too emphasizes that slaves, freedmen, friends, children, and wives often determined whether the *paterfamilias* would survive. (J. Osgood, *Caesar's Legacy: Civil War and the Emergence of the Roman Empire*, Cambridge, 2006, p. 80)

praemium operae: "The reward for the deed/work."

inter viatores tribunicios: These were the messengers of the tribunes, literally the men who traveled on the *via* to deliver edicts and requests of the *tribuni*. As Furneaux notes, this passage affords evidence that even the employees of the state officials had special places reserved for them. Fortunatus has his reward, however modest it might seem; in a culture obsessed with dignity and honor, the seating in the theater was a matter of great concern—and we are reminded yet again of the eminently theatrical nature of the whole proceeding: theater seating was especially important under the supreme imperial artist.

menses ... sequebantur: The Medicean has the singulars *mensis* and *sequebatur* here; Nipperdey emended to the plurals (Heubner prints *sequeba* <*n*> *tur*).

eundem: From *idem, eadem, idem*. The demonstrative underscores that April had been renamed; the same month was now in a sense both April and "Neroneus."

Neroneum: April was renamed "Neroneus." At XV, 74 Tacitus describes how April was given the cognomen of "Nero."

Claudii ... Germanici: May was now called "Claudius," and June, "Germanicus." When Nero had been adopted by Claudius in A.D. 50, he took the name "Nero Claudius Caesar Germanicus Drusus." Nero's mother was Agrippina the Younger, whose father was Germanicus. Caligula had renamed September *Germanicus*. For a convenient overview, see J. Rüpke, *The Roman Calendar from Numa to Constantine: Time, History, and the Fasti*, Malden, Massachusetts: Wiley-Blackwell, 2011. "So Commodus, by drawing upon his farrago of titles, was able to construct a year comprising the months—*Amazonius, Invictus, Pius, Felix, Lucius, Aelius ...*" (Jackson's Loeb note *ad loc.*). Julius Caesar was famous for his calendar reforms; Nero's would be of a more ephemeral quality.

testificante: Present participle from the deponent *testificor*. Orfitus "brought it to light" or "bore witness" (cf. *testis*), that is, as to why the names of the months were changed.

Cornelio Orfito: Servius Cornelius Scipio Salvidienus Orfitus; he served as consul in 51 under Claudius, and was proconsul in Africa under Nero.

censuerat: *Censeo, censere, censui, censum*, "to give an opinion/vote/decree/ judge." Tacitus does not give any indication why it was Orfitus in particular who should be involved in these calendar issues.

ideo: "For that reason."

transmissum: The exact meaning of this participle has been the subject of debate. Lipsius (followed by Halm) emended *Iunius* to *Iulius*, arguing that the point of the passage is that May was renamed "Claudius" and *July* "Germanicus," with June "passed over" (*transmissum*) because it was now considered an unlucky name. The problem is that there is no other extant use of *transmissum* in the sense of, "to pass over into a new name." *Iunium*, in any case, is Lipsius' emendation of the Medicean reading *iunctum*; the passage was apparently one that was prone to corruption and confusion. It seems likely that Nero would have wanted to change the name of "June" because of the executions of the Iunii; this at least gives a reason for the nomenclature alterations at this time. On the other hand, there is no good reason for why May was renamed (Furneaux observes that this detail may not have particularly bothered Orfitus).

interfecti: Supply *sunt*.

fecissent: Pluperfect subjunctive in a clause of alleged reason. "June" was allegedly now an inauspicious name because of the Iunii.

Chapter thirteen: Summation of the year and further disasters

foedum annum: Once again Tacitus employs the strong image of disgust and revulsion; the year A.D. 65 is condemned as being especially loathsome and odious on account of the many crimes of the *princeps*. The summation of the year will be another catalogue of woes and disasters.

etiam: "Also." There is an implicit criticism of Nero's view of his own divinity; the *princeps* tainted the year with his murders and foul crimes, while the gods seemed to voice their displeasure on the whole proceedings by storms and pestilence.

insignivere: For *insigniverunt*. Note here the view of Owen and Gildenhard:

> The gods, then, go beyond sending signs of warning. They cause havoc, and not only for the *princeps*. In the wake of the conspiracy of Piso, the wrath of the gods somehow encompasses all of Roman society. *Annals* 16.13.1-2 is particularly striking because it conflates divine anger with the savagery of the *princeps* ... And soon afterwards, Tacitus steps back from his account of the bloodshed caused by Nero to reflect on

his narrative and the impact it may have on the reader ... What these passages illustrate is the uncertainty principle.

(M. Owen and I. Gildenhard, *Tacitus, Annals 15.20-23, 33-34: Latin Text, Study Wids with Vocabulary, and Commentary*, Cambridge: Open Book Publishers, 2013, pp. 112–113). The wrath of the gods is a judgment on the Rome of the Caesars; it is an indictment not only of the *princeps*, but also of those who would either cooperate openly with him or consent by silence. The question also connects to the Stoic (and other) philosophical views on the action of the immortals, and to the problem of fortune/fate and chance that was raised in the very opening of the book, as Fortuna was said to be making sport of the would-be god Nero.

And so as a year ends, Nero evokes the wrath of the gods, a theme that dominates the opening sequence of Virgil's epic *Aeneid*. In that poem, the anger of Juno in the face of the *pietas* of Aeneas raises the question of the propriety of extreme divine rage and the problem of justice and due recompense for labors and struggle; in Tacitus, either the gods are punishing Rome for the actions of Nero and those who would collaborate with him either actively or in silence, or the world is witnessing the horror of how the gods of heaven seem to be cooperating with the god Nero in wreaking havoc for Rome.

vastata: Supply *est*.

turbine ventorum: "A whirlwind of winds," that is, tornadic type activity.

villas ... fruges: The asyndeton effectively expresses the action of the whirlwind that devastated Campania.

arbusta: Orchards or vineyards (cf. *arbor*, a "tree").

fruges: From *frux, frugis*, f., produce or fruit/crops. Derived from this is the indeclinable adjective *frugi* (cf. the dative of *frux*), with the meaning of "useful/honest" (cf. English "frugal").

passim: "Everywhere." The adverb comes from *pando, pandere, pandi, passum* "to spread out." One sometimes finds index or other such entries with the label *passim*, meaning that something occurs over a wide area or in a widespread fashion.

disiecit: The force of the prefix is that the action of the wind tore through and tossed whatever was in its path into "different" directions.

pertulit: The prefix is both directional and intensive.

urbi: A dative of respect, reference, or direction; the destruction spread even to areas near the city. Unqualified *urbs* usually refers to Rome.

in qua: Supply *urbe*.

omne mortalium genus: "Every kind of mortal thing," that is, both human and animal.

vis pestilentiae: "Autumn was always a sickly time in Italy"—Furneaux. Some scholars have tried to identify the specific nature of the pestilence (cholera?), but Tacitus gives precious little in the way of epidemiological clues.

depopulabatur: Deponent. The verb vividly highlights how there was literally a depopulation because of the force and power (*vis*) of the sickness. It can refer to the sacking of cities and the devastation of both human and animal resources; it can be used of both natural disaster (weather and storm), and of disease: "to rob, despoil" (cf. *OLD* s.v. 2).

nulla caeli intemperie: "With no disturbance of the sky." *Intemperies* describes any sort of meteorological trouble or hazard.

occurreret: Imperfect subjunctive in a generic relative clause. Pestilence afflicted the city, but the air quality, as it were, did not appear to be disturbed. The Medicean reads *occurret* here.

exanimis: Literally "breathless," that is, "dead."

itinera: "Journeys," and so by extension roads and byways. There were funerals and makeshift funeral rites everywhere. Tacitus may have had in mind the chilling conclusion of Lucretius' *De Rerum Natura*, of the great plague at Athens.

funeribus: *Funus* could refer either to a "funeral" or to the actual corpse.

periculo: Separative ablative. There was no age or gender that was free from the peril of the pestilence.

perinde: "In the same manner/just as/equally." The plague did not distinguish between slaves or citizens; the devastation and peril was equal for all.

ingenua plebes: *Ingenuus* is an adjective rich in connotation and range of meanings; it means "freeborn" and conveys a note of nobility and honor; it can also mean that something or someone is delicate and tender. Cf. English "disingenuous" for the opposite idea. The word refers also to that which is particularly appropriate for someone who is freeborn and noble, as it were (cf. *OLD* s.v. 3); it can describe the refined taste of the palate, or that which is modest and open in the sense of free from dissimulation and any hint of dishonesty or guile.

raptim: The root is from the notion of a quick snatching or taking away (*rapio, rapere*); the action of the pestilence was swift and sudden. Bartera suggests to me that the pestilence is meant to reflect Nero's actions; like a plague, he kills many men and women, of all ranks.

extingui: There may be a hint of the metaphor of the extinguishing of the lamp or light of life.

coniugum et liberorum: Tacitus returns to the theme of the family in death; the laments of spouses and children filled the city in the wake of the health disaster.

adsident: From *adsideo, adsidere, adsedi, adsessum*, literally "to sit next to someone/something."

eodem rogo: From the image of the family that committed suicide in the same room and with the same blade, we move to a terrifying picture of families in lament at funeral pyres, where the mourners are swiftly taken ill and quickly burned in the same place as those whom they were mourning. Cf. the repetition of *eodem* in Chapter 11.

equitum senatorumque interitus: Another jab of the historian at Nero; the deaths of senators and knights were less mournful (*minus flebiles*), despite their great number (*quamvis promisci*), since by virtue of the mortality that is common to all, they seemed to anticipate the savagery of the *princeps*. Put more directly, Nero would have executed many of the noblemen who fell victim to the plague anyway; the pestilence was an all too effective reminder of humanity's mortal state, and no one had much time to spend on tears for those who would have died sooner rather than later anyway. *Interitus* refers to that which is particular violent or unnatural, a death that is both before one's time and savage in its manner; by extension the noun can refer to anything that is ruined or in the process of being destroyed (*OLD* s.v. 2).

dilectus: Drafts or levies of troops.

Galliam Narbonensem: Narbonese Gaul, the Roman province that was situated in what today is the Languedoc and Provence in the south of France. This area was the first Roman province to the north of the Alps (121 B.C.), and was sometimes referred to as "Transalpine Gaul" or "Gaul on the other side of the Alps." The "other" Gaul was "Cisalpine," of Gaul on the Roman side of the mountains. The modern French name "Provence" retains the memory of *provincia*.

supplendis: Gerundive in a dative of purpose construction.

Illyrici: "Illyricum" was a province in what is today parts of Croatia, Bosnia and Herzegovina, and Albania; it was at this point actually divided into Pannonia and Dalmatia. "Illyria" was a region in the western Balkans that had been conquered by the Romans in the second century B.C.; Tacitus thus refers here to a relatively large region that had soldiers worn out both in years and by physical weakness and infirmity. The fact that the draft came from Narbonese Gaul, Africa, and Asia may hint at a loss in manpower in the wake of the plague.

sacramento: Ablative of separation. The word means "oath"; cf. "sacrament." Literally, the sense is to make something sacred or holy.

Lugdunensem: The modern Lyon. The "Lugdunese disaster" is not described here in detail; there has been some suspicion that a lacuna should be posited. According to Seneca (*Ep.* 91, 14) the city had suffered a catastrophic fire; there is some uncertainty as to the exact date of the fire. Nero's financial aid may have come as many as seven years after the conflagration; in any case, Tacitus makes clear that the money that was sent to Lyon was actually the same amount that had been sent to Rome to help with disaster in the capital.

quadragies sestertio: *Quadragies* means "forty times"; the total referred to here = 4,000,000 sesterces (forty times one hundred thousand). For large sums of money, the numeral adverb (in this case, *quadragies*) is interpreted with an understood *centena milia* (i.e., one hundred thousand). *Sestertium* (i.e., the neuter singular) is then used in the appropriate case (here ablative with *solatus est*; Nero "consoled them with …").

amissa: What had been lost in the fire.

urbis casibus: It would be most natural to take the "disasters of the city" as referring to what Tacitus has already described in this paragraph; the question then is when exactly the fire in Lyon took place. Possible (if less likely) is that Lugdunum had sent four million sesterces as some sort of reserve sum of money in case of trouble in the capital. It is possible that the paragraph ends on a note of sarcastic commentary on Nero's act of charity.

Chapter fourteen: A new year, horoscopes, and new intrigues

C. Suetonio: That is, Gaius Suetonius Paulinus, a celebrated military commander (and not the author of the lives of the Caesars). As usual, Tacitus notes the start of the new year (A.D. 66) with the mention of the consuls.

For a careful consideration of the consular information of Nero's reign, see P. A. Gallivan, "Some Comments on the Fasti for the Reign of Nero," in *The Classical Quarterly* 24.2 (1974), pp. 290–311. "His removal from Britannia by Nero does not seem to have done Suetonius Paulinus any lasting harm, since he achieved the consulship five years later (AD 66)" (N. Fields, *Boudicca's Rebellion AD 60-61: The Britons Rise Up Against Rome*, Oxford: Osprey Publishing, 2011, p. 22). He eventually supported Otho in the struggles of the Long Year; captured by Vitellius, he saved his life by claiming that he had deliberately sabotaged Otho's chances for victory. His ultimate fate remains unknown.

On the start of the new year, see S. Bartera, "Year-beginnings in the Neronian Books of Tacitus' *Annals*," in *Museum Helveticum* 68 (2011), pp. 161–181. This new year opens with references to imperial banishment; libelous poetry allegedly composed against the *princeps*; and, soon enough, mention of the fantastic world of Babylonian astrology and stellar prognostication.

Luccio Telesino: The manuscripts and older editions of Tacitus read simply *L.* here; the name is supplied from inscriptional evidence. Nothing much is known of Gaius Luccius Telesinus; we have no idea when he was born or when he died. Apparently he had philosophical interests; Jackson notes in his Loeb edition that he appears in Philostratus' early third-century novel of Apollonius of Tyana (IV, 40, 43; VII, 11; VIII, 7, 12).

Antistius Sosianus: The Antistii were a patrician family from Gabii, an ancient city of Latium some eleven miles due east of Rome. Antistius was praetor in A.D. 62. On the whole business of the supposed discovery of a plot against Nero, see S. H. Rutledge, *Imperial Inquisitions: Prosecutors and Informants from Tiberius to Domitian*, London-New York: Routledge, 2001, pp. 170–171.

factitatis: The verb is frequentative, and refers to actions that were taken over and over again, in repeated fashion.

in Neronem: "Against Nero."

carminibus probrosis: Scurrilous verses, libelous poetry. Once again Tacitus is never too far from making references to the arts and literature in his Nero books; Sosianus was officially exiled for scandalous writings about the *princeps*. *Probrosus* refers to that which is "attended with reproach, disgraceful, shameful" (*OLD*); it describes that which is abusive and designed to confer ill repute and opprobrium.

multatus: The participle of *multo, multare*, "to punish." The verb can be used with an "ablative of forfeit" to describe how one is fined or penalized (*OLD*);

reos: "Defendants." Anteius and Ostorius were at once reckoned among the condemned and the damned, not among those awaiting trial.

adeo ut: "To such an extent that ..." Matters were so bad for Anteius that no one would witness his will. Roman law required the presence of seven witnesses. On the general topic of legal matters in later Tacitus, advanced students may note the helpful study of J. W. Thomas, "Roman Criminal Law and Legal Narrative in the Neronian Books of the *Annals* of Tacitus," Dissertation Loyola University of Chicago, 1993.

testamentum: "Last will and 'testament.'"

Tigellinus: Ofonius Tigellinus, the notorious prefect of the praetorian guard from A.D. 62 to 68. Tigellinus was able to negotiate successfully the transition from Nero to Galba; he was sentenced to death by Galba's successor Otho, upon which he committed suicide. His early career was rather checkered; he was accused of adultery with both Agrippina the Younger and Julia Livilla. His connection to Nero came from his preoccupation with horse breeding.

supremas tabulas: "The last tablets," that is, the tablets that were covered in wax to facilitate writing. Tigellinus steps forward as a witness to Anteius' disposition of his goods, with the understanding that Anteius needed to commit suicide sooner than today, as it were; *auctor* indicates that Tigellinus was willing to step forward to be the first (and six more would then be more willing to follow). No one wanted to risk acting against the wishes of Nero.

hausto veneno: Literally, "with poison having been quaffed." Anteius takes a draft of some sort of poison; the slow acting nature of the toxin then compels him to open his veins.

eius: That is, of the *venenum*.

perosus: The prefix is intensive; Anteius was greatly frustrated and disgusted with how slowly the poison was taking to kill him.

Chapter fifteen: The death of Ostorius

longinquis: "Far off/distant." Ostorius was nowhere near Rome when he met his end, though not nearly as far off as in the distant province of Britannia where he had found military glory and a record of distinguished

it can be used more generally (with an "ablative of penalty" to describe some sort of punishment or penalty more generally).

ut dixi: Cf. *Annales* XIV, 48.

accepit: Once he "realized" or "understood." Sosianus learned a lesson from recent events, namely that informers stood to profit handsomely in the current climate of suspicion and show trials.

inquies: "Unsettled" and "restless." Sosianus was hardly the sort to remain quietly in exile.

occasionum haud segnis: The genitive indicates the fundamental relationship between two nouns; here the descriptive adjective *segnis* is given particular focus by a defining genitive: Sosianus was not sluggish or slow in taking advantage of opportunities. On referential genitives of this sort see E. C. Woodcock, *A New Latin Syntax*, London: Methuen, 1959, p. 57.

Pammenem: The name is Egyptian; for the class of those who might be labeled "astrologers," with reference to this figure, see J. B. Rives, "Magicians and Astrologers," in M. Peachin, *The Oxford Handbook of Social Relations in the Roman World*, 2011, p. 689. The Greek writer Aelian mentions this Pammenes in his *On Animals* (XVI, 42), where he notes that he was the author of a work *Concerning Wild Animals* that noted the existence in Egypt of scorpions with wings and a double sting, something he claims to have seen firsthand.

Chaldaeorum arte famosum: Pammenes was knowledgeable about the so-called art of the Chaldaeans. The Chaldaeans were a Semitic people who lived in southeastern Mesopotamia; they were celebrated for their skill in astrological and astronomical prognostications. For a useful study of the treatment of astrologers at Rome and the place of the practice in Roman life, see P. Ripat, "Expelling Misconceptions: Astrologers at Rome," in *Classical Philology* 106.2 (2011), pp. 115–154.

eoque: "Because of this," that is, his skill in preparing horoscopes and the like. The ablative is causal.

similitudine fortunae: They were both exiles, after all.

ventitare: The verb is frequentative; the messengers kept coming and going with frequency.

nuntios et consultationes: A so-called hendiadys, from the Greek for "one through two." The messengers and the consultations are essentially the same thing; *nuntii* regularly visited the exiled Pammenes in order to secure fortune-telling.

annuam pecuniam: The exile was apparently being supported with a yearly salary supplied by Anteius.

P. Anteio: Publius Anteius Rufus. There is inscriptional attestation that he was involved in the rebuilding of legionary headquarters at Burnum in Dalmatia (modern Croatia); he suffered *damnatio memoriae* or the "damnation of memory" in A.D. 66, but his name was later restored (after the death of Nero). See further A. Barrett, *Agrippina: Sex, Power, and Politics in the Early Empire*, New Haven, Connecticut: Yale University Press, 1996, p. 297; T. J. Cornell, ed., *The Fragments of the Roman Historians*, Oxford, 2013, p. 639:

> In the view of Peter and Bardon, Anteius had written an encomiastic biography of Ostorius which implicitly criticized Nero by contrast. The nature of the work is not clear… The context is of writings on future destiny. Anteius may have been a student of astrology. Tacitus does not even say that the work was written by Anteius; perhaps, as Griffin suggests, it had been sent to Pammenes by its subject.

habebat: The verb *habere* has a wide range of meanings, including "to consider" or "to regard." Antistius was well aware that Anteius was sympathetic to Agrippina, and that he was possessed of significant financial resources.

caritate: Ablative of cause. On the connection between Agrippina and Anteius, Ronald Martin notes: " … the governorship of Syria, with its powerful legions, was earmarked for another of her protégés, Publius Anteius. But, for whatever reason, Anteius was never allowed to take up his appointment; possibly it was felt too risky to allow one of Agrippina's supporters to have control of so large a legionary army" (*Tacitus*, London: Bristol Classical Press, 1994, p. 170 [corrected paperback reprint of the 1981 B. T. Batsford Ltd. original).

Nero appears to have particularly indulged his artistic aspirations without restraint after the death of his mother (cf. *Annales* XIV, 14–15); on the increasing ambitions of the *princeps* in this regard in his final years, note E. Champlin, "Nero, Apollo, and the Poets," in *Phoenix* 57.3/4 (2003), pp. 276–283.

eius: That is, Anteius'.

ad eliciendam cupidinem: Gerundive; great wealth served the purpose of eliciting desire and greed on the part of Nero to possess the riches of others.

multis exitio esse: The so-called double dative construction, with a [...] purpose and a dative of reference. What is sometimes referred to as t[...] of advantage and the dative of disadvantage is a variety of the re[...] dative. The double dative here would literally (and awkwardly) be r[...] "was for the purpose of destruction with reference to many," that [...] wealth had been the source of ruin for many before Anteius. Transl[...] the cause of ruin for many."

furatus: From *furor, furari*; Antistius stole the *libellos*.

genitalis eius: "Birthday." Pammenes had secret papers in which [...] day (and probably also the time) of birth was recorded, so as to ai[...] production of an accurate horoscope.

eventura: Literally, "the things that were destined to come." The part[...] future active.

Ostorii Scapulae: Publius Ostorius Scapula had served in Britain fro[...] 47 to 52; his son Marcus is the Ostorius referenced here (cf. *Annales* [...] and XIV, 48).

quae incolumitati eius conducerent: Literally, "which pertained [...] safety," that is, to Nero's security.

adlaturum: Supply *esse*. Antistius promised that if given temporar[...] from his exile, he would bring "great things" (*magna*) to Nero, ne[...] pertained to the emperor's well-being.

imminere: The basic meaning of the verb is to lean over or to [...] outward; by extension it can mean to threaten (cf. English "imminent[...] accompanied by a dative object (here *rebus*).

rebus: The affairs of state and government. Antistius writes to Ner[...] Anteius and Ostorius had designs on power and government.

scrutari: Deponent; Anteius is accused of "looking into" or "investig[...] the destinies of both Caesar and himself.

liburnicae: The Liburnians were a people of Illyria; their name was [...] to a type of light galley that they were famous for using, an exceptio[...] swift vessel. Nero does not wait for long once he receives news about po[...] threats to his rule.

propere: "Hastily."

vulgato eius indicio: Once Antistius' report was made known, re[...] followed at once.

accomplishment. He would need to return to his own country, as it were, in order to find death at the order of his *princeps*.

apud: Once again with its usual accusative object.

Ligurum: Liguria is a region in northwestern Italy; in antiquity the territory of the *Ligures* extended into what is today France.

id temporis: The accusative regularly expresses extent or duration of space or time. "At the moment," Ostorius was in Liguria.

eo: "There, to that place." The ablative is one of direction.

maturaret: Imperfect subjunctive in a relative clause of purpose. A centurion was dispatched to hasten along Ostorius' death. *Maturare* can refer both to bringing something to maturity and (by transference) to hastening something's moment in time (as here); cf. *OLD* s.v. 4.

festinandi: Gerund. *Festinare* refers to making haste and to performing something in a speedy fashion; it conveys the sense of brooking no delay and losing no time in the performance of some deed.

fama: The Latin *fama* has a wide range of meanings, including reputation, report, rumor, and fame. Ostorius was considered a far more formidable target than Anteius.

civicam coronam: The "civic crown" was an oak leaf crown that was earned by those who had slain the enemy and thus saved the lives of Roman citizens; the rescued *civis* would give witness to the act of rescue. Ostorious had performed manfully in Britannia.

ingenti corpore: Ostorius was powerful in size and body. The phrase is perhaps borrowed from Sallust (who has *corpore ingenti* of Mithridates at *Historiae* II, 77.1).

invaderet: Imperfect subjunctive. The verb in a fear clause is in the present or imperfect subjunctive in accord with the sequence of tenses.

reperta nuper coniuratione: "With the conspiracy recently having been discovered." Syme notes that *coniuratio* "shows fourteen instances in XV and XVI," in his consideration of verbal repetitions (*op. cit.*, p. 741).

exterritum: Once again the prefix is intensive. Nero lived in fear and terror that he would be the victim of some conspiracy; the paranoia was especially great in the recent wake of the uncovering of the alleged plot. *Pavidum* describes a man who was seemingly timid by nature; *exterritum* refers specifically and pointedly to the current mood of the *princeps*.

effugia: The escape routes or exits. The word is not particularly common; it occurs in both Lucretius and Livy. It can refer both to the means of escape, and to the act of making use of such exits.

aperit: "Unfolded" or "explained."

hostis: Accusative plural. A *hostis* was a public enemy, as opposed to an *inimicus* or personal one.

spectatam: Ostorius' heroism and courage had been demonstrated against the enemy on any number of occasions, and now he would turn that same *fortitudo* against himself (*in se*).

interruptae: Literally, "broken apart" (from *interrumpere*); cf. *intercisis venis* above (of Anteius' suicide). Furneaux notes that both of these expressions about the veins occur only here in Tacitus. Both of Nero's latest victims suffer somewhat botched suicides.

parum sanguinis: "Too little of blood." The severed veins did not release sufficient blood to cause a relatively speedy death.

hactenus: Usually written as one word, as here; *hac—tenus* means literally "to this point, thus far." Ostorius employed a slave in his suicide, but only for the purpose of having him hold a dagger firmly for the suicide. The adverb underscores how Ostorius tried to minimize the help of another in his final moments.

manu: Ablative with *usus* (with which supply *est*).

pugionem: A "dagger." Ostorius wanted to make sure that the weapon was held immobile (*immotum*), so as to ensure a swift death.

adpressit: The force of the prefix is that Ostorius pressed the hand of the slave toward him.

eius: That is, of the slave.

iugulo: *Iugulum* is properly the hollow oft the neck, collarbone, or throat; from this anatomical location's prominence in ancient suicides and murders, it came by extension to mean "slaughter/violent death." Ostorius took the hand of the slave that was wielding the dagger, and ran his neck into the blade. *Iugulo* could be dative, which would describe vividly the force with which Ostorius meets the dagger (i.e., a sort of dative of direction); it could also be ablative (so Furneaux).

occurrit: A brave final note for Ostorius; he literally "hastens to meet," even "runs toward" the point of the dagger.

Chapter sixteen: The historian's reflection

Etiam si: "Even if ..." Tacitus now begins an extraordinary authorial intervention, as he reflects and offers commentary on the seemingly interminable catalogue of victims of Nero's tyranny.

Tacitus makes verbal reference in this paragraph to the aforementioned image from the opening of Virgil's *Aeneid* to the anger of the gods and the divine powers or *numima* that sometimes seem bent on the destruction of Rome. In the Tacitean context, the anger of the gods cannot simply be passed over with this or that narrative of the capture of cities or the disasters incurred by an army; the deaths of senators and equestrians (and often their family members) have become a daily part of life in Rome under Nero.

bella externa: Foreign wars.

obitas ... mortis: "Deaths met/faced for the republic." *Obitas* is from *obeo*, *obire*; cf. English "obituary." There is a sense that the deaths were performed or executed for the state, as it were.

memorarem: The verb evokes the image of the historian as the guardian or custodian of memory. Tacitus preserves the record and recollection of the past, and by his detailed accounts of the savagery of the *princeps* he bestows the gift of memory on the victims, even as he creates a haunting image for those who would not stand up and resist despotism with all their ability.

satias ... taedium: The first noun is nominative, the second accusative. On the sense of weariness to which Tacitus refers, cf. the judgment of Furneaux: "The immediate outcome of the conspiracy [i.e., Piso's], as that of Seianus, was a prolonged and continuous reign of terror; and the Sixteenth Book, so far as we have it, closely resembles the dreary record of the Sixth, in its monotonous list of executions and enforced suicides" (p. 78).

> Many students of history and literature discover a narrow range of subjects in the *Annales* and voice their disappointment ... Hence an easy censure on the historian: he was obsessed with Rome, the Caesars, the Senate ... His vision was also narrow, and his sympathies ... Narrow also was his personal experience ... The *Annales* betray serious defects ... The historian himself has not received justice ... Above all, XVII and XVIII (if the author survived to compose them) must have answered many questions about the state of the Roman Empire—and quelled most objections. (Syme, *op. cit.*, pp. 766–767)

cepisset: Pluperfect subjunctive in a contrafactual condition. Tacits notes that even if he were relating deaths that had been suffered for the sake of the republic in foreign wars, a certain "satiety" and weariness would by now have set in for writer and reader.

honestos: "Noble" or "dignified" (not "honest"). The deaths of those who were slain under Nero were noble—though they were also depressing and full of gloom.

aliorum … aspernantium: Tacitus refers to readers who would disdain or cast off the constant accounts of one death after another, grim as the stories are (*tristis*), and multiplied in abundance (*continuos*).

at nunc: Barrett (in Yardley's translation) observes here that "Tacitus' train of thought in this section is far from clear." *At nunc* is an adversative temporal marker that refers to the case of Tacitus' description of the deaths suffered under Nero (in contrast to those one might read of in an account of the wars against Carthage or Pyrrhus). There may, too, be a hint of a reference to Tacitus' own day, a period that had seen a rebirth of tyranny and despotism under Domitian, an age that was perhaps all too aware of the tedium that a catalogue of deaths can bring.

patientia servilis: Tacitus is fascinated by the apparent willingness of free men to behave in the manner of slaves; cf. the prominent *At Romae ruere in servitium* of *Annales* I, 7 (the historian's description of the period after Augustus' death, on the accession of Tiberius in A.D. 14). *Patientia* has its root in *patior, pati, passum*, and expresses the notion of tolerance and extreme endurance. We may be reminded of the problem of those who, like Tacitus, lived through the days of their own tyranny under Domitian—and who may have survived in part because they did not speak out against the assaults on liberty and human dignity.

tantumque sanguinis … perditum: There is a hint of the Lucanian notion that the spilling of so much blood could easily have won an empire for Rome; instead the blood is shed in civil and domestic strife (and, in this case, not even in the course of an actual civil war).

domi: Locative.

maestitia: Sadness or gloom. One becomes not only weary and fatigued, but also miserably sad and despondent through the course of the long and grim reports of suicides and executions.

restringunt: The root meaning of the verb is to draw something back tightly, to bind and constrict it; from this comes the figurative sense of restraint and confinement, and the transferred notion of restricting the activity of something, for example, of the mind (cf. *OLD* s.v. 2). Tacitus notes that the *animus* becomes not only weary from the constant report of deaths, but also overwhelmed by sorrow and grief.

ista: The demonstrative *iste* can have a pejorative tone and contemptuous air; Tacitus knows that his subject may seem "distasteful" and unpleasant to his readers.

defensionem: The usual meaning is "defence" or "protection"; Yardley offers the rendering "indulgence." *Defensio* can also extend in meaning to describe the rationalization or justification of one's actions (*OLD* s.v. 3); it also occurs in legal contexts to describe the action taken to obtain recompense for a death.

exegerim: Perfect subjunctive in an expression of potentiality. *Exigo, exigere* means "to demand or require," but it has as wide a range of uses as we might expect from a compound of *agere*.

tam segniter pereuntis: "Those perishing/who perished so sluggishly." Tacitus here introduces a bit of a surprise, as he implicitly begs the pardon of the reader for not harshly indicting those who may seem to have died in such an atmosphere of acceptance and willful cooperation with tyranny, or at least for granting them the dignity of detailed obituaries. Tacitus could not bring himself to hate these casualties of Nero, and so he has afforded them the dignity of separate notice (a theme that will soon enough be developed more clearly). *Pereuntis* is accusative plural of the masculine present participle of *pereo, perire*.

And so the one request that Tacitus has in his authorial intervention is essentially that he be forgiven for not condemning those who seemed ready to go to their deaths like lambs to the slaughter. Furneaux considers the view of other scholars that *oderim* stands for *odisse videar*, the point being that Tacitus does not want to be liable to the charge of having a personal detestation of men he thinks died lazily and sluggishly. But the difference in meaning is not so great. Throughout, the emphasis is on the power of memory (*memorarem*); the historian can grant a modicum of honor and dignity to the dead by preserving their memory for posterity.

> It is more pertinent to ask what other course was open to those to whom flight and resistance were alike impossible, or to what support they could have appealed, when each member of the senate was trembling for himself, when even such ineffective popular feeling as had been displayed for Octavia lay at the command of no Roman noble, when plots such as that which had just failed so signally, were their sole resource. (Furneaux, p. 79)

Jackson in his Loeb edition notes prefers to consider the conjecture *oderint*; in his view Tacitus is asking the reader not to defend or to excuse the abject servility of those who died under Nero, but only that *they* not hate the victims.

ira illa numinum: "That wrath of the divine powers." We might recall the sentiments of the opening of Virgil's *Aeneid* about the anger of the gods and the offense to Juno's dignity; *illa* can refer to that which is especially noteworthy or famous.

in res Romanas: "Toward/with respect to/against Roman affairs."

ut in cladibus exercituum aut captivitate urbium: That is, the sort of things that would be the subject of historical accounts of *bella externa*. The reference to the capture of cities recalls the fall of Troy that is dramatically narrated by Aeneas in Book II of Virgil's epic; the destruction of that city was revealed by Virgil's Venus to be the direct result of divine anger against Priam's Troy.

semel edito: Literally, "with its having been related once." The verb *edo, edere* means "to give forth/discharge"; the *e* is long, in contrast to the short *e* of *edo, edere/esse, edi, esum*, "to eat."

detur hoc: "Let this be given ..." The subjunctive is jussive.

posteritati: "Posthumous report/reputation."

a promisca sepultura: "From undistinguished burial." Tacitus concludes his sentiments with another grim reflection, this time an image or association borrowed from the world of the grave. The famous are accorded the dignity of a separate funeral and their own requiem rites, and so in Tacitus' catalogue of death, they should be granted the respect of a separate funeral notice and individualized treatment. Tacitus has presented his sad commentary on the times: the historian is unable simply to move from military disaster to disaster, rather he must repeat the story of the trial and execution or suicide of noble men—and posterity should be granted the privilege of honoring their noble ancestors with separate obituaries (so Koestermann *ad loc.*). *Promiscus* is the regular spelling in Tacitus and Aulus Gellius; usually one finds *promiscuus*; it refers to that which is enjoyed or experienced, practiced or used by all without regard for status or wealth, to that which is "used by or available to the general public" (*OLD* s.v. 3). *Sepultura* describes the formal, ritualized disposal of remains.

traditione supremorum: "The handing down of their final moments."

propriam memoriam: "Their own memorial/memory."

Chapter seventeen: More deaths

Tacitus resumes his narrative with yet more of his catalogue of Neronian victims, including the first mention of the celebrated Gaius Petronius, and a reminiscence of the poet Lucan (whose death was narrated at XV, 70). Petronius' final hours will be very different from those of Thrasea that conclude the surviving portion of the book.

eodem agmine: "In the same battle line." *Agmen* need not refer to military maneuvers or tactics, but the language evokes something of the spirit of conflict and martial drama.

Annaeus Mela: Marcus Annaeus Mela, the father of the poet Lucan and brother of Seneca. The *Annaei* were a plebeian family that may have had freedmen origins; they were associated with literary pursuits (especially through the works of Seneca and Lucan).

Cerialis Anicius: Gaius Anicius Cerialis, who had been involved in intrigues in the days of the emperor Caligula (a topic Tacitus addresses at the end of this paragraph). According to Tacitus, Cerialis had been an informant who had divulged news of a conspiracy against Gaius Caligula; in Dio Cassius' *Roman History* (Book LIX), "Nicius" Cerialis is subjected to torture and dies under interrogation, while his son Sextus Papinius turns betrayer.

Rufrius Crispinus: This equestrian served as praetorian prefect under Claudius, a job that he lost under Agrippina (who appointed Burrus in his place). He married Poppaea (who would later marry Otho and Nero). His exile to Sardinia is mentioned at XV, 71. Barry Baldwin notes that "the name Crispinus is unhelpfully common in all periods of Roman history"; the Neronian prefect has been thought by some to have served to inspire the savagely indicted Crispinus of Juvenal's first and fourth satires. See further B. Baldwin, "Juvenal's Crispinus," in *Acta Classica* 22 (1979), pp. 109–114.

C. Petronius: The praenomen has been the source of controversy; Heubner prints *T*. for Titus. The Medicean reads *ac* here; *C*. is the conjecture of Wesenberg. This Petronius—who will receive his own detailed obituary in the next paragraph—has usually been associated with the author of the mysterious *Satyrica* or *Satyricon*. The origin of the name is discussed in detail by Chrys C. Caragounis in his *Peter and the Rock*, Berlin-New York, Walter de Gruyter, 1990, pp. 17–25. On the Tacitean treatment see further H. Haynes, "The Tyrant Lists: Tacitus' Obituary of Petronius," in *The American Journal of Philology* 131.1 (2010), pp. 69–100.

equites ... senatoria dignitate: See further here H. Hill, "'Equites' of Senatorial Rank," in *The Classical Quarterly* 23.1 (1929), pp. 33–36; note also the same author's "The 'Equites Illustres,'" in *The Classical Quarterly* 22.2 (1928), pp. 77–82. These were senators in terms of property/wealth qualifications; they needed only the special permission of the emperor to assume the *laticlavius* or broad purple stripe for their togas.

hic: That is, Crispinus.

accepto ... nuntio: Crispinus commits suicide as soon as he receives the order; we might recall Tacitus' recent remarks about the question of "sluggishness" in the matter of resisting tyranny.

Mela ... natus: Annaeus Mela was the brother of Gallio and Seneca.

Gallio: Lucius Iunius Gallio Annaeanus, who is perhaps best known for his mention in the *Acta Apostolorum*, where he was involved in a legal proceeding with the apostle Paul.

Seneca: Lucius Annaeus Seneca, the famous Seneca the Younger, one of the most celebrated writers and philosophers of the so-called Silver Age of Latin literature. His conviction and suicide in the wake of the Pisonian conspiracy is narrated in XV, 60–64.

petitione: A separative ablative; Mela "abstained from the seeking of honors." The basic meaning of *petitio* is an "attack," from which comes the sense of seeking to obtain or secure some goal or objective, and then the more particular instance of the work done on behalf of a candidate in an election (*OLD* s.v. 5).

adquirendae pecuniae: Gerundive in a purpose construction. *Iter* is regularly followed by a genitive expressing destination (*OLD s.v.* 4a).

procurationes: "Stewardships" or "administation."

administrandis principis negotiis: This is either an ablative or a dative; the latter would express purpose, the former would describe the particular aspect or respect in which Mela undertook administrative tasks. *Negotiis* refers to business dealings in particular (though not exclusively). Mela preferred to remain an equestrian and to amass large sums of money by assisting Nero in management of finances.

idem: That is, Mela.

Annaeum Lucanum: The poet Lucan, the author of the epic *Bellum Civile* or *Pharsalia*, and a poetic rival of the *princeps*. Lucan's epic is in ten books that may or may not be "complete"; for an introduction see F. M. Ahl, *Lucan: An Introduction*, Ithaca, New York: Cornell University Press, 1976; L. Fratantuono, *Madness Triumphant: A Reading of Lucan's Pharsalia*, Lanham, Maryland: Lexington Books, 2012; also S. Bartsch, *Ideology in Cold Blood: A Reading of Lucan's Civil War*, Cambridge, Massachusetts: Harvard University Press, 1997; E. Fantham, "A Controversial Life," in P. Asso, ed., *Brill's Companion to Lucan*, Leiden-Boston: Brill, 2011, pp. 3–20.

> We know from Statius' anniversary poem … that Lucan married Polla Argentaria … We neither know when Lucan and Polla were married … nor can we be sure that they had no children. We can be fairly sure that none survived into adulthood. This, then, was the end of the Annaei— but not of their memory—which was vindicated by their own and others' literary monuments. (p. 20)

grande adiumentum claritudinis: As much a praise of Lucan as a sarcastic remark about Mela; perhaps the best thing that ever happened to the latter is that he was the father of the great poet.

dum rem familiarem eius acriter requirit: Mela was particularly concerned with the disposition of Lucan's estate in the wake of his son's suicide. *Res familiaris* refers to one's property or estate.

Fabium Romanum: Fabius was apparently troubled by the meddling of Mela in Lucan's estate; it is likely that Fabius was one of the heirs of the property, and the odium that might have developed between the poet's late father and his friend is easy enough to understand.

adsimilatis … litteris: Fabius decides to implicate Mela in the Pisonian conspiracy by forging letters from Lucan.

opibus eius inhians: Literally, "gaping after his wealth." Nero completes the veritable ascending tricolon of apparent greed: Mela appears to have coveted the property of his late son, Fabius was also somehow involved in the question of the estate (less probable, though admittedly conceivable, is that on principled grounds he was offended by the father's machiantions)—and now Nero is covetous of the wealth that he had apparently not ordered to be seized after the suicide of Lucan.

erogabat: The verb means "to pay out" or to "expend." Mela commits suicide, but not before offering what would essentially be a bribe to Tigellinus and Cossutianus Capito, in the hopes that the rest of the money would remain for his heirs. Given what Tacitus adds next about the last testament, it appears that Nero and his agents were actively involved in the drafting of the will and its codicils.

Cossutianum Capitonem: Mela's son-in-law had served in the senate and been a governor in Cilicia; he was also a notorious Neronian informant (one of whose victims was Antistius).

tamquam … scripsisset: Heubner (following Draeger) encloses this aside in square brackets; it may be an explanatory gloss on what Mela's codicil actually stated.

nullis supplicii causis: Causal ablative. The codicil stated that Mela was not committing suicide because he had any reason to kill himself—in other words, he was innocent of any wrongdoing against Nero.

vita frui: The verb *fruor, frui, fructus sum* takes an ablative object. Mela complained in his will that while he was blameless, Crispinus and Cerialis were guilty and still enjoying the pleasure of life.

infensos principi: Alive and well, they were full of hate for Nero.

quia interfectus erat: "Because he had been killed." Crispinus was already dead; it is unclear whether or not Mela knew this, since Tigellinus and Cossutianus may have drafted the codicil with or without Mela's full knowledge.

ut interficeretur: "In order that he might be killed." A marvelous Tacitean antithesis; we might say that Mela's codicil killed two birds with one stone.

multo: Ablative of degree of difference. Not long after the will was published, Cerialis took its message to heart and committed suicide.

meminerant: A final detail or note about memory. Cerialis received less pity than Crispinus, Mela, and the others, because he had been involved in the betrayal of news about a conspiracy to Caligula. The exact date and circumstance of the conspiracy is unknown; Furneaux identifies it as one of A.D. 40.

Chapter eighteen: A retrospective of Petronius' character and habits

Here commences the most important surviving *testimonium* of the supposed author of the remains of the *Satyrica*, the novelist Gaius Petronius. The bibliography on Petronius grows ever space; the standard commentary now on the novel is that of Gareth Schmeling, *A Commentary on The Satyrica of Petronius*, Oxford, 2011; Schmeling has a helpful introduction and overview to the question of this mysterious author in the first chapter of Heinz Hofmann's *Latin Fiction: The Latin Novel in Context*, London-New York: Routledge, 1999. On the question of the identity of the author of the novel, fundamental is the posthumous 1971 Brill monograph of K. F. C. Rose, *The Date and Author of the Satyricon*, which has its origins in the late author's 1962 Oxford B. Litt. thesis under the great Petronian scholar J. P. Sullivan; note also Rose's "The Author of the *Satyricon*," in *Latomus* 20.3 (1961), pp. 821–825. H. D. Rankin provides a careful study of the Tacitean account of Petronius in his *Petronius the Artist: Essays on the Satyricon and Its Author*, The Hague: Martinus Nijhoff, 1971. Useful too is the collection of J. Prag and I. Repath, *Petronius: A Handbook*, Malden, Massachusetts: Wiley-Blackwell, 2009, especially Caroline Vout's article on the *Satyrica* and Roman culture. On how Petronius' suicide seems to fulfill his desires, while Seneca's death in Book XV seems to frustrate his, see C. Star, *The Empire of the Self: Self-Command and Political Speech in Seneca and Petronius*, Baltimore: The Johns Hopkins University Press, 2012, pp. 11 ff. For a sensitive study of the display of individuality inherent to Petronius' suicide in the Tacitean conception, see P. Toohey, *Melancholy, Love, and Time: Boundaries of the Self in Ancient Literature*, Ann Arbor: The University of Michigan Press, 2004, pp. 175 ff.

Marsh and Leon note that Petronius is one of the main characters in the novel (and derivative film) *Quo Vadis*.

C. Petronio: Nipperdey deleted the mark of the praenomen, given the question in *c.* 17 as to the correct name.

pauca repetenda sunt: Gerundive; "a few things must be recounted/related." Passive periphrastic.

somnum: The Medicean manuscript has *somnium*, which normally means a dream or a fantasy of some sort.

hunc: That is, Petronius.

ignavia ad famam proluerat: Laziness and indolence brought Petronius into high repute, just as for others industry and hard work. *Ignavia* refers specifically to neglect of one's work or business; it can also refer to a certain faintheartedness in the face of labor or duty, to a weakening of resolve in the face of crisis and upheaval (*OLD* s.v. 2–3).

habebatur: "He was considered/he was held to be."

ganeo: Not a particularly common word (though old; it occurs in Naevius and Terence, and may have a certain archaizing quality here); it describes in particular a glutton or debauched individual, particularly in the matter of eating overmuch and decadent consumption.

haurientium: The metaphor is from drinking or eating to excess (and thus continues the general sense of the metaphor that was implicit in *ganeo*); Petronius was not considered in the same class as those who wrecked their financial states and fortunes by abuse of their resources.

erudito luxu: We might translate this as, "of a studied luxury." Petronius was a master, in Tacitus' judgment, of turning excess and decadence into an elegant, cultured, and mannered pursuit of consumption and use of the pleasures of life. He was, in short, the epitome of class. We do well to remember that the "Petronian problem" is not simply one of whether or not Tacitus' Petronius is the Petronius of the *Satyrica*, but the degree to which we can trust the historian's account of the habits and manners of this Neronian victim. *Eruditus* implies a sophistication and attention to what he calls the demands of class and elegance. The ablative is of quality.

solutiora: Literally, "more loosened/unrestrained."

praeferentia: Present participle from *praeferre*, "to bear in front/bear before." Petronius' words and actions carried with them a certain "neglect" or "lack of concern" for himself (cf. Yardly's "nonchalance"). Tacitus' Petronius seemed utterly unconcerned with what people thought of his *dicta* and *facta*, and thereby seemed all the more honest and without guile (cf. *in speciem simplicitatis* below). The mannerism of Petronius was constructed so as to seem utterly unaffected, and therein was one of its most admired and respected virtues.

in speciem simplicitatis: Tacitus' entire presentation of Petronius is itself of what we might call be a studied simplicity, one in which the line between artifice and natural reflection and reflection is deliberately obscured. Here the historian says that Petronius' unrestrained words and actions were received by his audience as if they were a mark of *simplicitas*; lurking here is the idea that the allegedly unrestrained deeds and sayings were actually a deliberate ploy to appear "natural." On the possibility that the word *simplicitas* occurred in Petronius' own writings with reference to himself, see H. D. Rankin, "Did Tacitus Quote Petronius?," in *L'Antiquité classique* 37.2 (1968), pp. 641–643 (in response to H. Bogner, "Petronius bei Tacitus," in *Hermes* 76.2 [1941], pp. 223–224). There is pretense here, but in pursuit not of political domination, we might think, so much as the arts. Nonetheless, Petronius is very much a part of the Neronian, Caesarian world of dissimulation.

Simplicitas refers to a freedom from sophistication or elaboration (*OLD* s.v. 4 and 4b); it is an extended meaning from the basic sense of single-mindedness and simplicity of mind and heart.

proconsul tamen Bithyniae: The *tamen* is adversative; Tacitus' Petronius was actually quite competent in the administration of his province. The historian here presents an interesting twist on his narrative; Petronius is not some mere caricature of a lazy, shiftless seeker of pleasure, but a skilled executor of political and financial tasks. Pliny the Younger also served in Bithynia, which was located in modern Turkey in the northwest of Asia Minor, with a capital at Nicomedia.

mox consul: Furneaux notes that this would have been a suffect consulship, that is, one that was undertaken to complete the term of the *consul ordinarius* who for whatever reason had not finished his tenure. The date of Petronius' consulship is known to have been A.D. 61, thanks to a tablet from Herculaneum (J. P. Sullivan, "Petronius, Seneca, and Lucan: A Neronian Literary Feud?," in S. Byrne, E. Cueva, and J. Alvares, eds., *Essays in Honor of Gareth L. Schmeling*, Groningen: Barkhuis Publishing, 2006, p. 306–307, with commentary on what we know of Petronius' political career, and what can be reasonably surmised about his literary endeavors). Sullivan rightly notes that while Petronius was admitted to Nero's inner circle, he was apparently not on quite the same intimate terms as the prefect Tigellinus, who was clearly successful in remaining the favorite of the *princeps*.

parem negotiis: We might say in English, "equal to the task."

revolutus: *Revolutus* is the participle of *revolvo, revolvere*. Petronius is said to have "rolled/slid back" into *vitia* or vices, or at least to have imitated a life of vice and debauchery (*seu imitatione vitiorum*). The language once again introduces the notion of studied leisure and deliberate construction of a front and persona. On this passage note H. C. Schnur, "*Vitiorum Imitatio*: Tacitus on Petronius," in *The Classical Journal* 50.8 (1955), pp. 353–354.

inter paucos familiarium: "Among the few of the familiars," in literal translation; this is the inner circle of the *princeps*, the supposed partners of the emperor in vice and crime.

elegentiae arbiter: The famous title "arbiter of elegance," which gave rise to the habit of identifying the author of the *Satyricon* as "Petronius Arbiter." This was not an official title of Nero's court, we might think (though Furneaux does well to note that the title may have been playfully given to Petronius as a sort of pseudo-cognomen or agnomen); the point is that Petronius was regarded as the judge of whatever was to be considered "elegant" and refined. Furneaux finds it noteworthy that Tacitus nowhere makes any mention of Petronius' literary skills or talents; this very silence has given rise to the view of some that the Petronius of *Annales* XVI is not the author of the surviving novel. Jackson notes in his Loeb edition that Tacitus would never have lowered himself to consider Petronius' works "literature" in the strict sense.

Marsh and Leon note that the only attested holders of the name Arbiter were slaves and freedmen.

adfluentia: The exact grammatical use of this word is open to debate. Furneaux notes that it could be a "concise use of a causal ablative," that is, "in his extravagance, Nero thought that nothing was pleasant or soft ..." It could also be an ablative of specification with *molle*.

ei: That is, to Nero.

invidia: Tacitus returns to the theme of resentment and envious jealousy; Tigellinus came to despise Petronius for how Nero seemed to favor and depend on him.

adversus aemulum: "Against a rival."

scientia voluptatum: "The science of pleasures." Petronius turned the quest for *voluptates* into a veritable art form, into something that could be pursued with academic rigor and in zealous quest for knowledge. *Potiorem* is the comparative of *potis*; Tigellinus feared that Petronius was more capable in the art of pursuing debauchery.

cui ceterae libidines cedebant: "To which the rest of his pleasures yielded/ gave way." Nero's *crudelitas* is for Tacitus a defining characteristic of his personality; his other pursuits were nothing in comparison to his capacity and lust for savagery. "Tacitus writes history with the accent upon personality, penetrating to the deepest recesses in his search for motive" (R. Syme, *Tacitus*, Oxford, 1958, p. 526).

adgreditur: Tigellinus "solicited" or "laid claim" to Nero's cruelty. The paranoid emperor is easily manipulated by his praetorian prefect into finding a reason to terminate Petronius' quasi-employment at his court.

Scaevini: Flavius Scaevinus, who at XV, 49 is noted for his life of indolence and surrender to luxury. A praetorian tribune and quaestor, he had been implicated in the Pisonian conspiracy; his ultimate fate is left unrecorded by Tacitus.

obiectans: Throwing forth in Petronius' face, as it were; *Petronio* is dative after the compound verb.

corrupto ... servo: A slave was corrupted and turned informer against his master.

adempta defensione: The exact nature of the *defensio* is not specified; Petronius was apparently given no quarter or opportunity to make any case in his own favor—this accusation represented yet another foregone conclusion.

maiore parte familiae: The greater part of his staff of servants, etc. The Latin word *familia* typically referred to the slaves of a master's household, and did not include the "nuclear family" of parents and children with which the English word is associated.

Chapter nineteen: The death of Petronius

Forte ...: Tacitus does not make clear why exactly Nero had set out for Campania; it appears that Petronius was in his retinue, though the precise timing of when he fell into disfavor is not specified. He was detained at Cumae; Nero apparently proceeded along on his journey.

Cumas: Cumae, a locale made famous in Virgil's sixth *Aeneid* for the entrance to the underworld that Aeneas entered with the Sibyl. In the immediate context, Tacitus artfully presents Petronius on the verge of his own descent to Avernus; if this were really the place where Petronius met his end, then the historian could not have wished for a more fitting site. Cumae was in origin a Greek colony that was celebrated as a center of Hellenic culture and civilization in southern Italy.

progressus: From the deponent *progredior*.

illic: "There, in that place."

tulit: The verb *fero* has a wide range of meanings; in English we might say that Petronius no longer "brooked any delay."

ut libitum: "As it was pleasing." *Libet* is an impersonal verb. Tacitus' Petronius tries to present himself as retaining as much control over the circumstances as possible.

obligatas: Petronius opened his veins, and then had them bound up again so that he might not seem to have been compelled to commit suicide; his goal was for his death to appear as natural as possible in the face of the intolerable circumstances.

gloriam constantiae: The fame or glory of his steadfastness in the face of an unjust death. We might think of the Platonic account of the suicide of Socrates at the end of the *Phaedo*. Petronius had no interest in any philosophical or declamatory speech or dialogue by which he might appear to be a new Stoic hero. At the end of the extant book Thrasea will speak of the example of those who practiced *constantia* in the face of tyranny and threats to freedom; Petronius is presented as not actively seeking such glorious repute through his words, but earning it rather by silent example.

referentis: Accusative plural, "people/men discoursing/relating stories about …" Petronius' deathbed was not the locus for elevated conversation about the fate of the *anima*.

de immortalitate animae: Clifford Herschel Moore's classic work *Pagan Ideas of Immortality During the Early Roman Empire* (Cambridge, Massachusetts: Harvard University Press, 1918) remains a congenial introduction to a vast subject. The Epicureans argued for the annihilation of the *anima* and the eternal quality only of the constituent atoms of matter, while the Stoics were not so absolutely dismissive of the possibility of everlasting life for the soul. The Tacitean narrative of the suicide of Petronius stands in prefatory contrast to that of the Stoic Thrasea Paetus that follows soon after, and with which the surviving portion of this book breaks off.

In certain regards, the death of Petronius is invested with Epicurean sentiments that Lucretius might well have approved; the direct implication of Tacitus' narrative is that Petronius did not care about the ultimate disposition of his soul or its fate after dissociation from the body. Tacitus does not reveal later in this book what Thrasea thought in his last hours about the soul and its fate, but he is depicted as being earnestly engaged in conversation on the subject. Petronius, in striking contrast, is not even interested in achieving the glory associated with *constantia*.

sapientium placitis: Those sayings and teachings that brought pleasure to wise men, that is, to philosophers. There is for Petronius no room for any theological or eschatological speculation on the fate of the soul or the nature of the good life.

levia carmina: "Light" verses or poems. The genre or genres implied here would not include epic, but perhaps shorter lyrics and elegies, epigrams, and the like. There is probably no implicit criticism of the late epic poet Lucan, but rather a conscious decision to pursue the pleasure of lighter genres in his dying hours. *Levia carmina* are mentioned at Lucretius, *De Rerum Natura* V, 1380, where the poet discusses the rise of music and the development of the poetic arts from a more sophistication progression from the imitation of bird songs, etc.: *at liquidas avium voces imitarier ore/ante fuit multo quam levia carmina cantu/concelebrare homines possent aurisque iuvare* ("Music was fundamentally mimetic; men first imitated the songs of birds, and then proceeded to develop more sophisticated and technically demanding forms of music" (L. Fratantuono, *A Reading of Lucretius' De Rerum Natura*, Lanham, Maryland: Lexington Books, 2015, p. 389).

facilis versus: Perhaps "easy" lines of poetry, that is, verses that could be composed extemporaneously and without labored efforts. Marsh and Leon translate *facilis* as "racy," Yardley as "playful"; the two categories are not mutually exclusive, and the adjective's range of meanings permits either translation.

largitione … verberibus: Some slaves were rewarded with bequests and grants of wealth, while others were ordered to be beaten or flogged for past offenses (*verberibus*). Petronius is cast in the role of veritable underworld judge; before he enters the afterlife, as it were, he works out the just rewards and punishments of his staff.

iniit epulas: Literally, "he entered into the banquet."

somno: Dative after a compound verb.

coacta: Perfect passive participle from *cogo, cogere, coegi, coactum*, "to compel."

esset: Imperfect subjunctive; Petronius wanted the death that he was forced to suffer to appear to be one that was "fortuitous." Tacitus gives no indication in his dramatic depiction of the suicide as to how long the whole process took; his Petronius has time both to indulge in a banquet and in sleep.

ne … quidem: "Not even." Tacitus returns to the matter of the wills of the condemned. Petronius did not make any effort to praise either Nero or Tigellinus in his final testament, but instead took the opportunity to compose an account of the emperor's debaucheries and reprehensible debaucheries. Some have seen here a reference or allusion to the content of the *Satyrica*, the contents of which are somewhat difficult to reconcile with what Tacitus here ascribes to the "will" of Petronius.

quod plerique pereuntium: The *pereuntium* are those who are perishing, that is, the condemned who were expected to commit suicide. Most of them sought some concession for their families by making the terms of their will flattering and fawning toward Nero, Tigellinus, and other court favorites. Tacitus plays on the genitive plurals here and at *potentium*.

flagitia principis: Cf. Cicero's *sed iam stupra et flagitia omittamus: sunt quaedam quae honeste non possum dicere* (*Philippics* 2.47). *Flagitia* is a strong word; it is a term he employs not only for Nero's deeds, but also for the actions of the Christians (XV, 44).

sub nominibus: "It was an itemized account" (Marsh and Leon). Petronius named names, almost as if thereby shattering the dramatic illusion of Nero's theater.

exoletorum: The adjective *exoletus* refers to someone or something that is "worn out" or "used up"; in context, it refers to the sexual partners of Nero's depravity. Tacitus returns now and again to the image of the exhaustion and tired fatigue that sets in after too much pleasure and surrender to vice. Here it refers to male prostitutes, in contrast to the *feminae* who are also named.

novitatem cuiusque stupri: "The novelty of each act of vice." Again, the emphasis is on the unending quest for the original and the creative, an endeavor that is doomed to end in tired ennui with the whole pursuit of pleasure. *Stuprum* was a crime in Roman law; it referred to illicit sexual union with a woman. For a detailed consideration of the offense, see J. A. Brundage, *Law, Sex, and Christian Society in Medieval Europe*, Chicago-London: The University of Chicago Press, 1987, pp. 29–30. Neue is responsible for the correction of the manuscript *novitate*.

perscripsit: The prefix may refer to the depth of detail into which Petronius went in his narrative. Again, there is no indication of how long all of this took; if Tacitus is relating what actually happened, perhaps Petronius had been working on his manuscript for some time.

obsignata: "Sealed." Part of Petronius' joke may have been that the emperor was fascinated by what we might call a sort of pornographic literature, though here of course he was the star performer.

usui: Dative of purpose. Petronius broke his ring so that his seal could not be used to issue any orders or bequests in his name.

ad facienda pericula: Literally, "for the sake of dangers to be made" (gerundive in a clause of purpose). Petronius wanted to be sure that his *anulus* would not imperil anyone else; Tacitus' narrative emphasizes once again the element of control that Petronius tried to maintain over the proceedings. The *elegentiae arbiter* would offer an example of how a man of class and distinction meets his death. Pliny the Elder preserves the detail in his *Natural History* (XXXVII, 20) that Petronius owned a myrrhine vase that had been valued at 300,000 sesterces, which he destroyed so as to deprive Nero the chance to steal it.

Chapter twenty: Nero's reaction

Ambigenti: The basic meaning of *ambigere* is to go about in a circle, to wander; from this comes the idea of being in wonder or marvel about a certain thing. Nero receives the document under Petronius' seal, and wonders how his *elegentiae arbiter* could have known so thoroughly the catalogue of his debaucheries (the implication is that Petronius was not privy to all of Nero's vices and sexual crimes).

If Nero fancied himself a dramatic artist, then in some sense Petronius has upstaged him; in the game for control and dominance of the social and political arena, the late Gaius (or Titus) has more than managed to embarrass the *princeps*.

quonam modo: "In what way/manner."

noctium suarum ingenia: That is, the inventive acts of genius of his nights. Petronius wrote of all the novel and clever things that Nero had done in the pursuit of sexual gratification.

notescerent: The verb is inchoative/inceptive; Nero wondered how his nocturnal passions were becoming more widely known. There is a hint here of a sense of shame and awareness that the news of what was happening in the "privacy" of his court could be damning to his reputation.

offertur: "Is suggested" (Furneaux); the picture is of Nero contemplating the various ways in which his escapades could have become known, and finally settling on Silia as a likely source for the scandalous information.

Silia: As the wife of a senator, her participation (willing or not) in the emperor's nocturnal games was especially shocking.

haud ignota: "Scarcely unknown." The fear would be that if Silia had opened her mouth to Nero, then she might just as easily have told others, and she was, after all, well known because of her high rank. Her senatorial husband's identity is unknown.

ipsi: That is, to Nero himself, for use in every sort of perversion (*ad omnem libidinem*).

adscita: "Taken" or "accepted." Silia had been involved in all of Nero's perverse pleasures.

ac Petronio perquam familiaris: "And, what is more, she was quite well known to Petronius." Silia was a likely source for the information, given her relationship with Petronius. The force of the conjunction *ac* is that besides the fact that Silia was a sexual intimate of Nero, she was *also* someone with whom Petronius had more than a passing acquaintance—but this detail is almost given as an afterthought.

agitur in exilium: She was driven into exile. The *tamquam* clause with pluperfect subjunctive expresses the alleged reason for her banishment.

quae viderat pertuleratque: "What she had seen and experienced." The prefix is intensive; Silia had been a witness to exceptionally untoward things, and had been a participant in many sexual escapades.

proprio odio: The ablative expresses the cause or manner of Nero's action against Silia; this was a particularly personal and intensely felt hatred. Silia had been a sexual confidante and libidinous partner of the *princeps*, and she had betrayed the implicit confidence that he had placed in her. The ablative may express the Tacitean view that Silia was undeserving of the penalty, and that Nero was consumed with a very personal sort of desire for revenge.

Minucium Thermum: The Medicean reads *Municium*; the spelling given here is Ryck's correction. Nothing much is known of this ex-praetor; he may be the son of the Minucius of VI, 7 who was condemned and then turned informer. Tacitus does not make clear the exact connection, if any, between Silia and the Petronian matter and the persecution of Minucius; the brief note of his end provides a transition to the narrative of the fall of Thrasea Paetus and Barea Soranus.

praetura functum: The verb *fungor, fungi, functus sum* takes an ablative object. "A former praetor."

simultatibus: From *simultas, simultatis*, f., meaning "hatred" or "animosity." Nero and Tigellinus are depicted as sharing potential victims of rivalry and dissension. From the primary meaning of quarreling and feuds come the sense of a contest of a trial (*OLD* s.v. 2).

dedit: This is the correction of Rhenanus for the Medicean reading *deditum*.

libertus … detulerat: The freedman had brought in certain items of incriminating evidence about Tigellinus. Once again, the culture is one of informing and surrender of targets for gain; in this case, Thermus' *libertus* would suffer his own penalty along with his former master. The question of exact meaning hinges on the preposition *de*; either Tigellinus was himself being accused, or his *patronus* Thermus was being targeted for allegedly saying malicious things about the praetorian prefect.

criminose: Furneaux renders this adverb as "vindictively." Apparently he brought information that was then tested and extracted under torture; in the process of undergoing the *cruciatus*, he incriminated his master Thermus. As Furneaux notes, the *libertus* would have been rewarded and not savagely punished had he brought information about libelous sayings uttered by Thermus against Tigellinus.

cruciatibus: "Tortures."

ipse: That is, the freedman.

nece immerita: "By a death that was not merited."

luere: Historical infinitive. The freedman paid for his actions by the agonies of the torture he suffered; Thermus, meanwhile, was unjustly killed. *Luere* means to make expiation or to pay a penalty to satisfy the debt for some infraction.

Chapter twenty-one: Thrasea Paetus

Trucidatis ... viris: Ablative absolute. The phrase is soon balanced by *interfecto* ... The verb *trucidare* means to kill in an especially savage way; it is one of the stronger and harsher words in the vocabulary of slaughter and murder.

ad postremum: "In the end" or "finally." Tacitus casts the previous deaths as mere prolegomena to the real target, *virtus*—which he will identify with two men in particular. On the last movements of this book, see C. Edwards, *Death in Ancient Rome*, New Haven, Connecticut: Yale University Press, 2007, pp. 134 ff. The Thrasea narrative now dominates the remainder of the book; we have no way of knowing definitively how the rest of the book would have been developed.

virtutem ipsam: "Virtue itself," as if Paetus and Soranus personified *virtus* and were living exemplars of it. On the campaign against virtue see D. Hammer, *Roman Political Thought: From Cicero to Augustine*, Cambridge, 2014, pp. 348–349.

concupivit: The subject is Nero.

Thrasea Paeto: Publius Clodius Thrasea Paetus, the celebrated Stoic and father-in-law of Helvidius Priscus (who married his daughter Fannia). A native of Patavium, he was suffect consul in 56; Tacitus relates that he walked out of the senate when Nero succeeded in securing the death of his mother Agrippina (*Annales* XIV, 12), an episode that the historian returns to in the present passage. Like Cassius, he was known for celebrating the honor and memory of the assassins of Julius Caesar (Juvenal, s. V, 36). See further the detailed discussion at T. J. Cornell, ed., *The Fragments of the Roman Historians*, Oxford, 2013, pp. 535–537; note also C. Brooke, *Philosophic Pride: Stoicism and Political Thought from Lipsius to Rousseau*, Princeton, 2012, pp. 63 ff. (with consideration and analysis of the Tacitean narratives of Paetus). On the culture of insult against the emperor as referenced in both Tacitus and Dio Cassius (with extended consideration of Paetus), see J. E. Lendon, *Empire of Honor: The Art of Government in the Roman World*, Oxford, 1997, pp. 141 ff. On the "fortuitous" place of Thrasea in the closing sections of the extant Book XVI, see E. O'Gorman, *Irony and Misreading in the Annals of Tacitus*, Cambridge, 2006, pp. 176 ff. For a good overview with useful material, see R. M. Krill, "Nero's Senatorial Foe Thrasea," in *Social Science* 54.5 (1979), pp. 210–214; cf. also T. Strunk, "Saving the Life of a Foolish Poet: Tacitus on Marcus Lepidus, Thrasea Paetus, and Political Action Under the Principate," in *Syllecta Classica* 21 (2010), pp. 119–139. Books XII–XV have sixty-nine, fifty-eight, sixty-five, and seventy-four chapters, respectively; it is possible that the death of Thrasea came at the midpoint of XVI.

Barea Sorano: Quintus Marcius Borea Soranus was suffect consul in 52. See P. A. Brunt (*et al. ed.*), *Studies in Stoicism*, Oxford, 2013, p. 316, for arguments against the idea that Soranus was an adherent to Stoicism. For the possible connection of the Bareae Sorani to the family of the future emperor Trajan's family, see J. Barrett, *Trajan: Optimus Princeps, a Life and Times*, New York-London: Routledge, 1997, pp. 12–13.

olim: "For a long time now."

quod … egressus est: Tacitus gives the actual reason for the enmity: Thrasea walked out of the senate when the topic of Agrippina was raised for discussion. At XIV, 12 Tacitus offers the comment that Thrasea's walking out was a source of peril to himself (*ac sibi causam periculi fecit*), and that insofar as the other senators were concerned, it did not put forth the beginning of liberty (*ceteris libertatis initium non praebuit*)—a comment that Koestermann and others have taken to be especially critical of the sluggish senators who did not respond to the *exemplum* of a Thrasea.

cum … referretur: Imperfect subjunctive in a *cum*-clause expressing past time. Temporal *cum*-clauses normally employ the indicative when referring to present or future time.

quodque: Another reason is put forth for Nero's displeasure.

Iuvenalium ludicro: These games had been instituted by Nero in A.D. 59 to mark his coming of age.

> The Principate of Nero introduced a change of pace, and the two generations from his Juvenalian games to the death of Trajan represented an acme in the history of the ludic. Emperors never invested more in the Games at Rome than over this period, which saw a consolidation of their function in an imperial monarchy based on a semblance of popular consensus, and a successful blending of Greek and Roman historical traditions. (N. Purcell, "'Romans, play on!' city of the Games," in P. Erdkamp, ed., *The Cambridge Companion to Ancient Rome*, Cambridge, 2013, p. 456)

parum spectabilem: Litotes; Thrasea was literally "too little conspicuous" in the games. If he were there, he was perhaps clearly not interested in his attendance; we might recall the detail about the guards at the games whose task was to ensure that people were applauding correctly for the spectacle.

cetastis: "The Cetastian Games." There has been some question about this celebration, which apparently featured tragic acting; Fisher, for example, notes in his Oxford text critical apparatus that he has doubts about the first letter of the name. Cf. further here the lengthy, masterful article of J. Linderski, "Games in Patavium," in *Ktema* 17 (1992), pp. 55–76 (reprinted with significant addenda in *Roman Questions II: Selected Papers*, Stuttgart: Franz Steiner Verlag, 2007). Little can be adduced definitively about the Patavian games to which Tacitus refers ("The Patavines do not yield their secrets gladly. After our disquisition we do not necessarily know more about the Games in Patavium, but it is an informed aporia."—Linderski); one older theory was that the word should be rendered *caesticis* and have something to do with the *caestus* or boxing (cf. the drama of Virgil's *Aeneid* V)—a creatively fanciful idea (see, e.g., A. W. Van Buren, "Tacitus, *Annals* XVI.21," in *The Classical Review* 38.5/6 (1924), pp. 110–111). The many conjectures and ideas about the meaning of *cetastis*/the "correct" reading are found in L. Jacobs, "Ludi cetasti Patavinorum," in *Athenaeum* 67 (1989), pp. 275–281. Linderski draws attention to possible connections between *Cetasti* and games having to do with sea creatures such as dolphins (with possible associations to Virgil's depiction of the equestrian *lusus Troiae* in *Aeneid* V, and to Pompeian evidence for a *ludus serpentis*—cf. the Anchises serpent Virgil's Aeneas encounters in Sicily). Dio Cassius (LXII, 26) adds the detail that the Patavian festival was held every thirty years (probably with no connection to the tradition we find in Virgil, for example, that Ascanius ruled for that many years at Alba Longa).

Thrasea's offense with respect to the games was that he took an active part in *Cetasti* of his hometown while appearing to have neglected taking on a conspicuous role in Nero's Juvenalian *ludicrum*. Was there some implied rivalry or disrespect implied because of the associations of Thrasea's Patavium with Antenor, and Nero's possible connection of himself with Aeneas and the Trojan settlement at Pallanteum/Rome? Certainly, the appearance of Thrasea as a tragic actor would have been likely to inspire a sense of jealous anxiety in Nero, especially given the evidence that Thrasea was not interested in making sacrifice to the emperor's voice.

Troiano Antenore: Tacitus returns to allusions from the early mythological history of Rome and its neighbors. The Trojan Antenor was said to have arrived in Italy before Aeneas and his companion exiles; he was held to have been the founder of Patavium (the modern Padua in northern Italy). Useful still is the article of I. C. Thallon, "The Tradition of Antenor and Its Historical Possibility," in *The American Journal of Archaeology* 28.1 (1924), pp. 47–65; cf. L. Braccesi, *La legenda di Antenore da Troia a Padova*, Padua: Signum, 1984 (with the review of N. Horsfall in *The Classical Review* N.S. 37.2 [1987], pp. 228–230).

mitiora: Literally, "gentler things." Thrasea urged for a penalty less severe than death.

deum honores: "The honors of the gods." *Deum* is genitive plural.

sponte: "Of his own will." The Stoic hero had made clear his feelings about the whole charade of Poppaea's deification after her likely murder.

funeri: Dative with a compound verb.

sinebat: The imperfect may express a simmering grudge and resentment that Cossutianus would not forget.

praeter animum ad flagitia praecipitem: Another of Tacitus' briefly sketched, effective descriptions of personality. Cossutianus had a mind that was headlong, indeed reckless in the pursuit of shameful, criminal deeds.

quod … concidisset: Pluperfect subjunctive in a *quod*-clause of alleged reason.

eius: That is, Thrasea's.

Cilicum: "The Cilicians." Cilicia was a Roman province on what is today the southern coast of Turkey; it has been added to the Roman Republic's provincial sway by Pompey the Great as part of the achievements of his campaigns in the East.

repetundarum: The verb *repetere* literally means "to strike/attack again"; from this comes the transferred sense of bringing or taking something back. In the case of *pecuniae* or money that "was to be taken back," that is, *pecuniae repetundae*, the matter was one of extortion. Cossutianus had apparently stolen money from the Cilicians, and he was tried and compelled to repay the extorted funds. The genitive is a genitive of the charge; *pecuniarum* should be understood.

Cossutianus is thus possessed of a quite personal reason for wishing to see Thrasea fall.

Chapter twenty-two: Accusations of cossutianus

sollemne ius iurandum: "The solemn oath." The first of January (*principio anni*) was a day for the renewal of oaths and promises of allegiance. The *ius iurandum* referenced here is to the preservation of the *acta* or "acts" of the emperor and his predecessors.

nuncupationibus: A solemn, public pronouncement of vows. It appears that on the first of the month, there was a vow for the safety of the republic, and on the third for the preservation of the *princeps*.

quindecimvirali sacerdotio: There were fifteen official cults in Roman religion, with the three major ones being in honor of Jupiter, Mars, and Quirinus. Needless to say, all the priestly colleges would have been expected to have been involved in the rites surrounding the offering of vows.

aut caelesti voce immolavisse: The strangest of the charges against Thrasea: he was accused of not having made sacrifice to Nero's *caelestis vox* or "heavenly voice." "By 66 failure to listen to the imperial singing and strumming or to sacrifice to his heavenly voice could be mentioned the Senate as an indication of disloyalty." (Griffin, *op. cit.*, p. 162). The apparent establishment of a cult to the voice of the *princeps* may well represent the ultimate in the Neronian farce of stage and theater. For the charge of Thrasea's insult to Nero's voice, cf. Dio Cassius, LXII, 26.

vulgaribus ... consultis: Thrasea was always reliable and eager to do senatorial business, indeed even in seemingly trifling discussions and debates. Only relatively recently, Cossutianus notes, had he stopped even coming to the senate.

semet fautorem aut adversarium: Thrasea is said to have displayed himself (*ostenderet*) in the senate as either a supporter or an opponent of the various proposals that came before that body for deliberation; he was an old style parliamentarian, in other words—eager to participate in the work of the *curia*, and thus all the more conspicuous now for his absences. The suffix *met* may be related to the old ablative form of the first person pronoun *ego*, which was *met* or *med* in early Latin (compare the old ablative ending of the first declension, "ad," which is preserved in the compensatory lengthening of the final vowel). The suffix serves to intensify and highlight the pronoun; the effect is virtually impossible to render in English.

triennio: For a period of three years. The ablative can be used to express location both in space and in time. We are not certain exactly what the rules were about the enforcing of attendance for senatorial meetings at this time; Thrasea's absence, in any case, would have been a likely subject for additional charges.

nuperrime: "Most recently."

coercendos: Gerundive; literally, "to be restrained."

certatim concurretur: The language of hurried excitement, in this case in the pursuit of most questionable, indeed deplorable activities. The imperfect subjunctive is used here in a *cum*-clause expressing past time.

secessionem iam id et partis: The language of factionalism. Cossutianus argues that there is now a Caesar party and a Thrasea party; if the problem becomes more serious in terms of the number of adherents to the latter, then there would be open war.

audeant: Present subjunctive in the protasis of a future less vivid or "should/ would" condition. "If many should dare the same thing (*idem*) ..."

bellum esse: "It was outright war." (Yardley).

C. Caesarem: Gaius Julius Caesar.

inquit: Latin did not have quotation marks; the defective verb *inquam* served this function instead.

M. Catonem: Marcus Cato. This is Marcus Porcius Cato Uticensis, or Cato the Younger (95–46 B.C.), the great-grandson of Cato the Elder. Cato was known for his scrupulous adherence to the work of the senate, and to republican principles in the face of the widespread perception that Caesar was possessed of tyrannical ambitions. Cato and Caesar clashed during the Catilinarian conspiracy of 63 B.C.; he was later among the Pompeians in the great civil war that reached its climax at the battle of Pharsalus in 48 B.C. Cato ultimately committed suicide (April, 46 B.C.) after the disaster at the Battle of Thapsus. Cossutianus thus thrusts Nero and Thrasea into what some might consider quasi-stage roles; the two men are presented as reliving the great conflict between the republican principles of a Cato and what some saw as the revolutionary tyranny of Caesar.

avida discordiarum civitas: Cossutianus is made to play on Nero's nervous temperament; he paints a picture of a Rome that is always eager and zealous for discord and civil strife.

sectatores vel potius satellites: "Followers, or rather, agents." Cossutianus accuses Thrasea of having not so much adherents to his cause, but men ready to do his bidding. The ironies of the charge are rich.

contumaciam sententiarum: "The stubbornness of his opinions." Cossutianus describes a progressive adherence to Thrasea's position; first men imitate him in dress and appearance, and soon enough they subscribe fully to his views.

rigidi et tristes: "Stiff and grim." Stoic philosophers and adherents were sometimes accused of never appearing to be "happy."

quo … exprobrent: Relative clause of purpose.

tibi: Dative of reference.

lasciviam: "Playfulness." Cossutianus presents Nero as if he were some harmless, cheerfully impish, playfully mischievous sort—the perfect foil for the dour and grim reputation of Thrasea and his fellow Stoics.

huic uni: Dative of reference.

cura: This crucial word was added by Lipsius (and so the Oxford text italicizes it). Thrasea alone is said not to care about the safety and well-being of the *princeps*—and, perhaps even more damningly, he is said to hold Nero's art in no honor (*artes sine honore*). Once again, Tacitus is relentless in developing his theme of the perverse artist.

respuit: A strongly worded charge; Thrasea is said literally to be spitting back the prosperous, successful achievements of Nero's reign.

etiamne luctibus et doloribus non satiatur: It is one thing to reject benefits and blessings; it is another never to be satisfied with sorrow and misery.

eiusdem animi ... cuius: Genitive of characteristic; "it is of the same mind ...," etc. Cossutianus makes the seemingly extraordinary claim that the denial of Poppaea's divinity—which Tacitus has not mentioned until the Thrasea affair—is of a piece with the refusal to swear an oath to the *acta* of the divine Julius and the divine Augustus. Barrett (*ap.* Yardley) notes that it seems strange to leave Claudius out of the picture; given the immediately preceding reference to the conflict between Cato and Caesar, it may simply follow naturally that Cossutianus would reference Julius and his adopted son alone.

religiones: Religious practices and scruples (apparently not least among them being the veneration of Nero's voice). Cossutianus highlights the twin images of Roman religion and Roman law as veritable pillars of the state; Thrasea is cast in the role of perverter of the old order and reckless champion of new and revolutionary ways.

diurna: The *diurna* were a sort of ancient Roman newspaper; it was Caesar who in 59 B.C. had proposed that the deeds of the senate and the people should be published in digest form. Augustus had prohibited the publication of the *acta senatus*, but the *acta populi diurna* were released for the benefit of, for example, the citizens in the provinces. "Their name evidences their regularity (*diurna*—daily) and rhythmicity. It is likely that they were posted in a busy public place, such as the forum, where they would have an audience, could be examined, and from where copies could be taken. They were routinely displayed in places of movement." (D. Newsome, "Movement, Rhythms, and the (Re)production of Written Space," in G. Sears, P. Keegan, and R. Laurence, eds., *Written Space in the Latin West, 200 BC to AD 300*, London: Bloomsbury Ltd., 2013, p. 71).

curatius: Comparative adverb; "rather carefully."

ut noscatur: "In order that it may be known ..." Cossutianus argues that people in the province were reading reports merely to learn what affront Thrasea was committing against Nero's honor.

fecerit: Perfect subjunctive in an indirect question.

aut transeamus: Hortatory/jussive subjunctive. Cossutianus sarcastically says that the Romans should "go over" to Thrasea's way of thinking, if indeed it is better (*potiora*). Otherwise, the leader and founder of the movement (*dux et auctor*) should be taken away (*auferatur*, another jussive subjunctive).

nova cupientibus: Either a separative ablative or a dative of reference/possession. Thrasea is cast in the role of the champion of those who are zealous for new things, which, as usual in the Roman mind-set, means revolution and rebellion against the traditional order.

ista secta: "That sect." *Iste*, as often, carries a pejorative and highly critical note; Cossutianus need not be referring here to any particular school of philosophy or political science (e.g., the Stoics), but more generally to those who could be classified as "malcontents" by those looking to support the regime of the Caesars.

Tuberones: The members of this family are exhaustively surveyed in Cornell's *Fragments of the Roman Historians*, pp. 361 ff.; a Stoic Quintus Tubero is one of the speakers in Cicero's *De Re Publica*, while a Lucius Aelius Tubero was a friend of Cicero, and an historian like his son Quintus (though the exact extent of what father and son may have done in matters historical is open to debate). "No scholar considers the identification of these *Tuberones* as a problem ..." (F. R. Berno, "In Praise of Tubero's Pottery," in J. Wildberger and M. L. Colish, eds., *Seneca Philosophus*, Berlin-Boston, Walter de Gruyter, 2014, pp. 385 ff., with detailed consideration of the question).

Favonios: Marcus Favonius, who was an admirer of Cato the Younger, and an adherent to Cynic philosophy. Favonius opposed both the first triumvirate of Caesar, Pompey, and Crassus, and the second of Octavian, Antony, and Lepidus; he was proscribed and finally executed in 42 B.C. The Favonii and the Tuberones are held up as examples of where thinking such as Thrasea's is said to lead. Thrasea apparently wrote a biography of Cato (cf. Plutarch, *Cato Minor* 25, 37); Favonius was, as Griffin notes (*op. cit.*, p. 282), "an obscure follower of Cato," and it seems reasonable to conclude with her that Cossutianus is referencing Thrasea's work on Cato (which would have encouraged impressionable young men, as it were, to follow the example of the republican saint). See Griffin, p. 171 ff. for the question of whether or not it is reasonable to posit that there was a more or less organized "Stoic opposition" to Nero. The problems of whether or not the Stoic movement produced such opposition, and, if so, of why Stoic adherents in particular would have opposed Nero, is of prime importance to a study of the last years of the *princeps*.

Writing a life of the martyr Cato, like the honour shown to Cassius by A. Cremutius Cordus in his historical work ... was emblematic of approval of the republican cause and so could be taken to imply disapproval of the incumbent emperor ... By the time Plutarch wrote, however, after the death of Domitian and bracketing Cato with Phocion, a heroic Greek loser of the fourth century BC, the subject had lost its dangerous potency. (Cornell, *op. cit.*, p. 537)

For Thrasea's possible source material on the life of Cato, and the parallels that can be drawn between Thrasea and Socrates, see T. Duff, *Plutarch's Lives: Exploring Virtue and Vice*, Oxford, 1999, pp. 141–142.

veteri quoque rei publicae: The force of the argument is that even in what some might call the "good old days," there were complaints and arguments about all manner of political and social developments.

ingrata nomina: Names that brought no pleasure even in their own day.

ut imperium …: A typically sententious Tacitean expression; Cossutianus is made to argue that Thrasea and his ilk prefer liberty in order that they may overthrow the empire.

perverterint: Future perfect. Latin tense use follows a more strictly logical pattern and practice than English. Cossutianus argues that men like Thrasea are fundamentally disordered, and lovers of perpetual strife; if they succeed in subverting the empire, they will next attack freedom itself—with implications of constant civil strife and ongoing war.

> Tacitus emphasizes the irony of the situation by combining compounds of *vertere* with the transgressive *adgredientur* … The verbal cluster illustrates the extent to which the political discourse and words themselves have reached their acme of perversion during the reign of Nero. Such is a condition is of the utmost conceptual importance to Tacitus, who has previously posited the degeneration of eloquence in his *Dialogus* … The warping of the political discourse signifies the ultimate destruction of liberty. (F. S. L'Hoir, *Tragedy, Rhetoric, and the Historiography of Tacitus' Annales*, Ann Arbor: The University of Michigan Press, 2006, p. 83)

gliscere et vigere: *Gliscere* (cf. *c.* 3) is a favorite verb of Tacitus'; it describes the start of a process of swelling up or blazing forth.

passurus es: Future active participle in a periphrastic expression, literally, "If you are about to allow …"

nihil … scripseris: The perfect subjunctive can be used in a negative command. The perfect tense has completed aspect.

ipse: "You yourself," that is, Nero.

disceptatorem: "An arbitrator." Cossutianus cleverly urges Nero to let the senate be the deliberating and deciding body in the matter of Thrasea.

nobis: "For us." The dative is perhaps of reference (it also expresses possession); the senate is to handle the case, but the conclusion is, after all, foregone.

ira promptum: An ablative of respect; Nero praised how Cossutianus had a mind that was quick to anger (i.e., in a matter that deserved swift attention). Ritter deleted the ablative, which Heubner prints in brackets.

adicitque: Nero was happy with Cossutianus' speech, but he decided also to add Eprius as a backer of the charges against Thrasea, apparently because of the latter's skill. There need be no implied discredit on the emperor's part toward Cossutianus; Nero was worried about Thrasea's ability to rouse public support in his cause, and so he wanted to make sure that he had as much support as possible in his efforts to destroy him in the senate.

Marcellum Eprium: Titus Clodius Eprius Marcellus. His career after Nero's downfall is of particular interest; he rose to high favor during the reign of the Flavian Vespasian, only to be forced to commit suicide in A.D. 79 (the final year of Vespasian's rule). He figures in Book IV of Tacitus' *Historiae*, and in Book LXVI of Dio's *Roman History*; the exact circumstances surrounding his ruin are mysterious. On Eprius note E. Mary Smallwood, *Documents Illustrating the Principates of Gaius, Claudius, and Nero*, Cambridge, 1967, pp. 5 and 141.

acri eloquentia: Eprius is credited here as having particularly biting and bitter eloquence; Nero extolls the words of Cossutianus, and gives him the assistance of Eprius as the ideal prosecutor of the senatorial case.

Chapter twenty-three: The indictment of Barea Soranus

At: The adversative conjunction introduces a change of topic from the one accused to the other.

Ostorius Sabinus: Very little is known of this Roman equestrian; he is depicted as having sought the chance to prosecute Barea Soranus for actions taken while proconsul of Asia. *Ostorius* is the correction/supplement of Lipsius for the Medicean *torius*; M also reads *savinus* for *Sabinus*.

offensiones principis: *Offensio* refers to a sort of simmering resentment and indignation; below Tacitus notes that Soranus was, after all, accused of having been a friend of the ill-fated Rubellius Plautus.

iustitia atque industria: Ablatives of means. Soranus had increased Nero's sense of offense and indignation by virtue of the very justice and industry with which he exercised his government duties.

portui ... aperiendo: Gerundive. Soranus had personally undertaken the responsibility of seeing to the dredging of the harbor at Ephesus. Ephesus was a major city in southwestern Turkey, on the Ionian coast; it was famous for the Temple of Artemis that was counted among the seven wonders of the ancient world.

vimque: To be taken with *inultam*.

civitatis Pergamenae: "The Pergamene city-state." Pergamon had been bequeathed to Rome in 133 B.C. when its king, Attalus III, had died without an heir; at one time it was the capital of the Roman province of Asia.

statuas et picturas: Nero's freedman Acratus had been sent to steal artwork, both sculptures and paintings. Tyrants through history have been known to raid their empires for artistic plunder; in the context of Nero's reign, the theft takes on special significance, given the *princeps'* aspirations to be considered the consummate artist. Soranus clearly approved of the Pergamene decision to use force in preventing Acratus from plundering their treasures. Acratus was apparently Nero's regular merchant for stolen art; at XV, 45 he was involved in the same escapade after the great fire at Rome in A.D. 64.

amicitia Plauti: That is, friendship with Rubellius Plautus, who had been exiled to Asia in A.D. 60 and executed in 62. Tacitus thus provides both the personal reasons for Sabinus' desire to prosecute Soranus, and the official charges. Marsh and Leon note that "there was no military force stationed in the senatorial province of Asia, but a revolt begun there in favor of Plautus might be taken up by the legions of Syria."

ambitio conciliandae provinciae ad spes novas: Soranus was charged with the ambition of trying to bring over the province of Asia to his desire for revolution and revolt against Nero. The favor he had shown to the Ephesians and to Pergamon would be interpreted negatively as a desire to win over the local population to his political ambitions. For the references to Soranus' condemnation in Juvenal's third satire, see J. Uden, *The Invisible Satirist: Juvenal and Second-Century Rome*, Oxford, 2015, pp. 110–111.

tempus damnationi delectum: "The time chosen for the condemnation." There would be no question as to guilt or innocence.

Tiridates: On Tiridates' visit to Rome cf. *Annales* XV, 29–31. He was king of Armenia from A.D. 53, though with interruptions; Nero personally received him as his guest in the autumn of 66. For a convenient overview of Nero's foreign policy adventures, see Chapter 5, "Apollo in Arms: Nero at the Frontier," in E. Buckley and M. Dinter, eds., *A Companion to the Neronian Age*, Malden, Massachusetts: Wiley-Blackwell, 2013. On Tacitus' treatment of foreign potentates note A. M. Gowing, "Tacitus and the Client Kings," in *Transactions of the American Philological Association* 120 (1990), pp. 315–331. On Nero's and Vespasian's dealings with Armenia and the Armenian question, see P. M. Elwell, *Between Rome and Persia*, London-New York: Routledge, 2008, by 17. The early history of Roman involvement in the area is conveniently surveyed by R. Evans, *Roman Conquests: Asia Minor, Syria, and Armenia*, South Yorkshire: Pen & Sword Military, 2011.

accipiendo: Gerundive.

intestinum scelus: An internal crime. On the implications of the phrase and the language and vocabulary of imperial reaction to republican sentiment, see C. Damon, "*Inestinum Scelus*: Preemptive Execution in Tacitus' *Annals*," in B. Breed, C. Damon, and A. Rossi, eds., *Citizens of Discord: Rome and Its Civil Wars*, Oxford, 2010, pp. 261–272.

ut … obscuraretur: More carefully constructed theater. The time for the prosecution of Soranus was to be conflated with the arrival and reception of the Armenian king; Tacitus gives the weighted alternative that the point was either to obscure the internal conflict in Rome or so that Nero could display his own quasi-regal power by the destruction of great men.

quasi regio facinore: "As if by a regal/royal crime." Nero did not want to be outdone in the matter of monarchical prerogative by his eastern visitor (who was, of course, arriving as something of a suppliant); the prosecution and condemnation of Soranus (and of Thrasea) would provide the perfect way of demonstrating the power of the *princeps*.

Chapter twenty-four: Thrasea's reaction to the charges

omni civitate … effusa: Ablative absolute. Nero had met Tiridates in Naples, and was now returning with the king to Rome.

excipiendum … spectandum: Gerundives expressing purpose. All of Rome was preoccupied with the diversion of going out to see Nero and Tiridates; Thrasea, understandably enough, was preoccupied with responding to the dire actions taken against him—and, after all, he was barred from attending the festivities (which, we might think, he might have avoided being present for anyway).

occursu: A type of separative ablative. Thrasea was explicitly forbidden to be present for the dramatic events.

non demisit animum: Stoic fortitude. Another man might have become thoroughly despondent in the face of his impending fate; Thrasea calmly proceeds to writing a letter to Nero.

codicillos: The noun is used mostly in the plural; while it could mean the "codicil" of a will or testament, it also described a writing tablet or the writing thereon. *Codicillus* is a dimunutive of *codex/caudex*, literally "trunk of a tree" (denoting the bark that could be used for the fashioning of tablets for writing).

requirens obiecta: That is, seeking the exact nature of the charges. Thrasea seeks to compel Nero to lay out the case against him *in forma specifica*.

expurgaturum: Supply *esse*. Thrasea swore that he would respond in detail to the charges made against him, and that he would purge himself of any accusation of wrongdoing. Once again the prefix carries a note of intensity.

notitiam criminum: "Notice of the charges." Thrasea's letter to Nero highlights the distinction between rumor/innuendo and legal action.

diluendi: Gerund. The verb means to wash away or to dissipate and dissolve something. The language emphasizes the notion of washing oneself clean of the stain of guilt and ill repute.

habuisset: Pluperfect subjunctive in a subordinate clause in indirect discourse.

properanter: "Hastily/with eagerness."

spe: Furneaux takes this as an ablative of manner.

exterritum: "Thoroughly frightened." Tacitus has already highlighted Nero's easily spooked, timid nature; here the *princeps* is depicted as having the hope or expectation that Thrasea was so terrified by the turn of events that he had written something that greatly extolled the emperor, even as it offered proof of his own bad nature and criminal enterprise. Once again we might think of Nero as a stage manager; in this case, Thrasea would disappoint the director.

per quae extolleret ... dehonestaret: Imperfect subjunctives that express Nero's hopes and wishes, namely that the fame of the emperor would be extolled, and that Thrasea would besmirch his own reputation.

ultro: The adverb can mean "conversely, on the other hand"; Nero had hoped to defeat Thrasea easily and without much effort, and now he was not only deprived of his hope for victory, but also mired in his own anxiety.

quod: Namely, Nero's wish.

vultum ... spiritus et libertatem: Cossutianus had complained about the grim and dire looks of the Stoics; Nero now fears seeing Thrasea's resolute face, spirit, and commitment to freedom.

extimuit: A marvelous Tacitean reversal: Nero anticipated that Thrasea would be cowering in fear and eager to appease the *princeps*, and now he was the one who was utterly terrified at the prospect of facing Thrasea as he made his defense against the trumped up charges.

Chapter twenty-five: Thrasea's deliberations, part I

inter proximos: Presumably his closest friends and associates.

temptaretne ... an sperneret: Imperfect subjunctives in indirect questions. Thrasea consulted among his confidantes as to whether or not he should bother to mount a defense. The implication of *sperneret* is that he would see to his affairs and commit suicide. *Defensionem* refers to an appeal in the senate, or perhaps directly to the *princeps*.

diversa consilia: There were different opinions.

quibus ... placebat: The verb *placeo* takes a dative object. Some were of the opinion that Thrasea should enter the senate and make a case in his own defense.

securos esse de constantia eius: Infinitive in indirect discourse after *disserunt*. They said they were certain and without worry that he would maintain his consistency. *Eius* refers to Thrasea. The great Stoic philosopher and Neronian victim had written an entire essay *De Constantia Sapientis*, a work that Tacitus no doubt meant to recall in his report of the assurances of Thrasea's friends.

disserunt: This is Haase's emendation for the manuscript reading *dixerunt*, which was considered objectionable since it occurs in such proximity to *dicturum* (though ancient writers were less bothered by this sort of "repetition" than some moderns; cf. Syme: "How grave a view is to be taken of those repetitions? It is hard to say. But who can commend or approve the feeble 'se ostendere', twice in the *Historiae* (IV. 49. 2; V. 1. 1), banished from the *Annales* until Book XVI (10. 4; 18. 2; 22.1)?"—*op. cit.*, p. 741). *Disserere* once again refers to the careful arrangement of material in defense of a particular case.

dicturum: Supply *esse*. They said they he would say nothing except that which would increase his glory and reputation.

quo: A sort of ablative of means.

segnis et pavidos: Accusatives of substantive adjectives in indirect discourse. *Segnis* implies that one is sluggish and slow, perhaps from timidity; the word can be applied to one who has no energy and is in a state of torpor. *Pavidus* is more properly used of one who is suffering from fear.

secretum circumdare: Some of Thrasea's associates note that it is a mark of the timid and the fearful to put secrecy around their final actions (*supremis suis*). The noble Stoic should make a public spectacle of his defense, death and honor. *Circumdare* means to surround or to enclose; in this case, the charge is that some people close off their last moments and seek to escape the notice of the people.

aspiceret ... audiret: These imperfect subjunctives express the potentialities that could arise from Thrasea's presence in the senate; the people would see a man who was standing straight in the face of death, and the senate would a voice that seemed more than human.

obvius: Cf. *via*; that which is "obvious" is right in one's face, as it were. The Stoic hero should at the very least know how to die with dignity and honor. The prefix governs the dative object *morti*.

voces quasi ex aliquo numine supra humanas: Tacitus' report here no doubt means to recall the business of how Thrasea refused to make offering to the emperor's *caelestis vox*; Thrasea's friends are depicted as advising him that if he were to appear in the senate, his words would carry more than a human air and tone, indeed that they would seem to be the voice of some god. The Medicean reads *humanos*.

sin: "But if." The Medicean reads *si in* here.

insisteret: The subject is Nero. The imperfect subjunctive is used in the protasis of a present contrafactual condition.

memoriam honesti exitus: "The memory of a noble end." Once again the historian is concerned with the power of memory and recollection, and, as often, with the matter of what constitutes nobility, especially in the face of tyrannical threats to liberty.

ab ignavia per silentium pereuntium: Tacitus returns again to the question of the reputation of those who seemed to face the tyranny of the emperor without complaint. Thrasea's associates indicate that if he is indeed doomed, than it would be better if he were remembered for having made a courageous stand against tyranny, rather than submitting meekly to the outrages of Nero's rule.

Chapter twenty-six: Thrasea's deliberations, part II

opperiendum: Supply *esse*. Tacitus proceeds to detail the reasoning and thinking of those who thought that Thrasea should wait at his home and not venture to visit to senate.

de ipso Thrasea: "Concerning Thrasea himself." Those who wanted Thrasea to remain in his home were no less impressed with his constancy and nobility than those who were eager for a showdown in the senate.

eadem: "With an unexpressed verb of saying, upon which the following indirect discourse also depends." (Marsh and Leon).

ludibria … contumelias: The former refer mostly to words of mockery, the latter to insults and abuse. The fear of some was that Thrasea would be made a laughing stock by Nero's sycophants and those who were afraid of arguing contrary to the clear wishes of the *princeps*.

conviciis et probris: Separative ablatives. They believed that Thrasea should spare his ears the hearing of bitter opprobrium and insults.

promptos: Supply *esse*. Tacitus is reporting the sentiments of those who were remonstrating with Thrasea. Cossutianus and Eprius were not the only ones who were ready to commit crimes, they argued.

superesse: The verb here means "to exist in addition," that is, "there were also."

qui … ausuri sint: Relative clause of characteristic/generic relative clause. The fear was that someone might actually subject Thrasea to physical violence. *Ausuri* is Acidalius' emendation for the Medicean reading *angusti*; Heubner prints *ingest<ur>i <sint>* from the suggestions of other editors.

metu: Ablative of cause.

detraheret: Imperfect subjunctive used deliberately and with admonitory force.

potius: "Rather."

senatui: Separative ablative.

quid … decreturi fuerint: Indirect question with an active periphrastic. On the tense of the subjunctive Marsh and Leon note: "The perfect subjunctive form is used despite the contrary-to-fact condition and the dependence on a verb with a secondary tense. This use of the perfect subjunctive is occasionally found even in other writers when the apodosis of the condition is an indirect question, as here, or is introduced by *ut, cum,* or *quin.*"

inrita spe: Ablative of manner; the expectation that Nero would actually feel a sense of shame at the whole proceedings was void and to no effect.

agitari: The verb is the frequentative of *agere*, with just as wide a range of uses; it can mean to discuss or debate, to meditate upon or to turn over something in the mind, to toss about and "agitate."

ne … saeviret: Fear clause. *Saevitia* was, after all, a defining characteristic of Tacitus' Nero.

pignora: The basic meaning of *pignus* is a "pledge" or "surety." Here it refers to the other members of Thrasea's extended family.

eius: That is, Thrasea's.

intemeratus: "Undefiled" and "pure."

vestigiis et studiis: A sort of hendiadys; the "tracks" represent the path that was set out by Thrasea's Stoic models, while the *studia* are the pursuits of philosophical and other contemplation in which he absorbed their lesson. In *vestigia* there is also the sense that some men have already shown by the character of their last moments how one should live and die; Seneca in particular is perhaps referenced here.

Rusticus Arulenus: Quintus Iunius Arulenus Rusticus, tribune of the plebs in 66. For his life and works see the entry in *Fragments of the Roman Historians*, pp. 573–574; he apparently wrote of Thrasea, though after his execution in 93, his writings—the likely cause of the indictment—were burned. He is perhaps most famous for the stirring words of Tacitus in the second chapter of the *Agricola*: "We have heard that the panegyrics pronounced by Arulenus Rustics on Paetus Thrasea, and by Herennius Senecio on Priscus Helvidius, were made capital crimes, that not only their persons but their very books were objects of rage," etc. (Church and Brodribb, trs.).

flagrans iuvenis: We might say that he was a "hothead," certainly someone who was full of righteous indignation at the situation, and ready to risk perilous moves for the sake of honor. Rusticus' behavior would eventually see him killed under Domitian. Pliny the Younger paints a positive picture of the young Rusticus, with whom he was apparently close (*Epistulae* 1.5; 1.14; 2.18).

cupidine laudis: A Tacitean comment on motivation. Rusticus was eager to receive praise for his daring action; the line between praise and blame in such case can be difficult to discern.

se intercessurum: He proposed that he would interpose his veto as the *tribunus plebis*. Thrasea at once counsels him against a course of action that would likely not be able to save him, and which would imperil the young tribune (Rusticus was born *c.* 33).

cohibuit spiritus eius …: Thrasea moves at once restrain his vigorous spirit. *Spiritus* (accusative plural of a fourth declension noun) can refer to breathing and breath, but also to pride, arrogance, and vigorous energy.

vana et reo non profutura: "Things that would be pointless and of no profit/ advantage to the defendant." Tacitus' language once again introduces the idea of the contrast between substance and shadow; the proposed action of Rusticus would have no purposeful effect.

intercessori exitiosa: "Fatal to the interposer of the veto."

sibi actam aetatem: The dative is of reference; the future Stoic martyr declares that his own life has been lived.

non deserendum: Gerundive. Thrasea asserts that his *vitae ordo* must not be abandoned at this late stage.

initium magistratuum: The beginning of a career in public office.

integra quae supersint: "What remained was whole/integral." Thrasea argues that Rusticus' future would remain unsullied and safe, were he to refrain from any precipitous action. The adjective refers both to the youth of the tribune, and to the idea that if he takes cautious counsel now, he can preserve his reputation in the eyes of the powers that be.

multum ante secum expenderet: The subjunctive is deliberative and admonitory; Thrasea said that Rusticus should weigh out in his mind in advance what he should do. *Multum* is an adverbial accusative; with *ante* it has temporal force (cf. Yardley's "far ahead").

quod: In agreement with *iter*. Rusticus is urged to consider carefully what path/route he should take in such an age/circumstance (*tali in tempore*).

capessendae rei publicae: Gerundive. The verb *capessere* means to pursue or chase after with particular zeal, to catch or capture something. For the phrase cf. Nepos' life of Themistocles, *c.* 2: *Primus autem gradus fuit capessendae rei publicae bello Corcyraeo* ... The phrase thus refers to the management of the government and the execution of the duties of state; it gives no implication of seizing power for personal or tyrannical gain.

ceterum: This adverb is formed from the neuter singular of the adjective *ceterus* and can literally be rendered "as for the rest," that is, moreover, furthermore. It used to move the narrative/argument along to another point.

ipse: That is, Thrasea.

an: "Whether." Thrasea gives no immediate answer as to what he plans to do.

deceret: The verb is impersonal.

meditationi suae: "To his own meditation/private thought." Tacitus does not make it clear whether or not Thrasea had already reached a decision.

Chapter twenty-seven: The senate convenes

postera luce: Cf. *Historiae* V, 16.1; *posterus* means "following" or "next." The phrase is not at all common as a temporal marker.

armatae ... gladiis: Tacitus emphasizes how Nero made his will known in part through intimidation.

templum Genitricis Veneris: We might think of the opening of Lucretius' *De Rerum Natura*, with its invocation of Venus as the *Aeneadum genetrix* or "mother of the children of Aeneas." The temple of Venus as Mother was founded in 46 B.C. by Julius Caesar, who traced his descent from the goddess through the lineage of Aeneas and his son Iulus/Julus; in origin the temple was supposed to be an offering for the goddess to mark victory in the great battle at Pharsalus in which Caesar defeated Pompey. The temple served to signify and to remind the populace of the connection of the Julian family with the goddess and her son, one of the putative founders of Rome (or, one might prefer to say, one of the setters in motion of the long process by which Rome would be founded); Nero, like Julius Caesar, played on connections between the Julian family and the Trojan origins of Rome (cf. *inter al.*, his epic *Troica*).

> The temple of Venus ... was built of solid marble ... The statue of Venus Genetrix by Arcesilaus, which Caesar set up, in foro Caesaris ... was probably in the cella of the temple ... Later, Augustus is stated to have set up in the temple a statue of the deified Julius with a star above his head ... although some scholars believe that this is a mistake for the temple of divus Iulius in the forum. (S. B. Platner ..., *A Topographical Dictionary of Ancient Rome*, Oxford, 1926, p. 226)

insedere: For *insederunt*.

globus togatorum: "A throng of men in togas." These are possibly civilians, in contrast to the praetorian cohorts; legally there was no right for these men to have open weapons (*non occultis gladiis*), but there was certainly no one around who was about to move to do anything much about it. Furneaux considers them to be "soldiers in undress," on the grounds that with respect to having armed civilians, " ... it is hardly likely that such a precedent was sanctioned; and if it had been, we should expect Tacitus to have said more about it, or at least to have used such a word as 'civium' ..."

obsedit: The verb comes in close proximity after *insedere*: Rome looked as if it were a city under military occupation, and the senate as if it were a place under military siege and threat of invasion.

basilicas: In origin, a Roman *basilica* was simply an open building, usually one that was right next to a forum or public square. The word has come to be associated mostly with Christian churches (cf. Saint Peter's Basilica in the Vatican).

cunei militares: Literally, "wedge-shaped military formations." There were two praetorian *cohortes* at the temple of the goddess; armed civilians at the door of the senate, and elsewhere, units of soldiers in tight military formations. One might almost have the idea that Thrasea Paetus did not warrant such seemingly extreme preventative measures. Nero's Rome is under veritable military occupation.

inter quorum aspectus: The senators literally between their meeting place under the eyes of those who were armed and making threats (*minas*).

curiam: For the exact location of the meeting cf. Furneaux's note:

> This word might no doubt be used of any place in which the senate met, and Nipp. supposes it here to be used of the "templum Veneris" ... But there is no reason why we should not suppose the senate to have met in its usual place, the "Curia Iulia," built by Augustus on the site of the old house ... This supposition seems to enable us to give a clearer account of the disposition of the troops: the body of the "togati" is posted at the actual entrance of the "Curia"; other detachments ... are in places closely adjoining; and a far larger and more imposing force occupies, as a kind of fortress, the neighbouring temple and precinct, to be available in case of need.

oratio principis: Nero himself was not present, but he presumably wrote the speech that was delivered. Nero the stage performer is here replaced by Nero the orator.

per quaestorem: The quaestor was properly in charge of financial affairs and matters of economic business; it was the first step in the so-called *cursus honorum*, and those who held the office were allowed to be present in the senate. We do not possess definitive knowledge as to how Nero was using quaestors. Tacitus does not record the name of this particular messenger; Syme observes that "His identity might have been worth knowing, for he is the recipient of Thrasea's last message to the world ... Ought not the historian to have furnished the name of the quaestor? It is his way to let a name speak for itself, to make his point by significant allusion, eschewing the detail of annotation."—*op. cit.*, p. 745). It may be wishful thinking to imagine that Tacitus deliberately sought to deny Nero's messenger onomastic dignity; the courtier will play a significant part in the stage setting of Thrasea's suicide.

nemine nominatim compellato: Ablative absolute. No one was actually named; those expecting an opening salvo against Thrasea or Barea were to be disappointed. Instead, Nero's quaestor made a general attack on unspecified senators—a tactic that would no doubt have made some officials even more fearful than they already were. The general atmosphere was one of anxiety and dread that others would fall with the more well known targets.

arguebat: The speech chastised or chided them.

quod ... desererent: A *quod*-clause of alleged reason, giving the pretext for which Nero has turned his critical pen against the senate.

publica munia: "Public duties/responsibilities." Thrasea had been accused of not attending senate meetings for the last three years; Nero seizes on the attendance issue for making the charge of dereliction of duty.

eorumque exemplo: Ablative of means: Roman equestrians are said to be following the example of lazy senators.

verterentur: The Medicean has *uterentur*.

quid mirum: "What surprise" was it if/that ...?

haud veniri: An impersonal use of the passive. The reading is Lipsius' conjecture for *had veniri* of the Medicean; Acidalius suggested *haud adveniri*. The exact point of the complaint of Nero's letter is difficult to construe definitively. Those who achieved the consulship and priesthoods are accused of spending more time on their gardens than on their official duties; small wonder, then, that barely anyone comes from the most distant provinces to Rome. The point of reference may be to former holders of office who prefer to remain away from the capital; Furneaux takes it to refer to equestians who were neglecting their urban duties in the interest of making a profit in overseas ventures.

cum ... inservirent: A *cum*-clause expressing past time, with the usual imperfect subjunctive.

adepti: From the deponent verb *adipiscor, adipisci, adeptus sum*, "to obtain."

hortorum ... amoenitati: "The pleasure of their gardens." Gardens had long been an important part of cultured Roman life; one might think of the *Horti Lucullani* or "Gardens of Lucullus" that had been established by the celebrated Roman republican military commander. Gardens were important symbols and elements in Roman literature and the arts; for a sensitive appraisal and study, see V. E. Pagán, *Rome and the Literature of Gardens*, London: Bloomsbury Ltd., 2007. For a perceptive consideration of the role of gardens in Tacitean death scenes, note K. T. von Stackelberg, "Performative Space and Garden Transgressions in Tacitus' Death of Messalina," in *The American Journal of Philology* 130.4 (2009), pp. 595–624.

amoenitati: Dative with the compound verb *inservirent*.

velut telum: "As if it were a weapon." *Telum* refers properly to missile weapons, a spear or javelin; Nero's cronies and sycophants use the quaestor's speech as the perfect launching point for their attack on Thrasea.

corripuere: For *corripuerunt*.

Chapter twenty-eight: Cossutianus and Eprius
launch their attacks

faciente Cossutiano: Ablative absolute. Nero's dogs did not wait long to begin their savage indictments.

maiore vi:: "With greater force." The attack is crescendo-like; first Cossutianus makes his case, and then Eprius follows with increased intensity.

summam rem publicam agi: Hyperbole, but no doubt effective in context; Eprius argues that nothing less than the very heart of the republic was in jeopardy on account of the actions of certain individuals.

clamitabat: Frequentative (also inceptive); Tacitus had said that Eprius was possessed of *acri eloquentia*, and now Nero's hired speaker begins his bitter rant with a lashing list of accusations and editorializing comments.

contumacia: Ablative of means. Tacitus now reports the substance of Eprius' argument, namely that the stubbornness of inferiors was weakening the mercy and charity of the ruler. In other words, Thrasea was pushing Nero too far, and thereby endangering the very stability of the state.

mitis: Accusative plural with *patres*.

qui: To be taken with *sinerent* below in a generic relative clause/relative clause of characteristic. Eprius upbraids the senate for ignoring the allegedly serious crimes and offenses of the three men he now proceeds to name. Once again, Thrasea is for the moment studiously avoided, though he is in a sense everywhere.

desciscentem: The basic meaning of *desciscere* is to depart from something, to defect or to revolt, to desert or to deviate from someone or something.

Helvidium Priscum: The son-in-law of Thrasea Paetus. We are not certain about his exact fate under Nero; he was possibly if not likely exiled. He survived the tyrant, and became something of the *de facto* leader of those who remembered the example of his father-in-law. Priscus would eventually seek to prosecute Eprius; once Vespasian was in power, however, this effort failed, given that the new Flavian emperor was not interested in reprisals and acts of revenge and justice dating back to the Neronian age. Priscus was eventually exiled once again, and finally executed by command of Vespasian. This is likely the first mention of Priscus in the *Annales*; he is given a fuller notice by Tacitus at *Historiae* IV, 5.

in isdem furoribus: "In the same acts of madness and fury." An important element of the show trial is to condemn the accused for acts that simply defy explanation or defense; the target must be vilified for being full of anger and rage against the state and those who would be loyal to it.

Paconium Agrippinum: The Stoic philosopher Epictetus (I, 2, 12 ff.) preserves the story that this Paconius was asked once by Lucius Mestrius Florus whether or not he should take part in a festival of Nero. Paconius replied that he should. When then asked why he himself stayed away from such events, Paconius gave the answer that the question of whether or not he should attend never even occurred to him. The Medicean manuscript has *ragonium* here for *Paconium*; he may have served as proconsul in Crete. It is possible that he is the son of the Marcus Paconius who lost his life after the fall of Sejanus, though whatever Tacitus may have said about this would have occurred in one of the lost sections of the Tiberian *Annales* (at III, 67 he is in found in the role of accuser in the proceedings against Silanus). Again, it remains an open question whether or not the Stoicism of these men was a direct factor in their downfall. Priscus had a marriage connection to Thrasea, and Paconius was, as Eprius notes, perhaps a long-standing opponent of the house of the Caesars. Both men, in short, had more than enough to condemn them in these late days of Nero, Stoicism aside.

paterni in principes odii heredem: The sins of the fathers; the inheritance in this case is said to have been one of hatred and contempt for the imperial family.

Curtium Montanum: A third target is named. Juvenal lampoons a man of the same name in satires 4 (107, 131) and 11 (34); there he is a poor orator and a sycophantic parasite of Domitian. Two letters of Pliny are addressed to him (VII, 29; V, 6). He would live another day to attack the informer Marcus Aquilius Regulus (cf. Tacitus, *Historiae* IV, 43–43). "Curtius will have had good reason to go after one of Nero's instruments, having suffered degradation at the *delatores'* hands during Thrasea's ordeal" (Rutledge, *op. cit.*, p. 125).

detestanda: Gerundive. Once again the charge of writing scurrilous, scandalous poetry is raised: "the words would imply that he was a libelous satirist." (Furneaux).

factitantem: Frequentative. Syme notes that "the expression 'carmina factitare,' once in the first hexad (VI. 39. 1), recurs four times in the third (XIV. 48. 1; 52. 3; 66.2)." (*op. cit.*, p. 741).

eludere: Cf. English "elude/elusive"; in this case there is the particular force of the notion of a game and the mocking nature of Montanus' poetry.

requirere ...: Eprius proceeds to an ascending tricolon of wishes before he finally names Thrasea. He wants a consular man in the senate; a priest in votive offerings to be rendered, and a citizen in the swearing of oaths—unless, perchance, contrary to the institutions and traditions of Roman political and religious life, *Thrasea* has put on the part of a betrayer and enemy of all that is good and old-fashioned. A powerful sentence, which builds in force and vigor to the contrafactual conclusion *nisi ... Thrasea induisset.*

The charge of absence from senatorial proceedings continues; Eprius sarcastically observes that he is "looking for an ex-consul" precisely because Thrasea has been absent from senatorial proceedings for three years now.

maiorum: Genitive plural, "of our ancestors." Eprius highlights the antiquity of Roman institutions, and tries to cast Thrasea in the role of novel usurper of ancient rites, and upstart revolutionary against the established, traditional order.

induisset: The verb properly means to don something or put something on, that is, an article of clothing (compare the English, "to assume the mantle").

agere senatorem: We might say, "to play the senator." Eprius alludes to Thrasea's alleged great interest in the life and parliamentary procedure of the senate (at least before he stopped attending).

obtrectatores: "Detractors." Thrasea is now accused of having shielded against prosecution and criticism of those who complained about the *princeps.*

censeret quid corrigi aut mutari vellet: On the image of Thrasea as "corrector" or "emender" of the senate, see Syme, *op. cit.*, p. 725.

veniret: Deliberative subjunctive with admonitory force; Thrasea should come now and act the part of a senator, etc. *Solitus* is used to describe what was allegedly Thrasea's customary behavior.

perlaturos: Supply *esse*. Eprius says that everyone would more readily and easily bear the attacks and criticisms of Thrasea, were he to detail what exactly troubles him about Nero's rule. Instead, his silence makes it clear that he simply despises everything and is a perpetual curmudgeon.

singula increpantem: "Carping at every individual thing." Heubner prints *singula increpanti<s> v<oce>m* from the conjecture of Madvig; the Medicean has *increpatium.*

omnia damnantis: "Of the one damning everything." Thrasea was of course trapped whatever he did; by deciding against arrival at the senate, he opens himself up to the continued charge of not participating in senatorial deliberations, and of using *silentium* as a sign that he was simply displeased with Nero's reign in principle, rather than in this or that specific act that he wished to see corrected or changed. The game was rigged, and Thrasea refused to play.

pacem: The action against Thrasea, we might recall, was deliberately taken to coincide with the reception of the Armenian king Tiridates. Suetonius' life of Nero (*c.* 13) details how Nero meant to exhibit Tiridates to the people, and was prevented by inclement weather; at last, the praetorian cohorts were assembled around the temples in the Roman Forum, and Nero was seated on the curule chair and received the submission of the king. Nero was hailed as *imperator*, and after bringing the laurel wreath of victory to the Capitol, he went to close the doors of the temple of Janus and to proclaim peace throughout the world. Thrasea is thus accused of being an ingrate in such times of glorious pacification and Roman international glory.

illi: Dative of reference.

sine damno exercituum: "Without loss to the armies." In the immediate context of Tiridates' dramatic entry into Rome, the arguments of Eprius about world peace must have carried some credence with the audience.

ne: To be taken with *facerent*, at the close of a long admonition.

hominem … maestum: "This grim man." Once again there is a reference to the perpetually sour appearance of certain philosophical types; Thrasea is depicted as being miserable even in a time of national rejoicing.

fora theatra templa: Effective asyndeton. Thrasea is accused of treating the forums, theaters, and temples of Rome as if they were a desert (*pro solitudine*). One wonders if there is a deliberate allusion to the author's own celebrated *solitudinem faciunt, pacem appellant* from *Agricola*, where the Caledonian commander Calgacus makes his trenchant observation about the Romans. Thrasea is said to treat Rome as a desert wasteland precisely because he does not seem to be interested in visiting the capital much these days.

minitaretur: From the deponent *minitor, minitari, minitatus sum*, "to threaten." "As though Rome could not get along with him" (Marsh and Leon).

ambitionis pravae compotem: "In control or mastery of his depraved ambition." Eprius urges the senate not to allow Thrasea to have what he wants. For the adjective *compos* cf. the English legal use of *non compos mentis*, etc.

non illi consulta …: Another tricolon. Thrasea is said not to care for the decrees of the senate, for the magistracies and offices of Roman government, or even for the city herself.

videri: The decisions of the senate, etc., are literally "not seen" by Thrasea (who has absented himself for some time from that body); by extension and implication, he can thus be said to have no regard or concern for any of it.

abrumperet vitam: "Let him break away his life …" Eprius ends his attack with a remark that is savagely tinged with double meaning; on the one hand, there is the question of Thrasea's departure from the city, on the other, his departure from life itself.

exuisset: Echoing *induisset* above. Thrasea is now characterized for what he has taken off or doffed, as it were: not only love for the city of Rome, but even the very sight of the city. Thrasea had been accused of performing in tragic attire at the Cetastian Games in Patavium; here the accuser is depicted as continuing to employ and extend the metaphor. Tacitus' Thrasea, however, is someone whose stage presence looms large even when he is not actually in the theater.

Chapter twenty-nine: Senatorial reaction

per haec atque talia: "Through these and similar/such things."

torvus: "Grim" or "savage," especially in appearance and image. Eprius was like a wild animal in his savage indictment of his target.

voce vultu oculis: More effective asyndeton; Eprius was burning in voice, face, and eyes as he railed against Thrasea and his supporters.

celebritate periculorum: "From the frequency of perils/hazards"; the ablative is causal. The word order conveys something of the seemingly unending queue of prosecutions; *nota* and *sueta* are adjectives in agreement with *maestitia*. Customarily the senate was noted for its "customary" or "usual" despondency in the face of the frequent prosecutions and accusations; what happens now in the wake of Eprius' remarks is even more frightening. Rhenanus read *crebritate* here (followed by Nipperdey-Andersen, and Heubner's Teubner).

sed novus et altius pavor: "But a new and deeper fear."

cernentibus: A referential dative with possessive force; the senators were in absolute dread of future events as they saw the soldiers holding weapons.

simul: "At the same time."

ipsius Thraseae venerabilis species obversabatur: "The venerable image of Thrasea himself was directed toward them." Thrasea's associates had debated whether or not he should appear in the senate; as it turns out, his *species* is indeed present in the wake of Eprius' vicious assault. The intensive *ipsius* highlights the scene; Thrasea was himself not present in the senate, and yet he was. Thrasea's image serves as an accusing conscience for the Roman senators; the weapons of the soldiers and citizens also add to the sense of weariness on the part of the senate with how far things have gone.

species: A key word in the Tacitean vocabulary, as the historian seeks to explore the psychology of motivation and the interplay between truth and image, reality and falsehood. Interested readers may wish to consult here L. T. Pearcy, Jr., *Tacitus' Use of Species, Imago, Effigies and Simulacrum*, Dissertation Bryn Mawr College, 1973.

innoxiae adfinitatis: "For a harmless kinship/bond of affinity." Helvidius was pitied by some because he seemed to be about to pay a penalty because he was Thrasea's son-in-law. The genitive is of the charge.

poenas daturum: Future active participle in the normal Latin expression for "paying a price/penalty."

quid: Tacitus reports the substance of some of the comments that were made in the wake of the accusations.

obiectum: "Thrown in the face of," that is, hurled at as an accusation. Agrippinus was seen as suspect merely because of the history of his parent.

nisi tristem patris fortunam: "Except the grim fortune of his father." The recollection of the savage persecutions of the Tiberian years serves in part to link his reign with that of Nero.

quando: "Since." The pluperfect subjunctive *concidisset* provides the report of the cause of the father's fall that was put forth by some. *Et* is adverbial.

perinde: "In the same manner, just as."

saevitia: Ablative of cause.

enimvero: The conjunction often introduces a statement of corroborating evidence.

probae iuventae neque famosi carminis: Genitives of characteristic. Montanus was a youth of noble and upright character, someone who should not be identified as the author of a scandalous, infamous poem. Once again the historian introduces details about the arts and literature in his description of the excesses of Nero's reign. Marsh and Leon note, "This use of the descriptive genitive is rather bold."

quia protulerit ingenium: "Because he produced/brought forth talent." The perfect subjunctive is used in a clause of alleged reason. Montanus was condemned, some thought, because he had shown himself to be another potential poetic rival of the *princeps*. Nero's fears and anxieties in this regard are a recurring topic in Tacitus' account of his reign; the experience with Lucan is the most famous example.

extorrem: "As an exile."

agi: Passive infinitive, "was being driven." The present infinitive indicates that the action is occurring at the same time as that of the main verb.

Chapter thirty: Barea Soranus

interim: That is, while the senate was busy reacting to the tirade against Paetus.

ingreditur: Another prosecutor enters, as the drama proceeds to its next act.

Ostorius Sabinus: See above on *c.* 23.

orditurque: "He begins." The verb is also used to describe the beginning of the process of weaving, of laying the warp—though here any latent metaphor is likely barely felt.

quodque ... egisset: A *quod*-clause of alleged reason.

pro claritate sibi: "For fame/glory for himself." Soranus is accused of having managed his proconsulate more to better his own reputation than out of any sense of what the province needed. *Pro claritate* was emended to *popularitate* by Nipperdey-Andersen.

potius ... quam: "Rather ... then."

alendo: Gerund in an ablative of means: Soranus is said to have fostered and nurtured civil discord and sedition as a way of furthering his own image and repute. The reference would seem to be to affairs at Pergamon, but the charge may also have more general import.

civitatium: "Of the city-states."

vetera haec: "These were old charges."

et quo ... connectebat: The magic charge against Soranus' daughter is the "recent" (*recens*) one (some might call it the pretext), the charge by which Sabinus connected Servilia to the legal predicament of her father. We may recall how Thrasea's associates had urged him to take precautions to ensure the safety of his family. The *quo* is the correction of Gronovius for *quot* of the Medicean; Agricola suggested *quod*.

discrimini patris: "To the hazard/peril of her father."

quod ... dilargita esset: A *quod*-clause of alleged reason.

magis: Dative plural of *magus*, "mage/magician." Soranus' daughter was accused of giving money to magicians. It is uncertain how much of the charge of consulting magicians would have been concerned with perceived threats to Roman religion, as opposed to the fear of the use of magic in obtaining harmful results for some target of malefaction; for a helpful overview of legal and other considerations, see D. Collins, *Magic in the Ancient Greek World*, Malden, Massachusetts: Blackwell Publishing, 2008 (Chapter 5 is devoted to "Magic in Greek and Roman Law," with coverage of magic, witchcraft, the *Lex Cornelia*, and the eventual response of Christianity to magic and the occult). Furneaux considers the possibility that the reference here is more to astrology than to magic *per se* (i.e., into enquiries after horoscopes and the like)—but as he notes, "the charge appears from the context to be that of attempting not only to divine the result of the trial, but also... to influence it."

sane: The basic meaning of this adverb is "soundly/healthily" (cf. English "sane"); by extension it comes to mean "certainly" or "truly," "indeed."

pietate Serviliae: "Because of the loyalty of Servilia." *Pietas* describes the relations between gods and men, and between different associations of mortals (in particular, between parents and children). It was one of the most quintessentially Roman and admirable of traits (cf. Aeneas' signal characteristic of *pietas* in Virgil). The English "piety" does not adequately convey the (ultimately untranslatable) sense of the Latin. Servilia's *pietas* toward her father prompted her to consult fortune-tellers and mystics to see what was destined to happen to him; she acted rashly out of worry and anxiety for the safety of her parent.

id enim nomen puellae fuit: She had some connection to the Servilian *gens*. For a good introduction to the problem of the relationship of *filia* and *pater* in Rome, see J. P. Hallett, *Fathers and Daughters in Roman Society: Women and the Elite Family*, Princeton, 1984.

simul imprudentia aetatis: "And at the same time, with the imprudence of her age."

non tamen aliud ... quam: Servilia did not consult the magicians about anything other than the question of her father's safety, and whether or not Nero was able to be appeased and the senate open to a merciful judgment and fair verdict.

an placabilis Nero: Almost as if he were a god, as of course he fancied himself to be; the girl wanted to see if there were any means by which he could be placated.

cognitio senatus: "The examination/inquiry of the senate."

nihil atrox: Servilia wanted to know if there would be any dire outcome from the court proceedings, that is, whether or not her father would be condemned, and if so, how severely.

accita est: "She was summoned." One has the impression that Nero's henchmen were more than prepared for the drama of this day.

diversi: They were facing each other before the officials, and they were also, of course, quite different in appearance, age, and station in life.

ante tribunal consulum: The *tribunal* was a raised platform that was erected for the seats of the magistrates; by metonymy it could be used of any court of law (as in the English use of "tribunal"), and by extension for any raised eminence or height (such as a mound or embankment).

grandis aevo: We might say, "heavy in years." Tacitus composes another of his memorable stage scenes, as Barea Soranus and his daughter stand before the senate tribunal, the son-in-law and husband having already been banished in the inquisitions of the preceding year.

intra vicesimum annum: Servilia was not yet twenty years of age.

Annio Pollione: Cf. XV, 56 and 71; he had fallen and been exiled as a result of the Piso conspiracy.

viduata: "Widowed."

ne ... quidem: "Not even."

intuens: With the emphasis again on the power of sight and presence. Servilia did not even look at her father, out of a sense of shame that by being caught consulting magicians she had only increased his problems and burdened him with further hazards (not least the spectacle of his daughter dragged into the senate deliberation).

onerasse: That is, *oneravisse*.

Chapter thirty-one: Servilia

cultus dotalis: *Cultus* can refer to a style of dress and the manner of one's external appearance, one's apparel and vesture. *Dotalis* describes the "dotal" possessions that were part of a dowry (usually of the wife); it is a poetic adjective that is used by Virgil (cf. *Aeneid* IV, 104; IX, 737; XI, 369) and Ovid. Servilia's husband has been driven into exile; her accuser now asks if she has pawned the wedding presents in order to pay for magic spells.

monile: A necklace.

venum: A defective noun that is found only in the accusative and dative singulars in extant Latin. Here it expresses purpose; translate, "to sell."

dedisset: Pluperfect subjunctive in an indirect question.

faciendis magicis sacris: Gerundive.

contraheret: Imperfect subjunctive in a relative clause of purpose. The verb means literally "to drag or draw together," hence to "get," "cause," or "execute." It implies gathering money from different sources in order to be able to afford the magical spells and consultations.

strata: The participle is from *sterno, sternere, stravi, stratus*, "to spread or stretch out." In this case, she is literally throwing herself down on the ground.

humi: "On the ground." The form is either a locative or a local ablative.

longo ... fletu: Implying especially copious tears and crying. *Silentio* clarifies that Servilia was not making a loud display of her weeping, but maintained her silence until she began to speak.

altaria: Properly an altar for burnt offerings. Marsh and Leon note that *altaria* here may refer to the structure on which the altar proper was situated. Furneaux has a lengthy note on the question of the altars in the temple of Venus Genetrix and the *curia* of the senate, where there was a statue and altar in honor of the personified goddess Victoria.

complexa: From *complector, complecti, complexus sum*.

impios deos: With shades of reminiscence of the *pietas* with which she had been credited. *Impious deos* would refer perhaps to underworld or chthonic deities, denizens of the lower regions who would be willing to respond to the call to curse someone with black magic.

devotiones: "Curses." The word implies that something has been vowed to a particular underworld deity.

> Curse tablets, also known as *defixiones*, were normally inscribed, small, thin sheets of lead. They were often written in cursive script or in relief, the letters being impressed from the reverse side. Curse tablets were intended to influence, through supernatural means, the actions or welfare of persons, against their will. They were usually buried in the grave of a "person untimely dead" ... or in the chthonic sanctuaries or placed in wells.

(B. Hudson McLean, *An Introduction to Greek Epigraphy of the Hellenistic and Roman Periods from Alexander the Great down to the Reign of Constantine (323 B.C.–A.D. 337)*, Ann Arbor: The University of Michigan Press, 2002, p. 207. Tacitus describes the use of such tablets at *Annales* II, 69, in his famous description of their appearance in the last days of Germanicus, who fell ill in 19 and became convinced that Piso had used magic against him. Claudius' wife Agrippina (the mother of Nero) accused her rival Domitia Lepida of their use; Claudia Pulchra was tried for alleged employment of the tablets against Tiberius. See further J. Gager, *Curse Tablets and Binding Spells from the Ancient World*, Oxford, 1992, pp. 253 ff. Useful on the vocabulary of Roman magic is E. E. Burriss, "The Terminology of Witchcraft," in *Classical Philology* 31.2 (1936), pp. 137–145.

nec aliud … quam: "No other thing than ..."

infelicibus precibus: "Infelicitous prayers," that is, the sort of thing one would expect in a curse ritual.

tu, Caesar: Marsh and Leon note that the apostrophe is rhetorical; they suggest that there may have been a statue of Nero present. The *princeps* had sent his quaestor to give his opinion, perhaps out of concern for how the senate would react to the condemnations, perhaps to maintain his regal/divine distance from the unseemly proceedings.

servaretis: Imperfect subjunctive in what amounts to an indirect command. *Incolumem* is in apposition to *patrem*.

dignitatis insignia: "The insignia of dignity"; the phrase is Ciceronian. A useful overview of the rich field of Roman dress is *The World of Roman Costume* (eds. J. L. Sebesta and L. Bonfante), Madison: The University of Wisconsin Press, 2001, with detailed coverage in different papers on women's jewelry, the dress of brides, and the "colors and textiles" of costumes; note also the edited volume of Jonathan Edmondson and Alison Keith, *Roman Dress and the Fabrics of Roman Culture* (Toronto, 2008), with papers *inter al.* on public dress, the role of clothing in Roman coming of age rituals, costumes of statuary and portrait art, the dress of Roman girls, and the dress of women on Roman funerary monuments. Is Servilia hinting at the *dignitas* of her exiled husband in her dramatic appeal before the senate?

quo modo: As Marsh and Leon note, one must supply a verb such as *dedissem*.

poposcissent: Pluperfect subjunctive. The contrafactual sentiment is that just as Servilia gave her jewels and her rich garments away, so she would have surrendered her very life and blood, had they demanded it of her. The third person plural subject refers to unspecified accusers and the like of her father. There is a play throughout the passage on the notion of young girls as being especially attached to ephemeral treasures; Servilia is more than willing to surrender either riches or life to defend Soranus.

viderint isti: Perfect subjunctive used as an imperative.

> Third person present and, much less frequently, perfect subjunctive forms are used to express orders, instructions, and prohibitions. They are used in the headings of statutes ... They are also found in transition formulas—for example, in Varro and Pliny the Elder ... The negative particle is normally *ne*. Passive forms are found as well. It is not always easy to decide whether the utterance is in fact jussive and not a wish. (H. Pinkster, *The Oxford Latin Syntax, Volume I, The Simple Clause*, Oxford, 2015, p. 501)

quo ... quas: Introducing indirect questions. Servilia professes that she had no connection to the *magi* before this consultation, and that they themselves should offer testimony as to what their name should be, and what arts or skills they practice. "It is up to these men ... to tell you" (Yardley).

nisi inter numina fuit: A studied bit of cleverness, perhaps designed to appeal to the vanity and pretentions of the *princeps*; Servilia asserts that she made no mention of Nero in her prayers and invocations, except when she named the divine powers.

nescit tamen: As she closes her remarks in defense, Servilia displays the *pietas* for which she has already been noted; her father Soranus, she declares, had no knowledge of her actions.

Chapter thirty-two: The proceedings continue; the case of Egnatius

Loquentis adhuc ...: "Of the girl as she was still speaking ..." Soranus interrupts his daughter.

illam: "She/that girl," that is, Servilia.

secum: "With him."

profectam: Supply *esse*. The verb is from *proficiscor, proficisci, profectus sum*. The infinitives in indirect discourse report what Soranus interjected in his daughter's defense.

potuisse: Perfect infinitive. Soranus argues that Servilia was too young to have had an opportunity to come to know Plautus.

conexam: From *connecto, connectere, connexi, connectus*. Servilia is said not to have been connected to the charges against her husband.

separarent: Soranus says that the judges should separate the trials, as it were, and recognize that Servilia was guilty only of "excessive loyalty" (*nimia pietas*), and not of any of the more serious charges that were being leveled against her father (or husband before him).

quamcumque sortem: "Whatever" eventuality or "lot" of fortune. Soranus makes an impassioned plea for the life and safety of his daughter; he expresses no concern whatsoever for his own safety.

simul ... ruebat: A vivid and pathetic scene; as the father makes the final pleas for his daughter's life, he attempts to rush over to share an embrace.

in amplexus occurrentis filiae: "Into the embraces of his daughter as she ran toward him." Again, Tacitus heightens the pathos by introducing the memory of a scene that must have had many equals in these years.

interiecti lictores: The lictors stood between the two defendants, much like the bailiffs in a modern court. The *lictor* (the word may take its origin from the verb *ligare* and the notion of binding/ratifying; cf. the bundled rods/axes of the *fasces*) was in origin a sort of bodyguard for magistrates and civil officials; Livy records the tradition that Rome's first king Romulus had twelve of them. Even a quaestor had one lictor; the consul had twelve, as did the *princeps*. Certainly, there would have been many in the curia on this day.

utrisque: "For both." The lictors prevented the father and daughter from having physical contact.

obstitissent: Pluperfect subjunctive in a contrary to fact protasis.

datus ... locus: The trial proceedings continue with the testimony of the witnesses.

quantum ... tantum: Correlatives. It appears that the savagery of the prosecution speech elicited a fair amount of pity and consideration for the defendants (at least for Servilia); now the testimony of Publius Egnatius arouses wrath and anger.

P. Egnatius: Publius Egnatius Celer. Furneaux cites the evidence of Dio (LXII, 26) for the generous rewards that Egnatius won for his services to Nero on this day, and for his Phoenician origins (he was from Berytus, the modern Beirut).

Tacitus proceeds to offer a biting commentary on the nature of this "witness" and informer against his patron. Juvenal appears to have remembered the famous example of a student turning on his master; he may have alluded to the present case in this third satire (116 ff.), though some have considered the verses to be a later interpolation (Courtney notes in his *A Commentary on the Satires of Juvenal* (London: The Athlone Press, 1980; reprinted with minor revisions in the "California Classical Studies" series of the University of California at Berkeley Press, 2013) that "114–18 do not fit in quite smoothly and look like a later addition." Juvenal openly calls Egnatius a *delator*, which cannot be supported in any strict sense by Tacitus' account—though that is certainly the implication.

cliens: The relationship between patron and client was fundamental to Roman social life and order.

emptus: A blunt appraisal; Egnatius' services were paid for and bought.

ad opprimendum amicum: Gerundive in an expression of purpose. Tacitus throughout highlights Egnatius' betrayal of the noble state of *amicitia*.

auctoritatem Stoicae sectae: "The authority of the Stoic sect"; Yardley translates, "the magisterial gravity." A direct indictment of Egnatius for his Stoic pretenses; Soranus' *discipulus* affected to be a follower of Stoicism, when in fact he was venal, corrupt, and possessed of a soul that could be bought and sold.

praeferebat: Tacitus here returns to one of his favorite topics, namely the difference between appearance and reality. Egnatius appeared to have all the *gravitas* and respectable air of a Stoic philosopher, when in fact the surface image belied a much darker inner core.

honesti exercitus: Characteristic genitive. For all appearances, Egnatius seemed to be pursuing a noble exercise of the pursuit of virtue and philosophical wisdom. *Exercitus* often means "army" or military unit; in origin (cf. English "exercise") it refers to what which requires effort and exertion—in this case, the study of greater truths. The text is, however, vexed; *exercitus* is a correction of the manuscript reading *et exerciti* (and Heubner prints *et* in square brackets).

animo perfidiosus: The real traits of character are now fully unveiled, as Tacitus looks beneath the mask. Egnatius was "perfidious," that is, faithless particularly against those to whom he should have had special respect and concern (e.g., his *patronus* and *magister*). The intended contrast is with Servilia and her great *pietas* toward her father.

subdolus: Sneaky and tricky, untrustworthy and of questionable honor. It can be used of persons and their character (*OLD* s.v. b), or of natural states and conditions (*OLD* s.v. c).

occultans: Again, the emphasis is on what is concealed and hidden. Egnatius was avaricious and libidinous, but he hid this well from most of those who came into contact with him. *Occultare* describes the action of presenting something from being seen or heard; it can also describe the keeping secret of facts or intentions (*OLD* s.v. 3).

pecunia reclusa sunt: But later, all of Egnatius' true traits were exposed by money. The ablative is one of means.

dedit exemplum: Roman historiography has a strong moral dimension. *Exempla* are stories or images that illustrate different moral and psychological reactions to circumstances, "examples" that offer an illustration of conduct that should either be pursued or avoided. See further W. Turpin, "Tacitus, Stoic *exempla*, and the *praecipuum munus annalium*," in *Classical Antiquity* 27.2 (2008), pp. 359–404.

praecavendi: Tacitus uses Egnatius as an example of how one must be careful and cautious in dealing with other people; one must plan in advance for the possibility of being betrayed and mistreated by a seemingly honorable man. The accusatives that follow are direct objects of the gerund.

fraudibus involutos: Literally, "thoroughly wrapped up in tricks and fraud." Furneaux takes the image to be worse than one of mere hypocrisy; for him such a man as Egnatius is "so wholly perfidious as to wear its character on the surface."

flagitiis commaculatos: "Stained with crimes." There is a hint of the commonplace that the guilty feel something of a sense of shame in the presence of the just whose mere presence is an affront to their way of life; Tacitus has already used this image in his condemnation of Nero. *Commaculare* can carry a particular force of sullying a reputation or good name (*OLD* s.v. 2); the present passage is cited by *OLD* as an example of "to defile morally, contaminate" (s.v. 1c).

sic specie bonarum artium: Once again, Tacitus returns to the concept of *species* or image. The mask in this case is one of the pursuit of the "good arts" or the following of the tenets of philosophy in the matter of character and personal behavior.

falsos et amicitiae fallacis: Men such as Egnatius are "false" and "fallacious" with respect to friendship. The genitive, as often, shows the relationship between two nouns; *fallacis* is probably accusative plural and not genitive singular: "Not only does *fallere* mean *dissimulare*; it means *simulare* too … Hence has sprung the one other recorded example of *fallax* with a genitive" (A. E. Housman, in J. Diggle and F. R. D. Goodyear, eds., *The Classical Papers of A. E. Housman, Volume II, 1897–1914*, Cambridge, 1972, p. 522).

Tacitus does not bother to record the lying words and manipulated speech of Egnatius; he reports that the *testis* elicited the anger of the assembly, but in this case he does not dignify the speech with the gift (or curse) of memory.

Chapter thirty-three: The verdicts

honestum exemplum: "The noble example." Tacitus draws a sharp contrast with the immediately preceding case of Egnatius and his betrayal of Soranus; Cassius Asclepiodotus is an example of what a friend should be.

Cassii Asclepiodoti: Cassius Asclepiodotus. He is also mentioned in Dio's history (LXII, 26), where he is cited as being a native of Nicaea (the city later made famous for an ecumenical council of the early Christian church). For a study of such wealthy men in the Roman east, cf. J. M. Madsen, *Eager to* *be Roman: Greek Response to Roman Rule in Pontus and Bithynia*, London: Bloomsbury Ltd., 2009.

magnitudine opum: The emphasis on wealth and prestige only serves to highlight the great sacrifice of this true friend, and stands in striking relief with the avarice of Egnatius.

et in exilium actus: He was exiled for his unflagging support of Soranus. He would be rehabilitated under Nero's successor Galba.

aequitate deum: A biting bit of theological commentary that is open to different nuances and shades of interpretation. The ablative may be causal; the immortals are depicted as being equal minded in the matter of both good and bad examples of friendship and character. "Pessimistic" indeed as sentiments go (so Marsh and Leon)—and certainly possessed of the cynicism for which Tacitus is noted. Furneaux observes: "This sentiment is the most Epicurean ... that has been preserved to us of Tacitus, and would seem to show that such scepticism grew upon him towards the close of his work." Rather, it is likely that the historian is here offering a carefully constructed commentary on the Stoic beliefs of Thrasea and his followers; Egnatius had pretended to be an adherent to the same sect, and now, in the end, the gods are shown to be all too Epicurean and unconcerned with the relative merits and faults of the cast of characters in this particular court drama.

On *aequitas* cf. Syme (*op. cit.*, p. 755): " ... 'aequitas' emerged as an official legend under Vespasian ... it was dropped by Domitian, but at once installed again by Nerva ... The word is found only twice in the *Annales* (XV. 2. 3; XVI. 33. 1)."

documenta: A *documentum* is an object lesson or instruction. The gods are not moved by such studies, in implicit contrast to those mortals who take *amicitia* seriously, even to the point of exile and loss of wealth.

Thraseae ...: Tacitus abruptly moves from his brief reflection on the gods to the punishments of the mortals. There is no further discussion of testimony and deliberation; at once Paetus, Soranus, and Servilia are all given the poor freedom merely to choose the manner of their deaths.

Italia: A separative ablative. Helvidius and Paconius suffered the comparatively lesser penalty of exile.

patri concessus est: He was given a concession, as it were, for the sake of his father. Tacitus has not mentioned this father before, let alone why Nero should have been interested in sparing the son out of respect; Juvenal's fourth satire, however, concerns a Domitianic sycophant of the same name: "Montanus, specific identity uncertain ... Possibly Curtius Montanus, influential with Nero ... evidently another imperial survivor. He is presented as a long-time gourmand ... hence his paunch: he represents the luxurious side of court life." (S. Braund, *Juvenal: Satires, Book I*, Cambridge, 1996, p. 259).

praedicto ne in re publica haberetur: Furneaux takes *praedicto* as an ablative absolute; the condition imposed on Montanus was that he could no longer "be held/considered in the republic," that is, that he could no longer have public office or any sort of political career. "This would mean that he should not continue in the service of the state, should not hold any magistracy." (Furneaux). A sort of political banishment then, and exile from public life.

quinquagies: "Fifty times." Eprius and Cossutianus were each awarded five million sesterces for their troubles (fifty times the understood hundred thousand).

duodecies: "Twelve times." Ostorius received one million, two hundred thousand. "These enormous rewards given to accusers must have far exceeded the one-fourth of the property of the accused, which they could claim by law ... The smallest sum here mentioned is more than the minimum senatorial census."—Furneaux.

quaestoria insignia: The equestrian thus receives the mark of the lowest rung of the *cursus honorum*. The paragraph closes on a likely deliberate note of reminiscence of the girl Servilia's *dignitatis insignia* that she was willing to surrender in an act of *pietas* toward her father. Certainly, Tacitus leaves the reader with a stark reminder of the motivation behind the work of the busy Neronian prosecutors.

Chapter thirty-four: Socrates *Redivivus*: The reaction of Thrasea

Tum ad Thraseam: Tacitus changes the scene, as he commences his narrative of the reaction of Thrasea Paetus to the verdict of forced suicide.

in hortis agentem: Thrasea was in his garden; Tacitus thus returns to the image he had introduced at *c.* 27 above, where the senators were accused in Nero's speech of spending all their time on such pointless pursuits as the care and maintenance of their gardens. The contrast with the senate's meeting place and the throng of soldiers is great; the garden should be a place of peaceful reflection and philosophical study. We see here the direct evidence of Thrasea's decision to listen to those who counseled him to remain at home and await the verdict of his peers. *Agere* is used here without any authorial comment on the nature or productivity of Thrasea's garden time.

quaestor consulis missus: A quaestor had read the speech of Nero, and now a quaestor brings the news of the day's drama to Thrasea.

vesperascente iam die: "With the day now declining toward evening." The highly evocative image plays on the notion of the evening of life and the fall of night as a metaphor for the mortality of men. For the possible intertextual relationship of Thrasea's death scene with that of Seneca, and more generally the possible influences of Plato's *Phaedo* (with its account of the end of Socrates) and Thrasea's own writing on Cato, see J. Ker, *The Deaths of Seneca*, Oxford, 2009, pp. 60–61; Ker notes that the garden in which the suicide narrative opens has Epicurean associations, while the *porticus* to which Thrasea proceeds in *c.* 35 evokes Stoicism. Tacitus proceeds to another stage setting, as Thrasea functions as an implicit rival playwright and artistic producer to Nero.

"Thrasea's death, then, is something different from the death of Seneca, reproducing it but not repeating it, and recycling it more explicitly for a following generation." (Ker).

inlustrium virorum feminarumque: News had traveled quickly of Thrasea's peril; his house was filled with noble men and women.

coetus frequentis: Accusative plural. The Medicean reads *coetus frequenter*, with a correction to *coetus frequentes* (which Heubner prints, and which some [cf. Furneaux and Fisher's Oxford text] have interpreted as *frequentis* because of Tacitus' preference for that form of the plural); Ritter and Halm suggested *coetum frequentem*. "The plural denotes the separate groups composing the whole assemblage." (Furneaux).

egerat: The verb is used here in the sense of "to impel or drive together." The image that Tacitus crafts is of a veritable school for instruction in the way a Stoic martyr will meet his end.

maxime intentus: A sign of resolve and of calm in the face of impending death, we might think; Thrasea is portrayed as intently focused on his philosophical colloquy, though Tacitus offers no comment or conclusion as to the result of Thrasea's discussion.

Demetrio Cynicae: Demetrius the Cynic. A friend of Seneca the Younger, he enjoyed a long career as a teacher (cf. *doctori*) at Rome in the days of Caligula and Nero, and on into the reign of Vespasian; if he wrote anything, no trace of his works survives. He reappears in Tacitus (*Historiae* IV, 40) as a defender of Egnatius against Musonius Rufus; according to Dio (LXV, 13) he was exiled in 71 in a general Vespasianic purge of philosophers. There is some question as to whether or not he should be identified with Demetrius of Sunium, who is mentioned in Lucian. See further R. B. Branham and M-O. Goulet-Cazé, *The Cynics: The Cynic Movement in Antiquity and Its Legacy*, Berkeley-Los Angeles-London: The University of California Press, 1996, p. 393 (amid a useful catalogue of known Cynic philosophers); note also R. Finn, OP, *Asceticism in the Graeco-Roman World*, Cambridge, 2009, pp. 24–25.

The association of the name of the movement with the Greek word for "dog" has been connected to early insults of the Cynics and comparisons of their lifestyle to that of canines in the streets. For a convenient overview of the movement and the surviving writings associated with it, see Robin Hard's Oxford World's Classics edition of *Diogenes the Cynic: Sayings and Anecdotes, with Other Popular Moralists*, Oxford, 2012 (with introduction and detailed annotations). The relationship between Stoicism and Cynicism is explored in depth by J. M. Rist, *Stoic Philosophy*, Cambridge, 1977, pp. 54–80.

institutionis doctoris: Koestermann notes that *institutio* occurs only here in the sense of "Sekte," (i.e., *secta*).

ut coniectare erat: Literally, "as it was possible to conjecture." Marsh and Leon note that this is a "Greek use not found in classical Latin prose and very rare even in the prose of the Silver Age." The usage is likely intended for poetic effect; Syme comments: "a Graecism hard to parallel anywhere in prose … With every allowance made for a style changing as the history changed, it becomes hard to believe that all parts of the third hexad had been properly worked up …" (*op. cit.*, pp. 741–742). The basic meaning of *coniectare* is to throw a missile or to hurl a projectile; from this comes the sense of making an inference or a conjecture, etc. (*OLD* 2–4).

de natura animae …: It appeared that Thrasea was discussing the nature of the soul and the question of the dissociation of *anima* and *corpus*—in other words, exactly the sort of philosophical and "heavy" discussion of eschatology that Petronius had eschewed in the course of his long-drawn-out suicide. Thrasea was well aware that he faced almost certain compulsion to take his own life, and he preferred to spend his last hours engaged in discussion of "the last things" with Demetrius. *Dissocatio*, as Furneaux notes, is a relatively rare word in extant Latin. Tacitus does not give a clear picture of what Thrasea felt and thought in these last hours about the matter of the fate of the soul; the historian's account is full of irony.

intentione vultus: Once again, a detail about appearances and image. One could clearly see that Thrasea was intensely focused on hid philosophical discussion; there is a deliberate contrast between the life of the senate and the machinations of Nero's henchmen and the thoughtful contemplation of the noble Stoic on the verge of the *dissociatio* of his body and soul. Tacitus may have already pronounced his own Epicurean verdict on the whole matter in his authorial aside about the *aequitas* of the gods. The historian plays here on how the *vultus* reveals both much and precious little.

si qua: For *si aliqua*. If someone were heard more clearly, it was of a philosophical bent; Thrasea and Demetrius were apparently afforded privacy by the others, almost in the manner of a priest and condemned before execution.

Domitius Caecilianus: This close (*ex intimis*) friend of Thrasea is not mentioned anywhere else in extant Latin. Apparently, the quaestor made the announcement to Thrasea's friends, and now Domitius comes to bring the news.

censuisset: Pluperfect subjunctive in an indirect question. *Censere* has a wide range of meanings; the basic sense is to give one's opinion or judgment on something, to suppose or to make a judgment; it can mean to think wrongly about something (*OLD* s.v. 2). For a senator it was essentially a technical term to describe the expression of a recommendation, or the judgment of the senate as a whole in the form of a decree (*OLD* s.v. 4–5). From these uses comes the definition of "to assess" or set a value on something, as in an appraisal (*OLD* s.v. 7–8).

flentis queritantisque: Accusatives plural. Thrasea's friends are now dissolved in tears and complaints, recriminations against Nero, even, we might think; he urges them to look after their own welfare and to make quick exits from the house of the condemned man. *Queritantis* refers to a frequentative act of complaint, to loud and bitter words of indignation; it is a rare verb that has given occasion to conjecture and emendation. *OLD* notes, "several app. exx. of this word in MSS. have been changed by edd. to *quirito*."

facessere propere: The verb is frequentative; here with the adverb it seems to mean "to make a hasty departure," though as Furneaux notes, it occurs "here alone in Tacitus in the sense of 'abire.'" Koestermann cites Syme's classification of this use of the verb (*op. cit.*, pp. 741–742), where the question of "stylistic weaknesses" is raised. Thrasea had been advised by some of his friends that he should look after the fate of his family; here he fulfills that admonition, with the additional act of sparing his wife her own self-imposed end.

Arriam: Thrasea's wife. The story of her homonymous mother's devotion to her doomed husband was celebrated; she had been married to Caecina Paetus, who had been condemned to die for his part in the conspiracy of Camillus Scribonianus against Claudius in 42. The heroic self-sacrifice of the devoted wife of the Claudian era is noted in a famous letter of Pliny the Younger (III, 11; 16; see further J. M. Carlon, *Pliny's Women: Constructing Virtue and Creating Identity in the Roman World*, Cambridge, 2009, pp. 41 ff.). She is perhaps best known for the words that accompanied her suicide: *Paete, non dolet.*

temptantem mariti suprema: Literally, "testing the last things of her husband," an expression that is made clearer by *et exemplum Arriae matris sequi*, "and to pursue the example of her mother Arria." Once again Tacitus introduces the image of an *exemplum*, and in another context of family *pietas*. The language is somewhat compressed, though not to the point of obscurity.

monet: A different conclusion to the story of this Arria; Thrasea advises her that she should hold on to life and be a source of solace for their only daughter.

filiaeque: Fannia, who was married to the soon-to-be-exiled Helvidius Priscus.

subsidium unicum: One might recall the *viduata* and *desolata* daughter of Soranus; Fannia was about to lose both father and husband. The phrase is Livian (*Ab Urbe Condita* XXIII, 21.5.2); cf. Suetonius, *Iul.* 27.2.2. The detail continues the book's concern with the problem of *pietas* in family relations. There may be a military metaphor inherent in *subsidium*, the primary meaning of which is a gathering of soldiers for reserve purposes and reinforcement; from this comes the more general sense of assistance and the safeguard afforded by a particular individual to another (*OLD* s.v. 3–4). For *unicus* in contexts of loss and the death of loved ones cf. Catullus, *c.* 39.4-5 ... *si ad pii rogum fili/lugetur, orba cum flet unicum mater*; 73.5-6 *ut mihi, quem nemo gravius nec acerbius urget,/quam modo quae me unum atque unicum amicum habuit.*

Chapter thirty-five: Suicide and liberation

in porticum: "The colonnade around the peristyle of his house" (Marsh and Leon). From the gardens we move to the portico, with possible implicit philosophical commentary. As the suicide narrative progresses, the audience becomes smaller as we move from a sizable *coetus* to the few witnesses of Thrasea's end. "*Porticus* villas … evolved from a long narrow row of rooms opening on to a road or court … The addition of a colonnade, or *porticus*, parallel to the row of rooms, with doors opening on to the gallery, provided the basic design of the Roman *porticus* villa …" (A. G. McKay, *Houses, Villas, and Palaces in the Roman World*, Southampton: Thames and Hudson, 1975, p. 117).

a quaestore: The consul's quaestor, who was no doubt responsible both for delivering the sentence, and for making sure that it was executed.

laetitiae propior: "Nearer/closer to rejoicing." There may be a play on the aforementioned dour and grim features for which the Stoic Thrasea was known; at the end, in death, he is happier than one might think Nero would have wished him to be. Happiness is exceedingly rare in the *Annales*, and here it continues the development of the theme of *pietas*, as Thrasea feels relief and rejoices that he will not be part of a larger family tragedy.

quia …: Thrasea is informed of the judgment that his son-in-law Helvidius Priscus had been exiled; he is joyful on receipt of the knowledge that Priscus would not be forced to take his own life. Tacitus moves swiftly from the brief mention of Thrasea's happiness to the scene of his suicide. Helvidius, for his part, would live to see some chance for a modicum of vengeance over Eprius; on the great "duel" of the two men in the matter of the delegation to the new emperor Vespasian that Tacitus narrates at *Historiae* IV, 7 ff., see T. A. Joseph, *Tacitus the Epic Successor: Virgil, Lucan, and the Narrative of Civil War*, Leiden: Brill, 2012, pp. 173 ff.

Italia: Separative ablative.

dehinc: Literally, "from this place/time forth"; thus "then, next."

porrectisque … venis: Tacitus has Helvidius and Demetrius ushered in by Thrasea as the witnesses to the suicide; there may have been a slave/doctor present who would be responsible for the actual opening of the veins (though the image is of two arms and two "guests" for the grisly spectacle). In any case, the description presents a portrait of a man who is actively willing and engaged in the procurement of what he soon enough implies is a liberating act.

postquam cruorem effudit: Latin *cruor* means either blood or gore; it can also have a figurative sense of bloodshed and violent acts/murder. Here it refers to the blood that Thrasea proceeds to sprinkle on the ground.

humum super spargens: Thrasea dramatically turns his suicide into a quasi-religious ritual, as he sprinkles the ground with the blood of his arms. The preposition is in anastrophe, that is, it follows its object. The word *humus* properly means earth or soil; there is no clear indication here of whether or not the *cubiculum* had a dirt floor. Thrasea uses blood and not the water of Seneca; for the association of water with "generative" power and new life (with reference to the Tacitean account of Seneca's suicide), see R. B. Onians, *The Origins of European Thought: About the Body, the Mind, the Soul, the World Time, and Fate: New Interpretations of Greek, Roman, and kindred evidence also of some basic Jewish and Christian beliefs*, Cambridge, 1951, p. 480. It is difficult to determine the exact force of Tacitus' point about the blood of Thrasea that has replaced the (accidental) sprinkling of water by Seneca—but the student, as it were, as certainly surpassed the master for dramatic display.

propius vocato quaestore: "With the quaestor having been called closer." Thrasea summons Nero's *de facto* emissary; Tacitus may well have thought that the suicide of Thrasea was nothing less than an *exemplum* to Nero of what he himself would be forced to face in not so very long a time.

libamus …: "'We make a libation,' he said, 'to Jupiter the Liberator.'" The same action is described in Dio's history (LXII, 26), while the Juvenalian scholia (*apud* 5.36) depict Thrasea's asking a rhetorical question of Demetrius: *nonne tibi libare videor Iovi liberatori?*" The verb can describe the pouring of liquids in contexts more or less ritually significant (*OLD* s.v. 3).

Iovi liberatori: Both the act of the sprinkling and the invocation to Jupiter the Liberator remind one of Seneca's suicide (XV, 64), where the context is not of the splashing of blood from a suicide, but of the bathwater as Seneca seeks to hasten his already drawn out and more or less botched suicide process. For the Jovian title, see J. G. Cook, *Roman Attitudes Toward the Christians: From Claudius to Hadrian*, Tübingen: Mors Siebeck, 2010, pp. 34–35:

> The epithet … was used for Augustus in an oath of 6. C.E. and many other texts … In Athens there was a priest of Nero and of Zeus the Liberator in 61/62 … Coins identified Nero as Zeus the Liberator (Zeus Eleutherios). … During Domitian's reign, an inscription in Athens styled him also as Zeus the Liberator … Hadrian was called the son of Zeus the Liberator (i.e., Trajan) … Antony Raubitschek notes that the worship of Zeus the Liberator in Athens was due to the city's deliverance from Persian attack and that Trajan's victory over the Persians may be the source of the epithet … A possible example of irony at the end of Tacitus' *Annals* is a scene in which the Stoic senator Thrasea Paetus is

forced to suicide by Nero. In the last seconds of his life he sprinkles his blood on the ground and says ...

On suicide in general in Roman political life, with special reference to Seneca's end (also Lucan's and Petronius'), see T. D. Hill, *Ambitiosa Mors: Suicide and the Self in Roman Thought and Literature*, London-New York: Routledge, 2004. On the sometimes fine line between compulsion and freedom in such matters, see J. P. Wilson, "The Death of Lucan: Suicide and Execution in Tacitus," in *Latomus* 49.2 (1990), pp. 458–463. If Nero were associated with Jupiter the Liberator, then the play here may be on the "real" Jupiter liberating Thrasea from the tyranny of the fraud. A stirring account, at any rate, of the death of a Neronian political martyr; one might also consider the role of the god in the apotheosis of the Stoic hero Hercules. If Nero is *Jupiter Liberator*, then the suicide victim manages to define the terms of his liberation; the *arbitrium mortis* that he was afforded becomes a salvific act for him and an affront to the *princeps*.

specta, iuvenis: A striking bit of stage direction, with more of the Tacitean preoccupation with image, death *tableaux*, and the visual. Thrasea casts himself as the lead actor in his own production; the *iuvenis* is probably the Neronian quaestor, though it is possibly that Helvidius Priscus is the intended referent. Furneaux (followed by Barrett in Yardley) note that the quaestor should in theory have been at least twenty-five, while Priscus would have been at least thirty-seven by this point (but might have been considered a *iuvenis* by Thrasea); the whole scene gains in dramatic flair if the summoned spectator is the unnamed quaestor who was just admitted to the chamber, the "everyman," as it were, for the youth of Nero's day—and, again, also a veritable incarnation of Nero (since the official would have been expected to make a full report of what he saw and heard). Syme (*op. cit.*, p. 745) takes the *iuvenis* to be the quaestor; he notes that "Thrasea's injunction may not be irrelevant to the subsequent vicissitudes of the [unnamed] young man."

"Tacitus' position is that of the critic of ideology, which is not to say that he positions himself outside of it: for him, ideology is history; no alternative vision of an external reality exists in his texts." (Haynes, *op. cit.*, p. 19).

et omen quidem dii prohibeant: "And indeed may the gods avert the omen." The suicide has been converted by the star into a perversion of the rites of sacrifice in honor of the god; Jupiter, too, may well have been associated with Nero in the function of liberator and deliverer. The "omen" that Thrasea prays may be averted in part relates to the idea that the quaestor (let alone the others) should not witness such an act of sanguinary propitiation of the god in the context of a suicide. The splashing of water in the Senecan suicide narrative admittedly seemed more of an *omen* in the traditional sense than the deliberate spilling of blood here, but the point in the end may be much the same. The present "omen" is very different from the signs of alleged divine rage and wrath that are often cited by Tacitus. On the attitude of Tacitus to omens and the like, see R. Mellor, *Tacitus*, London-New York: Routledge, 1993, p. 49.

ceterum in ea tempora: Thrasea proceeds to note that the young man has been born into an age in which it is fitting to shore up or fortify the mind by examples of constancy (*constantibus exemplis*). Once again, the emphasis is on the morally instructive value of *exempla* of good and ill; the words drip with irony, as Thrasea notes that the tyranny of Nero makes it useful for young men to have the benefit of seeing acts of noble suicide such as the present scene. *Ceterum* once again introduces an additional element to the argument; it serves as a transitional adverb: "moreover/in addition/ furthermore." Again, we do well to remember that Nero would himself soon enough be called upon to offer an example of constancy. *Ea tempora* introduces the often-made contrast between past and present, republic and empire, even Augustan, say, and Neronian times.

constantibus exemplis: Such as what Tacitus has been offering throughout the book, and for the possible tedium of which he apologized. Thrasea offers his own suicide as an *exemplum* to the youth who found themselves born for times such as Nero's. Petronius was depicted as not being interested in furthering his own reputation for glorious constancy in the conversations he had before his own suicide.

> Thrasea's hope that he would be an example was realized. His biography was written by his friend, the Stoic Junius Arulenus Rusticus, who as a tribune of the plebs in 66 had wanted to veto the Senate's trial but had been prevented by Thrasea from making a useless sacrifice. However, his biographies of Thrasea and of Thrasea's son-in-law Helvidius Priscus brought him the death penalty under Domitian. Helvidius ... was exiled ... Both entered into the canon of Stoic "martyrs" along with Cato and Brutus who were so much admired by the philosopher-emperor Marcus Aurelius. (B. H. Warmington, *Nero: Reality and Legend*, New York: W. W. Norton & Company, Inc., 1969)

lentitudine ... adferente: "With the slowness of the death bringing serious agony ..." We might be reminded of the long torture of Seneca's end, though the breaking off the of the text prevents any sense of how the suicide narrative might have continued. Extreme pain was a classic test of Stoic perseverance

and philosophical endurance; in the present case, it comes deliberately as
a timely development after the mention of constancy and steadfast resolve.
The problem of pain and suffering is a commonplace of philosophy; Thrasea
serves now as a living and dying example of how to respond to the burden
of agony. *Lentitudo* is a relatively uncommon word in extant Latin; it occurs
in Cicero and the *Appendix Vergiliana*, also in Pliny the Elder and Velleius
Paterculus; in Tacitus it seems to have confined to the later books of the
Annales and the *Dialogus*. The noun can refer to flexibility and pliancy, and
also to stickiness and difficulty in movement; from this meaning comes
the sense of slowness of action, sometimes even apathetic feeling or lack of
concern (*OLD* s.v. 3).

Hutchinson offers an extended discussion of "death in prose," with
extended attention to the end of life motif in Tacitus.

> One may start by stressing that truth is vital to the impact of the deaths
> that he narrates. Their literary force rests above all on moral response, and
> the moral response is to be affected by our knowledge that these events
> are historically true and truly told, and by the discrimination and justice
> of the assessing narrator. Tacitus' treatment is intensely concerned with
> evaluation, and his language characteristically emphasizes the severity,
> the vehemence, and the nuanced finesse of his judgments. He presents
> death and behaviour in regard to death as contributing to the achievement
> of good or evil fame; this fame has a special character and reality when
> the deeds are unquestionably actual. (G. O. Hutchinson, *Latin Literature
> from Seneca to Juvenal: A Critical Study*, Oxford, 1993, p. 257)

obversis in Demetrium***: The asterisks in the critical editions indicate the
end of the text as we have it. It has been conjectured that *oculis* must have
been the next word, though the conjecture *obversus* has been suggested for
the manuscript *obversis*. The verb means "to turn so as to face"; there is no
hint here of its use in more hostile contexts (cf. *OLD* s.v. 2).

The Juvenalian scholia offer the text *atque singulis amicis oscula offerens
exanimatus est* after the comment to Demetrius about Jove the Liberator,
though it is unclear how much of the scholiast's text should be attributed to a
copy of Tacitus. We have no way of knowing if Tacitus interrupted his writing
here, only to resume it in a now-lost section; see further here R. P. Oliver,
"Did Tacitus Finish the *Annales*?," in *Illinois Classical Studies* 2 (1977), pp.
289–314. But one could scarcely hope for a more dramatically appropriate
"ending" to the *Annales*. As with Lucan's "unfinished" epic, so with Tacitus'
Annales there were efforts to complete the work; cf. Brotier's workmanly
attempt (now almost unknown), which crams a significant range of material
into a "finished" Book XVI of inordinate length.

Vocabulary

A

ab (prep. + abl.) ... *of, from, by, since*

abdo, abdere, adidi, abditus ... *to put away, hide*

abicio, abicere, abieci, abiectus ... *to cast away*

aboleo, abolere, abolevi, abolitus ... *to abolish*

abrogo, -are, -avi, -atus ... *to appeal, abrogate*

abrumpo, abrumpere, abrumpsi, abruptus ... *to tear, break away, burst*

abscindo, abscindere, abscidi, abscissus ... *to tear/break off; divide, separate*

absens, absentis ... *absent*

abstineo, abstinere, abstinui, abstentus ... *to keep back; refrain, abstain*

ac (conj.) ... *and*

accendo, accendere, accendi, accensus ... *to set on fire*

accido, accidere, accidi ... *to fall down; happen, take place, occur, befall*

accipio, accipere, accepi, acceptus ... *to receive*

accitus, -a, -um ... *summoned*

accommodo, -are, -avi, -atus ... *to fit, adapt, adjust*

accusatio, accusationis, f. ... *accusation*

accusator, accusatoris, m. ... *accuser*

accuso, -are, -avi, -atus ... *to accuse*

acer, acris, acre ... *sharp, keen, fierce*

ad (prep. + acc.) ... *to, toward, for*

addo, addere, addidi, additus ... *to add*

adeo ut ... *to such an extent that*

adfero, adferre, adtuli, adlatus ... *to bring to*

adficio, adficere, adfeci, adfectus ... *to do to, handle, treat, affect, impress, influence*

adfinitas, adfinitatis, f. ... *relationship by marriage*

adfligo or affligo, ad(f)fligere, ad(f)flixi, ad(f)flictus ... *to dash at, strike upon, throw down*

adfluo, -ere, -fluxi, -fluctus ... *to flow by, stream, abound*

adhuc (adv.) ... *until now*

adicio, -ere, adieci, adiectus ... *to throw to, to add*

adimo, -ere, ademi, ademptus ... *to take away*

adipiscor, adipisci, adeptus ... *to arrive at; obtain*

aditus, -us, m. ... *entrance*

adiumentum, -I, n. ... *aid, help*

adloquor, adloqui, adlocutus ... *to speak to*

admiro, -are, -avi, -atus ... *to admire*

adprobo, -are, -avi, -atus ... *to approve*

adpropero, -are, -avi, -atus ... *to hasten*

adquiro, adquirere, adquisivi, adquisitus ... *to acquire*

adscitus, -a, -um ... *taken, approved, accepted*

adsequor, adsequi, adsecutus ... *to pursue*

adsevero, -are, -avi, -atus ... *to affirm*

adsideo, adsidere, adsedi ... *to sit near*

adsiduus, -a, -um ... *occupied, persistent*

adsimulo, -are, -avi, -atus ... *to make like, liken*

adsto, adstare, adstiti ... *to stand near*

adsumo, adsumere, adsumpsi, adsumptus ... *to take up*

adulatio, adulationis, f. ... *flattery*

adulor, -ari, -atus ... *to fawn over, flatter*

adveho, advehere, advexi, advectus ... *to convey to*

advenio, advenire, adveni, adventus ... *to come to*

advento, -are ... *to advance, approach*

adversarius, -a, -um ... *opposite; hostile*

adversum (adv.) ... *against*

adversus, -a, -um ... *opposing, hostile*

aegre (adv.) ... *reluctantly*

aemulus, -I, m. ... *rival*

aequitas, aequitatis, f. ... *uniformity*

aequo, -are, -avi, -atus ... *to make equal*

aequus, -a, um ... *equal*

aetas, aetatis, f. ... *lifetime, age*

aevum, -I, n. ... *time, age*

Africa, -ae, f. ... *Africa*

ager, agri, m. ... *field*

agito, -are, -avi, -atus ... *to set in violent motion, urge on, shake, disturb*

agmen, agminis, n. ... *battle line; throng*

ago, agere, egi, actus ... *do, drive, conduct*

agrestis, agreste ... *rural*

alacritas, alacritatis, f. ... *eagerness, alacrity*

alias (adv.) ... *at other times*

alienus, -a, -um ... *foreign, strange*

alimentum, -I, n. ... *nourishment*

aliqui, aliqua, aliquod ... *some, any*

alius, alia, aliud ... *other, another*

alo, alere, alui, altus/alitus ... *to nourish, feed, support*

altaria, -ium, n. ... *high altar*

altitudo, altitudinis, f. ... *height, depth*

altus, -a, -um ... *high, deep*

ambigo, ambigere ... *to go around, avoid, hesitate, be in doubt, debate*

ambitio, ambitionis, m. ... *soliciting of votes; flattery*

ambitus, -us, m. ... *circuit; show, ostentation; bribery*

amicitia, -ae, f. ... *friendship*

amita, -ae, f ... *(paternal) aunt*

amoenitas, amoenitatis, f. ... *bliss, pleasure*

amoenus, -a, -um ... *pleasant, blissful*

amor, amoris, m. ... *love*

amoveo, amovere, amovi, amotus ... *to remove*

amplector, amplecti, amplexus ... *to embrace*

an (conj.) ... *whether*

angustia, -ae, f. ... *narrowness*

anima, -ae, f. ... *soul, breath of life*

animus, -I, m. ... *soul, life, mind*

annus, -I, m. ... *year*

annuus, -a, -um ... *of a year*

ante (prep. + acc.) ... *before*

antehac (adv.) ... *before this time*

Antenor, Antenoris, m. ... *Antenor*

antiquus, -a, um ... *ancient*

anulus, -I, m. ... *ring*

appello, -are, -avi, -atus ... *to call on by name*

aperio, aperire, aperui, apertus ... *to open; disclose, reveal*

apprimo, apprimere, appressi, appressus ... *to press close*

apud (prep. + acc.) ... *at, near*

aqua, -ae, f. ... *water*

ara, -ae, f. ... *altar*

arbiter, arbitri, m. ... *spectator; master*

arbustum, -I, n. ... *vineyard, plantation; (in pl.), trees*

arceo, arcere, arcui ... *to enclose; to hold off; hinder*

ardesco, ardescere, ardarsi ... *to be inflamed; grow furious*

arguo, arguere, argui, argutus ... *to make known, prove, disclose; accuse, complain of*

arma, -orum, n. pl. ... *weapons, arms*

armo, -are, -avi, -atus ... *to arm*

ars, artis, f. ... *skill; art*

arvum, -I, n. ... *field*

Asia, -ae, f. ... *Asia*

aspectus, -us, m. ... *sight, appearance*

aspernor, aspernari, aspernatus ... *to disdain, reject*

asporto, -are, -avi, -atus ... *to carry off*

atque (conj.) ... *and, what is more*

atrox, atrocis ... *savage, wild, cruel, fierce*

attineo, attinere, attinui, attentus ... *to hold near, hold back, retain, reach out to*

auctor, -is, m. ... *author, originator*

auctoritas, auctoritatis, f. ... *authority*

audeo, audere, ausus ... *to dare*

audio, audire, audivi, auditus ... *to hear*

aufero, auferre, abstuli, ablatus ... *to carry off*

augeo, augere, auxi, auctus ... *to increase*

auris, auris, f. ... *ear*

aurum, -I, n. ... *gold*

aut (conj.) ... *or*

avaritia, -ae, f. ... *greed, avarice*

averto, -ere, averti, aversus ... *to avert*

avia, -ae, f. ... *grandmother*

avidus, -a, -um ... *eager for, avid*

B

bal(i)neum, -I, n. ... *bath*

basilica, -ae, f. ... *portico, basilica; public building*

bellum, -I, n. ... *war*

bonus, -a, -um ... *good*

bracchium, -ii, n. ... *forearm*

brevis, breve ... *brief*

Britannia, -ae, f. ... *Britain*

C

cado, cadere, cecidi, casus ... *to fall*

caedes, caedis, f. ... *slaughter*

caelestis, caeleste ... *heavenly*

caelum, -I, n. ... *heaven, sky*

caerimonia, -ae, f. ... *religious ceremony*

Caesar, Caesaris ... *Caesar*

calx, calcis, f. ... *heel of the foot*

Campania, -ae, f. ... *Campania*

Cano, canere, cecini, cantus ... *to sing*

cantus, -us, m. ... *song*

capesso, capessere, capessivi/-ii, capessiturus ... *to seize eagerly*

captivitas, captivitatis, f. ... *captivity*

caritas, caritatis, f. ... *affection, esteem*

carmen, carminis, n. ... *poem, song*

Carthago, Carthaginis, f. ... *Carthage*

casus, -us, m. ... *fall; chance; calamity*

causa, -ae, f. ... *cause, reason*

cedo, cedere, cessi, cessus ... *to yield, give way, cede*

celebritas, celebritatis, f. ... *throng, crowd*

celebro, -are, -avi, -atus ... *to celebrate*

celer, celeris, celere ... *swift*

censeo, censere, censui, census ... *to assess, estimate; resolve; determine*

centurio, centurionis, m. ... *centurion*

cerno, cernere, crevi, cretus ... *to separate; decide; discern*

certamen, certaminis, n. ... *contest, game*

certatim (adv.) ... *eagerly, in rivalry*

certus, -a, -um ... *certain*

cervix, cervicis, f. ... *neck*

ceterum (adv.) ... *moreover*

ceterus, -a, -um ... *the remainder*

circa (adv./prep. + acc.) ... *around; among*

circum (adv.) ... *around, about*

circumdo, -dare, -dedi, -datus ... *to set around, surround*

cithara, -ae, f. ... *lyre*

civicus, -a, -um ... *civil*

civilis, civile ... *civil*

civis, civis, c. ... *citizen*

civitas, civitatis, f. ... *city-state*

clades, cladis, f. ... *disaster*

clamito, -are, -avi, -atus ... *to cry aloud, keep shouting* clamor, clamoris, m. ... *shout*

claritudo, claritudinis, f. ... *renown*

claudo, claudere, clausi, clausus ... *to shut in, imprison*

cliens, clientis, m. ... *client*

cogo, cogere, coegi, coactus ... *to compel*

codicillus, -I, m. ... *codicil; writing tablet; petition*

coeo, coire, coivi/coii, coitus ... *to come or go together*

coerceo, coerecere, coercui, coercitus ... *to enclose on all sides; restrain; coerce*

coetus, -us, m. ... *company, crowd*

cognitio, cognitionis, f. ... *judicial examination*

cognitus, -a, -um ... *known, acknowledged*

cognosco, cognoscere, cognovi, cognitus ... *to come to know*

cohibeo, cohibere, cohibui, cohibitus ... *to hold together, embrace; stop, hold in check*

cohors, cohortis, m. ... *cohort*

collega, -ae, m. ... *colleague*

colo, colere, colui, cultus ... *to care for; honor*

columna, -ae, f. ... *column*

commaculo, -are, -avi, -atus ... *to defile*

communis, commune ... *common, shared*

compello, -are, -avi, -atus ... *to accuse; compel, incite*

complector, complecti, complexus ... *to embrace*

compleo, complere, complevi, completus ... *to fill up, make full*

compos, compotis ... *master of, possessing*

compono, componere, composui, compositus ... *to compose, arrange*

concido, concidere, concidi ... *to fall down, be slaughtered/slain*

concieo, conciere, concivi, concitus ... *to bring together, move violently, rouse*

concilio, -are, -avi, -atus ... *to bring together*

concupio, concupere, concupivi, concupitus ... *to covet, long for*

condo, condere, condidi, conditus ... *to found; preserve*

conduco, conducere, conduxi, conductus ... *to draw together, collect; undertake; hire; bribe*

confingo, confingere, confinxi, confictus ... *to fabricate*

confusus, -a, -um ... *disordered, mingled*

coniectura, -ae, f. ... *conjecture*

coniunx, coniugis, c. ... *spouse*

coniuratio, coniurationis, f. ... *conspiracy*

coniveo, conivere ... *to shut the eyes; blink*

connecto, connectere, connexi, connectus ... *to tie to, connect*

conscius, -a, -um ... *aware of, knowing*

constans, constantis ... *steadfast, comstant*

constantia, -ae, f. ... *constancy, steadfastness*

consto, constare, constiti, constaturus ... *to agree, correspond, fit*

consuetudo, consuetudinis, f. ... *habit, custom*

consul, consulis, m. ... *consul*

consularis, consulare ... *having to do with the consulship*

consulatus, -us, m. ... *consulship*

consulo, consulere, consului, consultatio, consultationis, f. ... *deliberation, consultation*

consulto, -are, -avi, -atus ... *to consult, deliberate*

consultus ... *to meet and consider, deliberate, determine, conclude*

consultum (senatus), -I, n. ... *decree
of the senate*

consumo, -ere, consumpsi,
consumptus ... *to consume*

contineo, continere, continui,
contentus ... *to contain*

continuo, -are, -avi, -atus ... *to join;
extend, prolong, continue*

continuo (adv.) ... *immediately,
at once*

continuus, -a, -um ... *uninterrupted*

contra (adv./prep. + acc.) ... *face
to face; opposite; in opposition;
contrary to*

contraho, -ere, -traxi, -tractus ... *to
draw together, collect; bargain;
bring about*

contumacia, -ae, f. ... *obstinacy*

contumelia, -ae, f. ... *insult, abuse*

convicium, -ii, n. ... *loud noise; insult*

convinco, -ere, convici, convictus ...
to convict, refute

corona, -ae, f. ... *crown*

corrigo, corrigere, correxi, correctus
... *to set right, correct*

corpus, corporis, n. ... *body*

corripio, -ere, corripui, correptus ...
to seize, snatch

corrumpo, corrumpere, corrupi,
corruptus ... *to destroy, waste,
corrupt*

credo, credere, credidi, creditus ... *to
believe*

credulitas, credulitatis, f. ... *gullibility*

cremo, -are, -avi, -atus ... *to burn*

crimen, criminis, n. ... *crime;
accusation*

criminosus, -a, -um ... *reproachful*

cruciatus, -us, m. ... *torment,
misfortune*

crudelitas, crudelitatis, f. ... *cruelty*

cruentus, -a, -um ... *bloody*

cruor, cruoris, m. ... *blood, gore*

cubiculum, -I, n. ... *little room/
chamber*

cultus, cultus, m. ... *ornament,
adornment*

cum (conj.) ... *when, because, although*

cunctus, -a, -um ... *all together, entire*

cuneus, -I, m. ... *wedge; division of
seats in the theater*

cupido, cupidinis, f. ... *desire*

cupio, cupere, cupivi, cupitus ... *to
desire*

cura, -ae, f. ... *concern, anxiety*

curia, -ae, f. ... *senate-house*

custodia, -ae, f. ... *guard, custody,
watch*

D

damnatio, damnationis, f. ...
condemnation

damno, -are, -avi, -atus ... *to condemn*

damnum, -I, n. ... *loss*

de (prep. + abl.) ... *of, concerning,
about*

decerno, decernere, decrevi, decet,
decere ... *to be suitable, proper*

decretus ... *to decree, decide*

dedecus, dedecoris, n. ... *dishonor*

dedo, dedere, dedidi, deditus ... *to
give away, surrender*

deduco, deducere, deduxi,
deductus ... *to lead away*

defectio, defectionis, f. ... *defection;
rebellion*

defensio, defensionis, f. ... *defence*

defero, deferre, detuli, delatus ... *to
carry off; report, give account of*

defleo, deflere, deflevi, defletus ... *to
weep over*

deformitas, deformitatis, f. ... *ugliness*

dehinc (adv.) ... *from this time,
henceforth*

dehonesto, -are ... *to dishonor, disgrace*

dein(de) (adv.) ... *thereafter, thence*

deligo, -ere, delegi, delectus ... *to choose*

delinquo, delinquere, deliqui,
delictus ... *to fail, fall short, do
wrong*

deminuo, deminere, deminui,
deminutus ... *to diminish*

demonstro, -are, -avi, -atus ... *to show*

depello, depellere, depuli,
depulsus ... *to drive out, expel*

depopulor, depopulari,
depopulatus ... *to lay waste*

deporto, -are, -avi, -atus ... *to carry
off; in insulam deportari ... to exile*

descisco, desciscere, descivi,
descitus ... *to withdraw, revolt*

desolo, -are, -avi, -atus ... *to forsake*

destino, -are, -avi, -atus ... *to make
firm; assign; select; designate;
appoint*

desum, deesse, defui ... *to be absent*

detergeo, detergere, detersi,
detersus ... *to wipe off*

detestor, detestari, detestatus ... *to curse*

detraho, detrahere, detraxi,
detractus ... *to draw off, take
down, pull down, deprive*

deus, dei, m. ... *god*

deveho, devehere, devexi, devectus ...
to take away

devotio, -onis, f. ... *self-sacrifice;
cursing, curse formula*

dextra, -ae, f. ... *right hand*

dico, dicere, dixi, dictus ... *to speak*

dictito, -are, -avi, -atus ... *to say*

Dido, Didonis, f . ... *Dido*

dies, -ei, m. ... *day*

differo, differe, distuli, dilatus ... *to
carry apart; defer*

differtus, -a, -um ... *stuffed*

dignitas, dignitatis, f. ... *dignity*

digredior, digredi, digressus ... *to go
away, depart*

dilargior, dilargiri, dilargitus ... *to
give lavishly*

dilectus, -us, m. ... *levy, draft*

diluo, -ere, dilui, dilutus ... *to wash
away, dissolve*

dimitto, -ere, dimisi, dimissus ... *to
dismiss*

dirus, -a, -um ... *ominous*

disceptator, disceptatoris, m. ...
arbitrator

discordia, -ae, f. ... *discord*

discrimen, discriminis, n. ... *critical
moment; peril, risk*

disicio, disicere, disieci, disiectus ...
to scatter, tear asunder

dispergo, dispergere, dispersi,
dispersus ... *to scatter, disperse*

displiceo, displicere, displicui,
displicitus ... *to displease*

dispono, disponere, disposui,
dispositus ... *to arrange*

dissero, disserere, dissevi, dissitum ...
*to scatter or sow seed; examine,
argue*

dissimulo, -are, -avi, -atus ... *to keep
secret, conceal, dissemble*

dissociatio, dissociationis, f. ...
separation

distendo, distendere, distendi,
distentus ... *to stretch out*

distinguo, distinguere, distinxi,
distinctus ... *to separate, divide,
distinguish*

diurnus, -a, -um ... *daily*

diversus, -a, -um ... *different*

divinus, -a, -um ... *divine*

divitiae, -arum, f. pl. ... *riches*

divus, -a, -um ... *divine*

do, dare, dedi, datus ... *to give*

doctor, doctoris, m. ... *teacher*

documentum, -I, n. ... *document,
proof*

dolor, doloris, m. ... *sorrow*

domus, -I, f. ... *house*

donec (conj.) ... *as long as, while*

dono, -are, -avi, -atus ... *give confer*

dotalis, dotale ... *having to do with
a dowry*

dubius, -a, -um ... *doubtful*

duco, ducere, duxi, ductus ... *to lead*

dum (conj.) ... *while, as, as long as,
provided that*

duo, duae, duo ... *two*

duodecies (adv.) ... *twelve times*

dux, ducis, m. ... *leader*

E

edo, edere, edidi, editus ... *to give out; produce; publish; relate, disclose*

efficio, efficere, effeci, effectus ... *to bring to pass*

effigies, -ei, f. ... *likeness, effigy*

effodio, effodire, effodi, effosus ... *to dig up*

effugio, -ere, effugi ... *to flee away*

effugium, -I, n. ... *fleeing; means of escape*

effundo, effundere, effudi, effusus ... *to pour out*

egredior, egredi, egressus ... *to go out*

eiulatus, -us, m. ... *lamentation, wailing*

elegentia, -iae, f. ... *elegance, refinement*

elicio, -ere, elicui ... *to entice, lure out*

eloquentia, -ae, f. ... *eloquence*

eludo, eludere, elusi, elusus ... *to stop playing; escape, avoid*

emercor, emercari, emercatus ... *to buy up, bribe*

emo, emere, emi, emptus ... *to buy*

enim (conj.) ... *for instance, namely, because, indeed, certainly*

enitor, eniti, enixus/enisus ... *to struggle upwards*

epistula, -ae, f. ... *letter*

epulae, -arum, f. pl. ... *banquet*

eques, equitis, m. ... *equestrian*

ergo (adv.) ... *therefore, then*

erogo, -are, -avi, -atus ... *to pay out, expend*

eruditus, -a, -um ... *learned*

et (conj.) ... *and; (adv.) ... also*

etenim (conj.) ... *for, indeed, because*

etiam (adv./conj.) ... *still, and also, furthermore*

evado, evadere, evasi, evasus ... *to go out, escape, evade*

evenio, -ire, eveni, eventus ... *to come out, come forth, happen*

ex/e (prep. + abl.) ... *out of; from*

exanimis, exanime ... *lifeless*

excipio, excipere, excepi, exceptus ... *to take out, withdraw; receive, capture*

excrementum, -I, n. ... *excretion*

exemplum, -I, n. ... *example*

exequiae, -arum, f. pl. ... *funeral*

exerceo, exercere, exercui, exercitus ... *to keep busy, occupy; prosecute*

exercitus, -us, m. ... *army*

exigo, exigere, exegi, exactus ... *to drive out; complete; finish; demand; exact; conduct; finish; consider; spend (i.e., time)*

exilium, -ii, n. ... *exile*

exim (adv.) ... *thence, after that*

exitialis, -e. ... *destructive, fatal*

exitiosus, -a, -um ... *destructive, deadly*

exoletus, -I, m. ... *a boy favorite*

expectatio, expectationis, f. ... *expectation*

expecto, -are, -avi, -atus ... *to wait for*

expedio, expedire, expedivi, expeditus ... *to extricate; explain; be profitable*

expello, -ere, expuli, expulsus ... *to expel; banish*

expendo, expendere, expendi, expensus ... *to weigh, weight out; reckon; ponder; consider; decide*

exprimo, exprimere, expressi, expressus ... *to press out; represent, copy, express*

exprobro, -are, -avi, -atus ... *to reproach, blame*

expromo, expromere, exprompsi, expromptus ... *to show forth, display; disclose, state*

expurgo, -are, -avi, -atus ... *to cleanse, purify*

exscindo, exscindere, excidi, excissus ... *to annihilate, destroy*

ex(s)olvo, -ere, -olvi, -olutus ... *to set loose*

externus, -a, -um ... *foreign*

exterreo, exterrere, exterrui, exterritus ... *to strike with terror*

extinguo, extinguere, extinxi, extinctus ... *to put out, extinguish*

extollo, extollere ... *to lift up, raise*

extorris, extorre ... *banished, exiled*

exul, exulis, c. ... *exile*

exuo, exuere, exui, exutus ... *to take off; divest*

F

facesso, facessere, facessi, facessitus ... *to perform*

facilis, facile ... *easy*

facilitas, facilitatis, f. ... *ease*

facinus, facinoris, n. ... *deed, achievement; bad deed, outrage*

facio, facere, feci, factus ... *to do, make*

factito, -are, -avi, -atus ... *to do frequently/persistently*

facundia, -ae, f. ... *eloquence*

fallax, fallacis ... *false, fallacious*

falsus, -a, -um ... *false*

fama, -ae, f. ... *report, rumor, reputation*

familiaris, familiare ... *domestic, private*

famosus, -a, -um ... *celebrated, famous; scandalous*

fatigo, -are, -avi, -atus ... *to weary, tire out*

fatisco, fatiscere ... *to fall apart; grow weak*

fatum, -I, n. ... *fate; destiny; destruction; death*

fautor, fautoris, m. ... *supporter*

femina, -ae, f. ... *woman*

fero, ferre, tuli, latus ... *to bring, bear, carry*

ferrum, -I, n. ... *iron; sword*

fessus, -a, -um ... *tired*

festinatio, festinationis, f. ... *haste*

festino, -are, -avi, -atus ... *to hasten, hurry*

fides, -ei, f. ... *faith, trust*

filia, -ae, f. ... *daughter*

filius, -ii, m. ... *son*

fingo, -ere, finxi, fictus ... *to fashion, shape*

finis, finis, m. ... *end; boundary*

firmo, -are, -avi, -atus ... *to strengthen*

flagitium, -ii, n. ... *shameful act*

flagito, -are, -avi, -atus ... *to demand*

flagro, -are, -avi, -atus ... *to burn, blaze with passion*

flebilis, flebile ... *lamentable*

flecto, -ere, flexi, flexus ... *to bend*

fletus, -us, m. ... *weeping*

foedo, -are, -avi, -atus ... *to disgrace*

foedus, -a, -um ... *disgraceful, shameful*

forma, -ae, f. ... *form; loveliness*

forsitan (adv.) ... *perhaps*

fortasse (adv.) ... *perhaps*

forte (adv.) ... *by chance*

fortitudo, fortitudinis, f. ... *strength*

fortuitus, -a, -um ... *fortutitous*

fortuna, -ae, f. ... *fortune, chance*

forum, -I, n. ... *forum, open space*

frango, frangere, fregi, fractus ... *to break*

frater, fratris, m. ... *brother*

fraus, fraudis, f. ... *deceit, fraud*

frequens, frequentis ... *regular, frequent, filled*

fruor, frui, fructus ... *to enjoy*

frustra (adv.) ... *in error; in vain*

frustror, frustrari, frustratus ... *to frustrate, deceive*

frux, frugis, f. ... *fruit, produce, crop*

fungor, fungi, functus ... *to perform, discharge*

funus, funeris, n. ... *funeral; corpse*

furor, furari, furatus ... *to steal*

G

Gallia, -ae, f. ... *Gaul*

ganeo, ganeonis, m. ... *glutton, wanton*

gaza, -ae, f. ... *treasure*

gemma, -ae, f. ... *gem*

gener, generi, m. ... *son-in-law*

genetrix, genetricis, f. ... *mother*

genitalis, genitale ... *having to do with birth*

genu, -us, n. ... *knee*

genus, generis, n. ... *race, origin, kind*

gero, -ere, gessi, gestus ... *to bear about, carry, wear; carry out, wage*

gestus, -us, m. ... *gesture*

gigno, gignere, genui, genitus ... *to produce, give birth*

gladius, -ii, m. ... *sword*

glisco, -ere ... *to swell or spread gradually*

globus, -I, m. ... *globe; throng, crowd*

gloria, -ae, f. ... *glory*

gnarus, -a, -um ... *expert, skilled*

grandis, grande ... *great, powerful, weighty*

gratus, -a, -um ... *pleasing, beloved*

gravidus, -a, -um ... *swollen, heavy; pregnant*

gravis, grave ... *serious; heavy*

gravitas, gravitatis, f. ... *heavy; dignity*

H

habeo, habere, habui, habitus ... *to have, hold; consider*

habitus, -us, m. ... *habit, character, disposition*

hactenus (adv.) ... *so far, thus far*

haud (adv.) ... *by no means*

haurio, -ire, hausi, haustus ... *to draw out; drain; drink in*

heres, heredis, c. ... *heir*

hic, haec, hoc (demonst. pron./adj.) ... *this*

histrio, histrionis, m. ... *actor*

hortor, hortari, hortatus ... *to encourage*

hortus, -I, m. ... *garden*

hostis, hostis, c. ... *stranger, foreigner; public enemy*

humanus, -a, -um ... *human*

humus, -I, f. ... *earth, ground*

I

iaceo, iacere, iacui ... *to lie, be at rest*

iam (adv.) ... *already, now*

ictus, -us, m. ... *blow*

idem, eadem, idem ... *same*

ideo (adv.) ... *for that reason, therefore*

igitur (conj.) ... *therefore*

ignavia, -ae, f. ... *sloth, idleness*

ignis, ignis, m. ... *fire*

ignotus, -a, -um ... *unknown*

ille, illa, illud (demonst. pron./adj.) ... *that*

illic (adv.) ... *there, in that place*

Illyricus, -a, -um ... *Illyrian*

imago, imaginis, f. ... *image*

imitatio, imitationis, f. ... *imitation*

immanitas, immanitatis, f. ... *hugeness; savageness*

immensus, -a, um ... *immense, vast*

immeritus, -a, -um ... *undeserved*

immineo, imminere ... *to overhang; be intent upon; be near to*

immobilis, immobile ... *unmoving*

immolo, -are, -avi, -atus ... *to make a sacrifice; immolate*

immortalitas, immortalitatis, f. ... *immortality*

immotus, -a, -um ... *immovable, unmoving*

impar, imparis ... *unequal*

imperator, imperatoris, m. ... *commander, emperor*

imperatorius, -a, -um ... *having to do with the empire/emperor*

imperium, -ii, n. ... *command, empire*

impetro, -are, -avi, -atus ... *to achieve, obtain, procure*

impexus, -a, -um ... *uncombed, unkempt*

impius, -a, -um ... *wicked, impious*
impollutus, -a, -um ... *unstained*
imprudentia, -ae, f. ... *imprudence*
impudicitia, -ae, f. ... *immodesty*
in (prep. + acc.) ... *into; (prep. + abl.)
... in, on*
inanis, inane ... *empty*
incestum, -I, n. ... *incest*
incipio, incipere, incepi, inceptus ...
    to begin
incolumis, incolume ... *safe*
incolumitas, incolumitatis, f. ... *safety*
increpito, -are ... *to chide, scold*
incuria, -ae, f. ... *neglect*
inde (adv.) ... *from that place, thence*
indefessus, -a, -um ... *unwearied*
index, indicis, c. ... *informer, witness*
indicium, -ii, n. ... *indication,
    evidence, disclosure*
indignus, a, -um ... *unworthy*
induco, inducere, induxi, inductus ...
    to lead in
indulgeo, indulgere, indulsi, indulsus
    ... *to indulge, favor*
induo, induere, indui, indutus ... *to
    put on, assume*
industria, -ae, f. ... *industry, diligence*
indutus, -us, m. ... *a putting on;
    apparel*
ineo, inire, inivi/inii, initus ... *to go
    into, enter*
inermis, inerme ... *unarmed*
inexpertus, -a, -um ... *without
    experience*
infamia, -ae, f. ... *ill fame, bad report*
infans, infantis, c. ... *infant*
infaustus, -a, -um ... *unlucky, baleful*
infelix, infelicis ... *unlucky,
    unfortunate, ill-omened*
infensus, -a, -um ... *hateful*
inferior, inferius ... *lower, further
    down*
infero, inferre, intuli, inlatus ... *to
    carry in*

ingenium, -ii, n. ... *talent, genius*
ingens, ingentis ... *huge*
ingenuus, -a, -um ... *native; noble*
ingruo, -ere, ingrui ... *to come
    violently, assault forcefully*
inhio, -are, -avi, -atus ... *to gape at*
inhonestus, -a, -um ... *dishonorable*
iniquitas, iniquitatis, f. ... *iniquity;
    guilt*
initium, -ii, n. ... *beginning*
inludo, inludere, inlusi, inlusus ... *to
    make sport of*
inlustris, inlustre ... *lighted;
    distinguished; illustrious*
innecto, innectere, innexui, innexus
    ... *to twist; entangle; join*
innocens, innocentis ... *innocent*
innoxius, -a, -um ... *harmless*
inquam ... *to say*
inquies, inquietis ... *restless*
inquiro, inquirere, inquisivi, inquisitus
    ... *to search after, inquire*
inritus, -a, -um ... *undecided, of no
    effect*
inrogo, -are, -avi ... *to propose in
    opposition (legal term); to impose;
    inflict*
inscribo, inscribere, inscripsi,
    inscriptus ... *to inscribe*
inservio, inservire, inservivi,
    inservitus ... *to serve, defer to*
insideo, insidere, insedi ... *to sit
    upon; settle; occupy*
insignio, insignire, insignivi,
    insignitus ... *to distinguish*
insignis, insigne ... *distinguished (as
    noun, cf. Eng. "insignia")*
insisto, insistere, institi, - ... *to stand
    on, follow, pursue, press on*
insons, insontis ... *innocent*
inspicio, inspicere, inspexi, inspectus
    ... *to inspect, examine*
instituo, instituere, institui, institutus
    ... *to institute*

institutio, institutionis, f. ... *institute*

institutum, -I, n. ... *institution; decree*

insto, instare, institi, instaturus ... *to stand upon; press upon; demand*

insula, -ae, f. ... *island*

insum, inesse, infui ... *to be in or upon*

insumo, insumere, insumpsi, insumptus ... *to take for, apply; assume*

insuper (adv.) ... *above; besides*

integer, integra, integrum ... *entire, whole, complete*

intemeratus, -a, -um ... *inviolate*

intemperies, intemperiei (found only in acc. and abl.), f. ... *excess; inclemency*

intendo, intendere, intendi, intentus ... *to stretch out; be zealous in*

inter (prep. + acc.) ... *between, among*

interea (adv.) ... *meanwhile*

intercedo, intercedere, intercessi, intercessus ... *to intervene*

intercisus, -a, -um ... *cut*

interficio, interficere, interfeci, interfectus ... *to kill*

interiectus, -a, -um ... *placed between*

interim (adv.) ... *meanwhile*

interitus, -us, m. ... *destruction*

interrogo, -are, -avi, -atus ... *to inquire*

interruptus, -a, -um ... *broken*

intersum, interesse, interfui, interfuturus ... *to be between*

interverto, intervertere, interverti, interversus ... *to turn aside, embezzle, squander*

intestinus, -a, -um ... *inward*

intimus, -a, -um ... *inmost, intimate*

intra (adv./prep. + acc.) ... *within, inside*

intro, -are, -avi, -atus ... *to enter*

introeo, -ire, -ivi ... *to go in, enter*

intueor, intueri, intuitus ... *to look upon*

inultus, -a, -um ... *unavenged*

invado, invadere, invasi, invasus ... *to enter; invade*

invideo, invidere, invidi, invisus ... *to cast an evil eye on; envy, grudge, be prejudiced against*

invidia, -ae, f. ... *envy, jealousy*

invoco, -are, -avi, -atus ... *to invoke, call on, pray to*

involvo, involvere, involvi, involutus ... *to roll, wrap up*

ipse, ipsa, ipsum (intensive pron.) ... *self*

ira, -ae, f. ... *anger; wrath*

iracundia, -ae, f. ... *anger; rage*

is, ea, id (demonst. pron./adj.) ... *this, that*

ita (adv.) ... *in this manner, so, thus*

Italia, -ae, f. ... *Italy*

iter, itineris, n. ... *journey, path, way*

iubeo, iubere, iussi, iussus ... *to order*

iudex, iudicis, m. ... *judge*

iugulum, -I, n. ... *neck, throat*

Iuppiter, Iovis, m. ... *Jupiter*

iuro, -are, -avi, -atus ... *to swear*

ius iurandum, iuris iurandi, n. ... *oath*

iustitia, -ae, f. ... *justice, equity*

iuvenis, iuvenis, c. ... *young person*

iuventa, -ae, f. ... *youth*

iuvo, iuvare, iuvi, iutus ... *to help*

iuxta (adv./prep. + acc.) ... *nearly, near/close to, adjoining*

L

labor, labi, lapsus ... *to slip, glide*

labor, laboris, m. ... *work, labor*

laetor, laetari, laetatus ... *to rejoice*

laetus, -a, -um ... *happy, joyful*

lamenta, -orum, n. pl. ... *wailing, laments*

largior, largiri, largitus ... *to bestow*

largitio, largitionis, f. ... *largess*

lascivia, -ae, f. ... *wantonness*

lascivio, lascivire, lascivivi, lascivitus
... *to be wanton*

later, lateris, m. ... *brick, ingot*

latus, -a, -um ... *wide, broad*

laudo, -are, -avi, -atus ... *to praise*

laus, laudis, f. ... *praise*

lectulus, -I, m. ... *small couch/bed*

legatio, legationis, f. ... *embassy,
legation*

legio, legionis, f. ... *legion*

lego, legere, legi, lectus ... *to choose,
select; collect, gather*

lenitas, lenitatis, f. ... *smoothness,
gentleness*

lentitudo, lentitudinis, f. ...
sluggishness

levis, leve ... *light; frivolous*

lex, legis, f. ... *law*

libellus, -I, m. ... *little book;
pamphlet; diary; indictment*

liberator, liberatoris, m. ... *liberator*

liberi, -orum, n. pl. ... *children*

libertas, libertatis, f. ... *freedom*

libertus, -I, m. ... *freedman*

libet, libere, libuit/libitum ... *it is
pleasing*

libido, libidinis, f. ... *lust, pleasure*

libo, -are, -avi, -atus ... *to pour out as
a libation*

liburnicus, -a, -um ... *having to do
with a Liburnian*

licet, licere, licitum ... *it is permitted*

lictor, lictoris, m. ... *lictor*

Ligures, Ligurum, m. pl. ... *Ligurians*

litterae, -arum, f. pl. ... *document,
letter*

locus, -I, m. ... *place*

longinquus, -a, -um ... *far off*

longus, -a, -um ... *long*

loquor, loqui, locutus ... *to speak*

luctus, -us, m. ... *grief, mourning*

ludibrium, -I, n. ... *mockery*

ludicer, ludicra, ludicrum ... *playful,
sportive*

ludicrum, -I, n. ... *game*

Lugdunensis, Lugdunense ... *having
to do with Lugdunum*

luo, luere, lui ... *to loose, atone for,
expiate, suffer, undergo*

lustralis, -e ... *having to do with
purification*

lustrum, -I, n. ... *a purificatory
sacrifice performed every five
years; a period of five years*

luxuria, -ae, f. ... *luxury*

luxus, -us, m. ... *luxury*

M

maestitia, -ae, f. ... *grief, sorrow*

magicus, -a, -um ... *magical*

magis (adv.) ... *more*

magnitudo, magnitudinis, f. ...
magnitude

magnus, -a, um. ... *great*

malus, -a, -um ... *bad, evil*

manus, -us, f. ... *hand*

maritus, -I, m. ... *husband*

materia, -ae, f. ... *material*

matrimonium, -ii, n. ... *matrimony*

maturo, -are, -avi, -atus ... *to hasten*

meditatio, meditationis, f. ...
contemplation, meditation

memini, meminisse ... *to remember*

memoria, -ae, f. ... *memory*

memoro, -are, -avi, -atus ... *to call to
mind, speak of, recall*

mens, mentis, f. ... *mind*

mensis, mensis, m. ... *month*

mentio, mentionis, f. ... *mention*

mereo(r), merere/mereri, merui,
meritus ... *to deserve*

metallum, -I, n. ... *mine*

metus, -us, m. ... *dread, fear*

miles, militis, m. ... *soldier*

militaris, militare ... *having to do
with the military*

mina, -ae, f. ... *threat*

minax, minacis ... *threatening*

ministerium, -ii, n. ... *service; duty*

ministro, -are, -avi, -atus ... *to attend, serve*

minitor, minitari, minitatus ... *to threaten*

miraculum, -I, n. ... *miracle, portent*

mirus, -a, -um ... *wonderful, marvelous*

misceo, miscere, miscui, mixtus ... *to mix*

miser, misera, miserum ... *unfortunate, wretched*

miseratio, miserationis, f. ... *pity, mercy*

misericordia, -ae, f. ... *pity, mercy*

miseror, miserari, miseratus ... *to lament, pity*

mitis, mite ... *gentle, soft*

mitto, -ere, misi, missus ... *to send*

modestus, -a, -um ... *temperate, sober*

modo (adv.) ... *only*

modus, -I, m. ... *mode, manner*

mollis, molle ... *soft*

momentum, -I, n. ... *movement; motion; moment*

moneo, monere, monui, monitus ... *to advise, warn*

monile, monilis, n. ... *necklace*

mora, -ae, f. ... *delay*

morbus, -I, m. ... *sickness*

morior, mori, mortuus ... *to die*

moror, morari, moratus ... *to delay*

mors, mortis, f. ... *death*

mortalis, mortalis ... *mortal*

mortalitas, mortalitatis, f. ... *mortality*

mos, moris, m. ... *custom, habit*

mox (adv.) ... *soon*

muliebris, muliebre ... *womanly*

multitudo, multitudinis, f. ... *multitude*

multo, -are, -avi, -atus ... *to punish, fine*

multus, -a, -um ... *much, many*

munia, -orum, n. pl. ... *duties, functions*

municipium, -ii, n. ... *municipality; free town*

munus, muneris, n. ... *service; gift, present*

muto, -are, -avi, -atus ... *to change*

N

nam (conj.) ... *for, certainly*

Narbonensis, Narbonense ... *Narbonese*

naris, naris, f. ... *nose*

nascor, nasci, natus ... *to be born*

ne (conj. + subj.) ... *that not, lest*

nec/neque (adv./conj.) ... *and not, nor*

necessitas, necessitatis, f. ... *necessity, the inevitable*

neglegentia, -ae, f. ... *lack of concern, negligence*

negotium, -ii, n. ... *affair*

nemo, neminis, c. ... *no one*

nepos, nepotis, m. ... *grandson, descendant*

neptis, neptis, f. ... *granddaughter*

Nero, Neronis ... *Nero*

nescius, -a, -um ... *unknowing*

nex, necis, f. ... *violent death, murder*

nihil (indeclinable), n. ... *nothing*

nimius, -a, -um ... *excessive*

nimium (adv.) ... *too much*

nisi (conj.) ... *if not, unless*

nobilis, nobile ... *noble*

nocturnus, -a, um. ... *nocturnal*

nomen, nominis, n. ... *name*

nominatim (adv.) ... *by name*

non (adv.) ... *not*

nondum (adv.) ... *not yet*

nosco, -ere, novi, notus ... *to come to know*

notesco, notescere, notescui ... *to become known*

notitia, -ae, f. ... *note, fame, knowledge*

novitas, novitatis, f. ... *novelty*

novus, -a, -um ... *new*

nox, noctis, f. ... *night*

nudus, -a, -um ... *bare, naked*

nullus, -a, -um ... *no*

numen, numinis, n. ... *divine power*

Numidae, -arum, m. pl. ... *Numidians*

nuncupatio, nuncupationis, f. ...
public pronunciation

nuncupo, -are, -avi, -atus ... *to call
by name*

nuntio, -are, -avi, -atus ... *to announce*

nuper (adv.) ... *recently*

O

ob (prep. + acc.) ... *towards, to; on
account of; instead of*

obeo, obire, obivi, obitus ... *to go to
meet*

obiecto, -are, -avi, -atus ... *to oppose;
charge, accuse with*

obicio, obicere, obieci, obiectus ...
*to throw before, offer, oppose,
reproach*

oblectamentum, -I, n. ... *pleasure*

oblittero, -are, -avi, -atus ... *to erase,
cause to be forgotten*

obnitor, obniti, obnixus ... *to press
on; struggle with*

obnoxius, -a, -um ... *guilty; servile,
obedient*

obscuro, -are, -avi, -atus ... *to make
dark, obscure*

obsequium, -ii, n. ... *indulgence,
compliance*

obsideo, obsidere, obsedi, obsessus
... *to stay, besiege*

obsigno, -are, -avi, -atus ... *to seal up*

obsto, obstare, obstiti ... *to be opposite*

obtego, obtegere, obtexi, obtectus ...
to cover over

obtempero, -are, -avi, atus ... *to
comply*

obtero, obterere, obtrivi, obtritus ...
to trample, crush

obtrectator, obtrectatoris, m. ...
detractor

obversor, -ari, -atus ... *to make an
appearance*

obverto, obvertere, obverti, obversus
... *to turn towards*

obvius, -a, -um ... *ready, at hand*

occasio, occasionis, f. ... *opportunity,
occasion*

occulto, -are, -avi, -atus ... *to hide,
conceal*

occultus, -a, -um ... *hidden, obscure*

occurro, occurrere, occurri, occursus
... *to run to, meet; oppose; remedy;
reply; offer*

oculus, -I, m. ... *eye*

odor, odoris, m. ... *odor*

odi, odisse ... *to hate*

odium, -ii, n. ... *hatred, odium*

offensio, offensionis, f. ... *a striking
against; disfavor; misfortune;
failure*

offero, offerre, obtuli, oblatus ... *to
offer*

officium, -ii, n. ... *duty*

olim (adv.) ... *once upon a time, at
that time*

omen, ominis, n. ... *omen*

omitto, omittere, omisi, omissus ...
to omit

omnis, omne ... *all, whole, every*

onero, -are, -avi, -atus ... *to burden*

opperior, opperiri, opertus ... *to wait*

opprimo, opprimere, oppressi,
oppressus ... *to press down, oppress*

(ops), opis, f. ... *wealth, resources*

opus, operis, n. ... *work*

opus est ... *there is need of*

oratio, orationis, f. ... *speech*

orator, -is, m. ... *orator*

ordior, ordiri, orditus ... *to begin,
undertake*

origo, originis, f. ... *origin*

orior, oriri, ortus ... *to arise*

ortus, -us, m. ... *birth*

os, oris, n. ... *mouth*

ostento, -are, -avi, -atus ... *to show, exhibit*

P

palam (adv.) ... *openly*

par, paris ... *equal*

parens, parentis, c. ... *parent*

paro, -are, -avi, -atus ... *to prepare*

pars, partis, f. ... *part; faction*

parum (adv.) ... *too little*

parvus, -a, -um ... *small*

passim (adv.) ... *at random, scattered about, in every direction*

pater, patris, m. ... *father*

paternus, -a, -um ... *paternal*

patior, pati, passus ... *to endure*

patres (conscripti), m. pl. ... *senators*

patronus, -I, m. ... *patron*

patruus, -I, m. ... *(paternal) uncle*

paupertas, paupertatis, f. ... *poverty*

pavidus, -a, -um ... *fearful, trembling*

pavor, pavoris, m. ... *fear*

pax, pacis, f. ... *peace*

pecunia, -ae, f. ... *money*

per (prep. + acc.) ... *through*

perago, peragere, peregi, peractus ... *to go through, finish*

percussor, percussoris, m. ... *murderer*

perdo, perdere, perdidi, perditus ... *to destroy, ruin, lose*

pereo, perire, perii/perivi, periturus ... *to pass away, vanish, be lost, disappear*

perfero, perferre, pertuli, perlatus ... *to bear through; announce; endure to the end*

perfidiosus, -a, -um ... *faithless*

pergo, pergere, perrexi, perrectus ... *to proceed*

periculum, -I, n. ... *danger*

perinde (adv.) ... *in the same manner*

permitto, permittere, permisi, permissus ... *to allow, permit*

permoveo, permovere, permovi, permotus ... *to move deeply, influence*

pernicies, -ei, f. ... *calamity*

perorno, -are, -avi, -atus ... *to adorn constantly*

perosus ... *hating greatly*

perquam (adv.) ... *extremely, exceedingly*

perscribo, perscribere, perscripsi, perscriptus ... *to write in detail*

persono, -are, personui ... *to resound*

perverto, pervertere, perverti, perversus ... *to overturn, overthrow*

pestilentia, -ae, f. ... *pestilence, plague*

petitio, petitionis, f. ... *a blow; solicitation for office, candidacy, canvassing*

Phoenissa (adj. f.) ... *of Phoenicia*

pictura, -ae, f. ... *painting*

pietas, pietatis, f. ... *sense of duty, loyalty*

pignus, pignoris/-eris, n. ... *pledge; hostage; children*

placabilis, placabile ... *able to be appeased*

placitus, -a, -um ... *pleasing, agreeable*

plausus, -us, m. ... *applause*

pleb(e)s, -is, f. ... *common people*

plerusque, -a, -um ... *a very great part*

plus, pluris ... *more*

Poenus, -a, -um ... *Punic/ Carthaginian*

pondus, ponderis, n. ... *weight*

pono, ponere, posui, positus ... *to put, place*

populus, -I, m. ... *people*

porrigo, porrigere, porrexi, porrectus ... *to stretch out*

portus, -us, m. ... *harbor*

posco, poscere, poposci ... *to demand urgently*

possum, posse, potui ... *to be able*

post (prep. + acc.) ... *after, behind*

posthac (adv.) ... *after this, henceforth*
posteritas, posteritatis, f. ... *posterity*
posterus, -a, -um ... *following, next*
postquam (conj.) ... *after that*
postremo (adv.) ... *at last, finally*
postremus, -a, um ... *last; next, following*
potens, potentis ... *powerful*
potestas, potestatis, f. ... *power*
potior, potioris ... *more capable*
potius (adv.) ... *rather, preferable, more*
praebeo, praebere, praebui, praebitus ... *to proffer, offer*
praecaveo, praecavere, praecavi, praecautus, *to be precautious*
praecello, praecellere ... *to surpass, excel*
praeceps, praecipitis ... *headlong, precipitous, hasty*
praecipuus, -a, -um ... *special, peculiar*
praeda, -ae, f. ... *booty*
praefectus, -I, m. ... *prefect*
praeficio, praeficere, praefeci, praefectus ... *to set over, place in command*
praegravis, praegrave ... *very heavy*
praemium, -ii, n. ... *reward*
praeposterus, -a, -um ... *in reverse order*
praeruptus, -a, -um ... *hasty, rash*
praesens, praesentis ... *at hand, present*
praetereo, -ire, -ii, -itus ... *to go by, pass over*
praetorius, -a, -um ... *praetorian*
praetura, -ae, f. ... *praetorship*
praevalidus, -a, -um ... *very strong*
praevenio, praevenire, praeveni, praeventus ... *to come before, anticipate*
pravus, -a, -um ... *crooked; wicked; perverse*
precor, precari, precatus ... *to pray*
prex, precis, f. ... *prayer*

primo (adv.) ... *at the beginning, at first*
primum (adv.) ... *at first, first*
primus, -a, -um ... *first*
princeps, principis, m. ... *first man, leader*
principium, -ii, n. ... *beginning*
prior, prius ... *former, prior, first*
privatus, -a, -um ... *private*
pro (prep. + abl.) ... *for, on behalf of, in front of*
probrosus, -a, -um ... *shameful*
proclamo, -are, -avi, -atus ... *to proclaim*
proconsul, proconulis, m. ... *proconsul*
proconsulatus, -us, m. ... *proconsulship*
procuratio, procurationis, f. ... *superintendence; caring for*
profugus, -a, -um ... *exile*
prodigo, -ere, prodegi ... *to squander*
proditor, proditoris, m. ... *betrayer*
prodo, prodere, prodidi, proditus ... *to put forth, reveal; disclose, betray*
profero, proferre, protuli, prolatus ... *to bring forth*
profligator, -oris, m. ... *wanton, spendthrift*
progredior, progredi, progressus ... *to proceed*
prohibeo, prohibere, prohibui, prohibitus ... *to forbid*
proinde (adv.) ... *therefore, accordingly*
promiscus, -a, -um ... *indiscriminate*
promissum, -i., n. ... *to hold back, prohibit*
promitto, -ere, promisi, promissus ... *to promise*
prompte (adv.) ... *readily*
promptus, -a, -um ... *ready, prompt*
properanter (adv.) ... *hastily*
properus, -a, -um ... *quick, hasty, speedy*
propinquus, -a, -um ... *near*

propior, propius ... *nearer; closer*

proprius, -a, -um ... *proper, peculiar*

prosum, prodesse, profui, profuturus ... *to profit, serve*

protego, protegere, protexi, protectus ... *to protect, shelter*

provenio, -ire, proveni, proventus ... *to come forth*

provincia, -ae, f. ... *province*

proxime (adv.) ... *nearest, next*

prudens, prudentis ... *prudent, thoughtful*

publico, -are, -avi, -atus ... *to make public*

publicus, -a, -um ... *public*

pudor, pudoris, m. ... *shame*

pugio, pugionis, m. ... *dagger*

pugna, -ae, f. ... *fight*

punio, punire, punivi, punitus ... *to punish*

Q

quadragies (adv.) ... *forty times*

quaero, quaerere, quaesivi, quaesitus ... *to seek*

quaestor, quaestoris, m. ... *quaestor*

quaestorius, -a, -um ... *having to do with a quaestor*

quamvis (adv./conj.) ... *however much; although*

quantus, -a, -um ... *how much, how many; how big*

quasi (adv.) ... *as if*

-que (conj.) ... *and*

queritor, queritari ... *to complain strongly*

queror, queri, questus ... *to complain, lament*

qui, quae, quod ... *who, what*

quia (conj.) ... *because*

quidam, quaedam, quoddam/ quiddam (indef. pron.) ... *certain*

quidem (adv.) ... *indeed*

quies, quietis, f. ... *quiet*

quin (conj.) ... *but, indeed, in fact*

quindecimviralis, quindecimvirale ... *having to do with the quindecimvirs*

quinquagies (adv.) ... *fifty times*

quinquennalis, -e ... *occurring every fifth year*

quippe (adv./conj.) ... *by all means; for in fact*

quisque, quaeque, quidque (adj./ indef. pron.) ... *whatever, each, every, every one*

quondam (adv.) ... *formerly, once*

quoque (adv.) ... *also*

R

raptim (adv.) ... *hastily*

ratio, rationis, f. ... *reckoning, account tally*

recens, recentis ... *recent*

recito, -are, -avi, -atus ... *to recite*

recludo, recludere, reclusi, reclusus ... *to unclose, disclose, reveal*

recordor, recordari, recordatus ... *to call to mind*

reddo, reddere, reddidi, redditus ... *to give back*

refero, referre, rettuli, relatus ... *to bear back, return, retire, retreat, give back, restore*

regius, -a, -um ... *royal*

regnum, -I, n. ... *kingdom*

religio, religionis, f. ... *religion, superstition*

relinquo, relinquere, reliqui, relictus ... *to leave behind*

reliquus, -a, -um ... *remaining*

remigium, -ii, n. ... *rowing apparatus, oars; oarsmen*

remitto, remittere, remisi, remissus ... *to send back*

removeo, removere, removi, remotus ... *to remove*

reor, reri, ratus ... *to think, reckon*

reperio, reperire, repperi, repertus ... *to find*

repeto, -ere, -ivi, -itus ... *to strike again; call to mind; to demand restitution; sue for recovery of money*

requiro, requirere, requisivi, requisitus ... *to seek again, need, require*

res, rei, f. ... *thing*

res novae, f. pl. ... *revolution*

resido, -ere, resedi ... *to sit down*

respergo, respergere, respersi, respersus ... *to sprinkle over*

respuo, respuere, respui ... *to spit back; cast off, expel*

restringo, restringere ... *to bind back, tighten*

retineo, -ere, retinui, retentus ... *to restrain, hold back*

reus, -a, -um ... *accused; (as substantive), defendant*

revolvo, -ere, -volvi, -volutus ... *to roll back, unroll, return*

rex, regis, m. ... *king*

rigidus, -a, -um ... *stiff, rigid*

ritus, -us, m. ... *rite, liturgy*

rogus, -I, m. ... *funeral pile; grave*

Roma, -ae, f. ... *Rome*

Romanus, -a, -um ... *Roman*

rostra, -orum, n. ... *speaker's platform*

rudis, rude ... *rough, coarse*

rumor, -is, m. ... *rumor*

ruo, ruere, rui, ruiturus ... *to rush down, go to ruin, hasten on*

rursum (adv.) ... *backward, on the contrary, in turn*

S

sacer, sacra, sacrum ... *holy, sacred*

sacerdos, sacerdotis, m. ... *priest*

sacerdotium, -ii, n. ... *priesthood*

sacramentum, -I, n. ... *oath of allegiance*

saepe (adv.) ... *often*

saevio, -ire, -ii, -itus ... *to rage, be furious, violent*

saevitia, -ae, f. ... *savagery*

salus, salutis, f. ... *safety*

sanguis, sanguinis, m. ... *blood*

sapiens, sapientis ... *wise, prudent*

sapienter (adv.) ... *prudently*

Sardinia, -ae, f. ... *Sardinia*

satelles, satellitis, c. ... *attendant, follower*

satias (only nom. sg.), f. ... *satiety*

satio, -are, -avi, -atus ... *to satisfy*

satis (adv.) ... *enough*

scaena, -ae, f. ... *stage*

scelus, sceleris, n. ... *crime*

scientia, -ae, f. ... *knowledge*

scribo, scribere, scripsi, scriptus ... *to write*

scriptor, scriptoris, m. ... *writer*

scrutor, scrutari, scrutatus ... *to investigate, examine*

secessio, secessionis, f. ... *withdrawal, secession*

secretum, -I, n. ... *hidden thing, secret*

secta, -ae, f. ... *sect; doctrine*

sector, sectari, sectatus ... *to follow*

secundus, -a, -um ... *following, next; favorable*

securus, -a, -um ... *free from care*

sed (conj.) ... *but*

sedile, sedilis, n. ... *seat*

seditio, seditionis, f. ... *sedition, civil discord*

segnis, segne ... *slow, slack*

segnities, -ei, f. ... *sluggishness*

semen, seminis, n. ... *seed*

semper (adv.) ... *always*

senatorius, -a, -um ... *senatorial*

senatus, -us, m. ... *senate*

senectus, senectutis, f. ... *old age*

sententia, -ae, f. ... *opinion, judgment*

sepero, -are, -avi, -atus ... *to separate*

sepultura, -ae, f. ... *burial*

sequor, sequi, secutus ... *to follow*

serius, -a, -um ... *serious, grave*

servilis, servile ... *slavish*

servo, -are, -avi, -atus ... *to preserve*

servus, -I, m. ... *servant*

sestertius, -ii, m. ... *sesterce*

severus, -a, -um ... *austere, strict*

sexus, -us, m. ... *sex, gender*

silentium, -ii, n. ... *silence*

sileo, silere, silui ... *to be silent*

similitudo, similitudinis, f. ... *similarity*

simultas, simultatis, f. ... *enmity, rivalry, animosity*

simplicitas, simplicitatis, f. ... *simplicity, naturalness*

simul (adv.) ... *at the same time*

singuli, -ae, -a ... *one at a time, single*

sino, sinere, sivi, situs ... *to let down, set; permit; allow*

socrus, -us, c. ... *father- or mother-in law*

soleo, -ere, solitus ... *to be accustomed*

solitudo, solitudinis, f. ... *desert, wilderness*

solitus, -a, -um ... *customary, ordinary*

sollemnis, sollemne ... *solemn*

solor, solari, solatus ... *to console*

solvo, solvere, solvi, solutus ... *to unbind, loosen, release, set free*

somnium, -ii, n. ... *dream*

somnus, -I, m. ... *sleep*

sors, sortis, f. ... *lot; destiny; fate*

spargo, spargere, sparsi, sparsus ... *to sprinkle*

species, -ei, f. ... *aspect; sight; pretense; pretext*

spectabilis, spectabile ... *visible; remarkable*

spectaculum, -I, n. ... *spectacle*

specto, -are, -avi, -atus ... *to look at, examine*

specus, -us, m. ... *cave, pit*

sperno, spernere, sprevi, spretus ... *to spurn, shun*

spes, spei, f. ... *hope, expectation*

spiritus, -us, m. ... *breath, spirit*

sponte (adv.) ... *freely, willingly*

statim (adv.) ... *regularly; immediately*

statua, -ae, f. ... *statue*

statuo, statuere, statui, statutus ... *to set up; establish; set forth*

sterno, sternere, stravi, stratus ... *to spread out; postrate*

stipator, stipatoris, m. ... *attendant, follower*

sto, stare, steti, statum ...

studium, -I, n. ... *inclination, eagerness; object of desire*

stuprum, -I, n. ... *disgrace, dishonor*

suadeo, suadere, suasi, suasus ... *to persuade*

subdolus, -a, -um ... *subtle, deceitful*

subeo, subire, subii, subitus ... *to come under, go under, approac, submit to*

subiecto, -are, -avi, -atus ... *to throw under*

subsidium, -ii, n. ... *aid, help*

subtraho, subtrahere, subtraxi, subtractus ... *to draw off, carry off, remove*

sudor, sudoris, m. ... *sweat*

suetus, -a, -um ... *accustomed*

sufficio, -ere, suffeci, suffectus ... *to supply; to adequate; yield*

-, sui (reflexive pron.) ... *himself*

sum, esse, fui, futurus ... *to be*

summus, -a, -um ... *highest*

super (prep. + acc./abl.) ... *above; beyond; in addition to*

superstes, superstitis ... *standing by, surviving*

suppleo, supplere, supplevi, suppletus ... *to supply*

supplicium, -ii, n. ... *supplication; death penalty; punishment*

supra (adv./prep. + acc.) ... *above; before; more; beyond*

supremus, -a, -um ... *highest; last*

suus, -a, um ... *his own*

T

tabula, -ae, f. ... *board; writing tablet; writing, record, document, statute; will, testament*

taedium, -ii, n. ... *tedium; weariness*

talis, tale ... *such, of such a kind*

tandem (adv.) ... *at last*

tamen (adv.) ... *nevertheless*

tamquam (adv.) ... *just as, as if*

tantus, -a, -um ... *so great, so much*

tarditas, tarditatis, f. ... *slowness*

telum, -I, n. ... *weapon*

tempestas, tempestatis, f. ... *season, weather, time, tempest*

tempto, -are, -avi, -atus ... *to try, attempt*

tempus, temporis, n. ... *time*

tenuis, tenue ... *slim, meager*

testamentum, -I, n. ... *will, testament*

testificor, testificari, testificatus ... *to call to witness*

testis, testis, c. ... *witness*

theatrum, -I, n. ... *theater*

timeo, timere, timui ... *to be afraid, fear*

timor, timoris, m. ... *fear*

togatus, -a, -um ... *civilian*

tolero, -are, -avi, -atus ... *to tolerate, endure*

tormentum, -I, n. ... *siege engine; instrument of torment*

torvus, -a, -um ... *grim, savage*

tot ... *so many*

traditio, traditionis, f. ... *tradition, handing down*

trado, tradere, tradidi, traditus ... *to hand over*

tragicus, -a, -um ... *tragic*

traho, trahere, traxi, tractus ... *to drag*

transeo, -ire, -ivi, -itus ... *to go over, cross over; hasten over; pass over*

transigo, -ere, -egi, -actus ... *to drive through; spend, pass (time)*

transmitto, transmittere, transmisi, transmissus ... *to send across, transmit*

tres, tria ... *three*

tribunal, tribunalis, n. ... *judgment-seat*

tribunicius, -a, -um ... *having to do with a tribune*

tribuo, tribuere, tribui, tributus ... *to assign, attribute, confer*

triennium, -ii, n. ... *period of three years*

triremis, -is, f. ... *trireme*

tristis, triste ... *sad, grim*

tristitia, -ae, f. ... *sadness*

Troianus, -a, -um ... *Trojan*

trucido, -are, -avi, -atus ... *to cut to pieces, slaughter*

trux, trucis ... *harsh, savage*

tumulus, -I, m. ... *burial mound*

tunc (adv.) ... *then*

turbidus, -a, um. ... *disordered*

turbo, -are, -avi, -atus ... *to disturb*

turbo, turbinis, m. ... *whirlwind*

Tyrus, -i., f. ... *Tyre*

U

ubertas, ubertatis, f. ... *abundance*

ullus, -a, -um ... *any, some*

ultra (adv.) ... *beyond; additionally*

ultro (adv.) ... *spontaneously, of one's own accord*

unde (adv.) ... *from which place, whence*

unicus, -a, -um ... *sole, only*

urbs, urbis, f. ... *city*

usus, -us, m. ... *use, experience*

usque (adv.) ... *all the way; until, up to*

ut (conj. + indicative) ... *as, when; (+ subj.) ... in order that*

uterque, utraque, utrumque ... *each, either, each one, the other*

utilitas, utilitatis, f. ... *usefulness, utility*

utor, uti, usus ... *to use*

uxor, uxoris, f. ... *wife*

V

vaco, -are, -avi, -atus ... *to be free, empty*

vacuus, -a, -um ... *empty*

vaecordia, -ae, f. ... *madness*

valeo, valere, valui, valiturus ... *to be strong, be able*

valetudo, valetudinis, f. ... *health*

vanitas, vanitatis, f. ... *vanity*

vasto, -are, -avi, -atus ... *to devastate, lay waste*

-ve ... *or*

veho, vehere, vexi, vectus ... *to convey*

vel (conj.) ... *or*

velo, -are, -avi, -atus ... *to cover, veil*

velut (adv.) ... *just as*

vena, -ae, f. ... *vein*

venenum, -I, n. ... *poison*

venerabilis, venerabile ... *venerable*

veneror, venerari, veneratus ... *to venerate*

venia, -ae, f. ... *kindness, indulgence, favor, pardon*

ventito, -are, -avi, -atus ... *to come often*

ventus, -I, m. ... *wind*

venum, n. ... *that which is sold*

Venus, Veneris, f. ... *Venus*

verber, verberis, n. ... *lash, whip*

verbero, -are, -avi, -atus ... *to beat, lash*

verbum, -I, n. ... *word*

verecundia, -ae, f. ... *modesty*

versus, versus, m. ... *verse*

verto, vertere, verti, versus ... *to turn, turn back, direct*

verus, -a, -um ... *true*

Vespasianus, -i ... *Vespasian*

vesperasco, vesperascere ... *to become evening*

vestigium, -ii, n. ... *footstep; track*

vestis, vestis, f. ... *clothing*

vetus, veteris ... *old*

vetustus, -a, -um ... *aged, ancient*

viator, viatoris, m. ... *traveler; attendant*

vicesimus, -a, -um ... *twentieth*

vicinus, -a, -um ... *neighboring*

victoria, -ae, f. ... *victory*

viduus, -a, -um ... *widowed, bereft*

vigeo, vigere, vigui ... *to be vigorous, lively*

villa, -ae, f. ... *farmhouse, villa*

vincio, -ire, vinxi, vinctus ... *to bind*

vinc(u)lum, -I, n. ... *chain*

violentia, -ae, f. ... *violence*

vir, viri, m. ... *man*

virtus, virtutis, f. ... *virtue*

vis (irregular noun), f. ... *strength, force*

viso, visere, visi, visus ... *to look at with attention*

vita, -ae, f. ... *life*

vitium, -ii, n. ... *vice*

vito, -are, -avi, -atus ... *to avoid, shun*

vivo, vivere, vixi ... *to live*

vocabulum, -I, n. ... *designation, name*

voco, -are, -avi, -atus ... *to call*

voluntarius, -a, -um ... *voluntary*

voluptas, voluptatis, f. ... *pleasure*

votum, -I, n. ... *votive offering, prayer*

vox, vocis, f. ... *voice*

vulgo, -are, -avi, -atus ... *to make public, divulge*

vulgus, -I, n. ... *crowd*

vultus, -I, m. ... *face, visage*

Bibliography and Further Reading

Ahl, F. *Lucan: An Introduction*. Ithaca-London: Cornell University Press, 1976.

Ash, R. *Ancient in Action: Tacitus*. London: Bristol Classical Press, 2006.

Ash, R. *Tacitus: Histories Book II*. Cambridge: Cambridge University Press, 2007.

Ash, R., ed. *Oxford Readings in Tacitus*. Oxford: Oxford University Press, 2012.

Ash, R., et al., eds. *Fame and Infamy: Essays on Characterization in Greek and Roman Biography and Historiography*. Oxford: Oxford University Press, 2015.

Asso, P., ed. *Brill's Companion to Lucan*. Leiden–Boston: Brill, 2011.

Bartera, S. *A Commentary on Tacitus, Annals 16.1-20*. Dissertation Virginia, 2008.

Braund, S. H., tr. *Lucan: Civil War*. Oxford: Oxford University Press, 1992.

Braund, S. *Seneca: De Clementia, Edited with Text, Translation, and Commentary*. Oxford: Oxford University Press, 2009.

Burnand, C. *Tacitus and the Principate: From Augustus to Domitian*. Cambridge: Cambridge University Press, 2012.

Cary, E., tr. *Dio's Roman History VIII: Books LXI-LXX* (Loeb Classical Library). Cambridge, MA: Harvard University Press, 1925.

Champlin, E. *Nero*. Cambridge, MA: Harvard University Press, 2003.

Chilver, G. E. F. *A Historical Commentary on Tacitus' Histories I and II*. Oxford: Oxford University Press, 1979.

Cornell, T. J., ed. *The Fragments of the Roman Historians* (3 vols.). Oxford: Oxford University Press, 2013.

Courtney, E. *A Companion to Petronius*. Oxford: Oxford University Press, 2001.

Damon, C. *Tacitus: Histories I*. Cambridge: Cambridge University Press, 2003.

Dudley, D. *The World of Tacitus*. Boston-Toronto: Little, Brown, and Company, 1968.

Edwards, C. *The Politics of Immorality in Ancient Rome*. Cambridge: Cambridge University Press, 1993.

Edwards, C. *Death in Ancient Rome*. New Haven, CT: Yale University Press, 2007.

Fisher, C. D., ed. *Cornelii Taciti Annalium ab Excessu Divi Augusti Libri*. Oxford: Oxford University Press, 1906.

Fratantuono, L. *Madness Triumphant: A Reading of Lucan's Pharsalia*. Lanham, MD: Lexington Books, 2012.

Furneaux, H. *Cornelii Taciti Annalium ab Excessu Divi Augusti Libri, Vol. II, Books XI-XVI*. Second Edition revised by H. F. Pelham and C. D. Fisher. Oxford: Oxford University Press, 1907.

Goodyear, F. R. D. *The Annals of Tacitus, Volume I (Annals 1. 1-54)*. Cambridge: Cambridge University Press, 1972.

Griffin, M. T. *Nero: The End of a Dynasty*. London: B. T. Batsford, 1984 (reprinted by Routledge, 2000).

Haynes, H. *Tacitus on Imperial Rome: The History of Make-Believe*. Berkeley–Los Angeles–London: The University of California Press, 2003.

Heubner, H., ed. *P. Cornelius Tacitus, Tom. I: Annales*. Stuttgart–Leipzig: Teubner, 1994 (corrected edition of the 1983 original).

Jackson, J., tr. *Tacitus V: Annals XIII-XVI* (Loeb Classical Library). Cambridge, MA: Harvard University Press, 1937.

L'Hoir, F. S. *Tragedy, Rhetoric, and the Historiography of Tacitus' Annales*. Ann Arbor: The University of Michigan Press, 2006.

Luce, T. J., and Woodman, A. J., eds. *Tacitus and the Tacitean Tradition*. Princeton, NJ, 1993.

Malloch, S. J. V. *Tacitus: Annals 11*. Cambridge: Cambridge University Press, 2013.

Marsh, F. B., and Leon, H. J. *Tacitus: Selections from His Works*. New York: Prentice-Hall, Inc., 1936 (corrected reprint, Norman: The University of Oklahoma Press, 1963).

Martin, R. *Tacitus*. London: B. T. Batsford, Ltd., 1981 (reprinted with corrections Bristol Classical Press, 1994).

Matyszak, P. *The Sons of Caesar: Imperial Rome's First Dynasty*. London: Thames & Hudson Ltd., 2006.

Mellor, R. *Tacitus*. London–New York: Routledge, 1993.

Mellor, R. *Oxford Approaches to Classical Literature: Tacitus' Annals*. Oxford: Oxford University Press, 2010.

Mendell, C. W. *Tacitus: The Man and His Work*. New Haven, CT: Yale University Press, 1957.

Miller, N. P. *Tacitus: Annals XV*. London: Methuen, 1973 (reprinted by Bristol Classical Press, 1994).

Morgan, T. *Popular Morality in the Early Roman Empire*. Cambridge: Cambridge University Press, 2007.

O'Gorman, E. *Irony and Misreading in the Annals of Tacitus*. Cambridge: Cambridge University Press, 2006.

Pagán, V. E., ed. *A Companion to Tacitus*. Malden, MA: Wiley-Blackwell, 2012.

Prag, J., and Repath, I., eds. *Petronius: A Handbook*. Oxford: Oxford University Press, 2009.

Rolfe, J. F. C., tr. *Suetonius, Volume II* (Loeb Classical Library). Cambridge, MA: Harvard University Press, 1914 (revised edition by D. W. Hurley, 1997).

Roller, M. *Constructing Autocracy: Aristocrats and Emperors in Julio-Claudian Rome*. Princeton, NJ, 2001.

Romm, J. *Dying Every Day: Seneca at the Court of Nero*. New York: Alfred A. Knopf, 2014.

Rudich, V. *Political Dissidence under Nero: The Price of Dissimulation*. New York–London: Routledge, 1993.

Rudich, V. *Dissence and Literature under Nero: The Price of Rhetoricization*. New York–London: Routledge, 1997.

Rutledge, S. *A Tacitus Reader: Selections from Annales, Historiae, Germania, and Dialogus*. Mundelein, IL: Bolchazy-Carducci Publishers, Inc., 2014.

Rutledge, S. H. *Imperial Inquisitions: Prosecutors and Informants from Tiberius to Domitian*. New York–London: Routledge, 2001.

Schmeling, G. *A Commentary on the Satyrica of Petronius*. Oxford: Oxford University Press, 2011.

Shotter, D. *Nero (Lancaster Pamphlets)*. London–New York: Routledge, 1997.

Sinclair, P. *Tacitus the Sententious Historian: A Sociology of Rhetoric in Annals 1–6*. University Park: Pennsylvania State University Press, 1995.

Smallwood, E. M. *Documents Illustrating the Principates of Gaius, Claudius, and Nero*. Cambridge: Cambridge University Press, 1967.

Sullivan, J. P. *The Satyricon of Petronius: A Literary Study*. Bloomington–London: Indiana University Press, 1968.

Syme, R. *Tacitus* (2 vols.). Oxford: Oxford University Press, 1958 (reprinted Sandpiper Books Ltd., 1997).

Syme, R. *Ten Studies in Tacitus*. Oxford: Oxford University Press, 1970.

Tresch, J. *Die Nerobücher in den Annalen des Tacitus: Tradition und Leistung*. Heidelberg: Carl Winter, 1965.

Walker, B. *The Annals of Tacitus: A Study in the Writing of History*. Manchester: Manchester University Press, 1952.

Walsh, P. G., tr. *Petronius: The Satyricon*. Oxford: Oxford University Press, 1997.

Warmington, B. H. *Suetonius: Nero*. London: Bristol Classical Press, 1977.

Woodcock, E. C. *Tacitus: Annals XIV*. London: Methuen, 1939 (reprinted by Bristol Classical Press, 1992).

Woodman, A. J., tr. *Tacitus, The Annals, Translated with Introduction and Notes*. Indianapolis–Cambridge: Hackett, 2004 (reviewed by R. B. Rutherford, *Bryn Mawr Classical Review* 2005-07-15).

Woodman, A. J., ed. *The Cambridge Companion to Tacitus*. Cambridge: Cambridge University Press, 2009.

Yardley, J. C. *Tacitus, The Annals: The Reigns of Tiberius, Claudius, and Nero*. With an Introduction and Notes by A. A. Barrett. Oxford: Oxford University Press, 2008.

Index